The Political Economy of Austria

*A Conference Sponsored Jointly by the
American Enterprise Institute for Public Policy Research
and the Austrian Institute (New York)*

The Political Economy of Austria

Edited by Sven W. Arndt

American Enterprise Institute for Public Policy Research
Washington and London

Library of Congress Cataloging in Publication Data
Main entry under title:

The Political economy of Austria.
  (AEI symposia; 82D)
     1. Austria—Economic policy—1945–   —Addresses,
essays, lectures.   I. Arndt, Sven W.   II. Series.
HC265.P64   1982   338.9436   82-11661
ISBN 0-8447-2241-3
ISBN 0-8447-2240-5 (pbk.)

AEI Symposia 82D

Printed in the United States of America

Panelists

Sven W. Arndt
Professor of Economics and Director
Applied International Economics Section
University of California, Santa Cruz

Jacques R. Artus
Assistant Director
Research Department
International Monetary Fund

Barry P. Bosworth
Senior Fellow
The Brookings Institution

William H. Branson
Professor of Economics
Woodrow Wilson School, Princeton University
National Bureau of Economic Research

Felix Butschek
Deputy Director
Austrian Institute for Economic Research

Jacob S. Dreyer
Deputy Assistant Secretary for International Economic Analysis
U.S. Treasury Department

Johann Farnleitner
Head, Legal Department
Austrian Federal Economic Chamber

William Fellner
Resident Scholar
American Enterprise Institute

Marvin H. Kosters
Resident Scholar
American Enterprise Institute

Fritz Machlup
Professor of Economics
Princeton University

R. Timothy McNamar
Deputy Secretary
U.S. Treasury Department

Thomas Nowotny
Consul General of Austria (New York)

Henry Owen
The Consultants International Group

Phillip Rieger
Director, Austrian National Bank

Herbert Salcher
Minister for Finance, Austria

Friedrich Schimpf
Austrian Trade Commissioner

Erich Schmidt
Head, Economics Department
Austrian Federation of Trade Unions

Karl Herbert Schober
Ambassador of Austria to the United States

Hans Seidel
Secretary of State
Ministry of Finance, Austria

Erich Spitäller
European Department
International Monetary Fund

Jan Tumlir
Director of Research
General Agreement on Tariffs and Trade (GATT) Secretariat

Karl Vak
President
Zentralsparkasse und Kommerzialbank

Henry Wallich
Member, Board of Governors
Federal Reserve System

Thomas D. Willett
Horton Professor of Economics
Claremont Graduate School

Milton Wolf
Former U.S. Ambassador to Austria

*This conference was sponsored by
the American Enterprise Institute for Public Policy Research
and the Austrian Institute (New York)
and held at the American Enterprise Institute
in Washington, D.C., on October 1–2, 1981*

Contents

PART TWO

MICROECONOMIC ISSUES: STRUCTURE AND PERFORMANCE

Preface

There is much in the economic challenges encountered by Austrian society during the past several decades that is ordinary and typical. We note the familiar tensions between full employment and adequate growth in living standards, on the one hand, and price stability and external balance, on the other. We observe a variety of complex and only partly settled questions involving economic structure, the division of labor between public and private sectors, the allocation of resources, and the distribution of income.

Although the problems may have been orthodox and commonplace, the manner and success with which they were managed are not. This is true especially at the macroeconomic level where Austria outperformed its neighbors and trading partners by substantial margins. This departure from orthodoxy is evident as well in the economic and social environment, at the center of which we find the social partnership. This complex set of institutions and procedures is designed to enable Austria's social groups to resolve in compromise the issues that lead to civil strife and industrial confrontation elsewhere.

Austria's extraordinary record and the social arrangements and practices that made it possible warrant close examination. To this end, the Austrian Institute in New York and the American Enterprise Institute sponsored a conference in the early autumn of 1981. Its object was to enable Austrian practitioners to tell their story to an audience of American and international civil servants, of business leaders, and of academics.

The papers collected in this volume were written in the main by Austrian policy makers and by those who advise them; the perspective is clearly that of the insider. The authors were selected by the Austrian sponsors of the conference, in which connection we owe a special debt of gratitude to Consul General Thomas Nowotny in New York and to Dr. Heinz Kienzl at the Austrian National Bank. The discussants were chosen by the editor in order to offer a critical counterpoint. Gottfried Haberler kindly agreed to expand his discussant's remarks into a longer essay.

As always, an undertaking of this magnitude benefits substantially from the efforts and contributions of many talented and dedicated individuals. Among them Dr. Fritz Cocron of the Austrian Institute, Consul General Nowotny, Dr. Kienzl, and Thomas Johnson and Eduardo Somensatto of AEI made crucial contributions at various stages of the enterprise. An additional measure of thanks goes to Ed Somensatto for invaluable assistance in editing and preparing the volume for publication.

Part One
Macroeconomic Policies and Issues

Introduction

Sven W. Arndt

The difficulty with fixed exchange rates is that they become obsolete. As time passes and economic conditions change, the equilibrium exchange rate also changes. As the gap between actual and equilibrium rates widens, policy conflicts intensify. The architects of Bretton Woods were fully aware of the problem and believed that they had taken care of it when they provided for periodic parity realignments. In leaving such adjustments to the discretion of governments, however, they overestimated the ability of governments to undertake timely and meaningful parity realignments. Bretton Woods collapsed because countries were not able to coordinate their macroeconomic policies so as to validate existing exchange rates; and when divergent economic developments required parity shifts, countries were unable to respond in a timely and appropriate fashion.

Still, the search continues for an optimal combination of fixed and floating rates. In Austria the schilling is anchored to the deutsche mark by means of an adjustable peg, but floats freely against all other currencies. In this part, the experiences that led to the so-called hard currency policy and the intellectual considerations that provide its foundation are examined in papers by Hans Seidel, by Gottfried Haberler, and by Stephan Koren.

A rigid exchange rate reduces uncertainty and cuts transactions costs. The resultant savings can be substantial for very open economies. Further, if a country tends to be more subject to inflation than its neighbors, fixing currency values is seen as a way of importing price stability. Tying the schilling to the currency of low-inflation Germany is viewed by many Austrians as a means of establishing price discipline at home.

Arguments in favor of fixed exchange rates are frequently accompanied by arguments against floating rates, which are then, often illegitimately, employed as reasons against parity changes in an adjustable-peg system. One of these arguments is reminiscent of the ancient

3

"elasticity pessimism" in asserting that trade elasticities may be too low, thus making exchange rates a useless or at best very inefficient instrument for payments adjustment. After reviewing the available evidence, Thomas Willett concludes that elasticity pessimism is unwarranted in the case of Austria.

A more sophisticated argument against exchange rate changes invokes the so-called vicious circle hypothesis, according to which devaluation at best provides only temporary relief. First, higher prices of imported materials and other inputs lead to higher prices of home-produced goods, thus reducing or eliminating the price advantages created by devaluation. Second, the absence of money and exchange rate illusion in wage setting implies that devaluation will be followed relatively quickly by nominal wage increases tending to dilute or emasculate the restorative powers of exchange rate adjustments.

The first argument is often embedded in the hypothesis that a small open economy is limited in its power to influence the prices of traded goods and that this inability has far-reaching consequences for economic behavior and economic policy. This hypothesis is central to the Austrian version of the Scandinavian open-economy model developed and tested by Helmut Frisch. It attempts, in streamlined terms, to capture the essential features of the Austrian scene in a two-sector open-economy model in which the sector producing tradable goods is fully "exposed" to the harsh winds of foreign competition, while the domestic sector, made up mainly of government, construction, and services, remains relatively "sheltered" and thereby less influenced by forces that would enhance productivity and moderate wage and price pressures.

Enlightened economic policy must, as Frisch points out, take into account the political constraints of the day. In addition, it must be cognizant of the structural limitations on freedom of action. One of these is the country's position along the "openness" spectrum. The question of whether Austria is mainly small and open or large and closed is at the heart of much of the policy debate; it is also essentially an empirical question. In his examination of the evidence presented by Frisch, Willett concludes that Austria falls somewhere in the middle of the spectrum and thus should possess meaningful price-setting independence. According to this evidence, therefore, Austrian policy retains a measure of control over the real exchange rate.

The vicious circle hypothesis has enjoyed widespread acceptance in Western countries, where it is also widely misunderstood and misapplied. In asserting that causation runs along a one-way street from exchange rates to prices, many supporters of the hypothesis confuse joint variation with causality by supposing that every observed exchange rate change is somehow the first event in a chain of events. Although exogenous exchange rate movements have indeed been observed, there are many other instances in which prices and exchange rates have moved jointly in response to other disturbances.

Moreover, even where an exchange rate change is exogenous, it can produce at most a finite rise in domestic prices and not an ongoing process or vicious circle. The circle is generated by domestic institutional and governmental responses that accommodate and perpetuate the disturbance. The dynamics of the circle are typically driven by political pressures aiming to deflect or postpone the often painful adjustments needed to correct the disequilibrium. In such situations, politics simply overrules economics; and although this does not make the problem less real, it crucially alters the range of viable solutions.

It is clear that Austrian policy makers are skeptical about the effectiveness of exchange rate adjustments in light of a perceived absence of money illusion in the labor market coupled with anxiety about the potentially deleterious consequences of exchange rate volatility for the social partnership. This skepticism is a decidedly un-Keynesian view of the world, one that raises doubts about the Keynesianism which is said to have characterized Austrian macroeconomic policy during the period in question. Few notions, after all, were more central to postwar Keynesian analysis than employment policy based on real wage manipulation by means of price adjustment. This suggests that there may be diverse ways of classifying the intellectual underpinnings of given policies; and some of these are explored by Seidel for Austria. As Haberler suggests, however, many specific policy maneuvers were consistent with Keynesian as well as monetarist perceptions of reality.

The hard currency policy tends to be viewed by many as a prerequisite for effective incomes policy. As such, this view recalls the notion of balance of payments as discipline that served to underpin arguments for fixed exchange rates in earlier times. With the schilling pegged to the deutsche mark, Austrian wages and prices must follow the patterns set by Germany if, at the given exchange rate, payments problems with Germany are to be avoided. At the same time, the motion of the Austrian schilling relative to other currencies is determined in critical ways by the movement of the deutsche mark in world currency markets. Any tendency for Austrian inflation to exceed German inflation beyond certain permissible margins brings with it impaired competitiveness and trade imbalances vis-à-vis Germany and against the rest of the world as well.

It is generally accepted that exchange rates will move in response to differential inflation. If the exchange value of the Austrian schilling in other countries is influenced by relative German inflation and if

5

inflation in Austria exceeds inflation in Germany, the schilling will appreciate relative to other currencies by more than is warranted by Austrian inflation. The effect of such appreciations is deflationary and thus complicates the government's ability to honor its strong commitment to full employment.

During the 1970s, the rate of inflation in Austria exceeded the German rate. Austria's competitiveness declined, and the bilateral trade balance reflected these developments. At the same time, the deutsche mark appreciated sharply against other currencies for much of the 1970s, pulling the schilling up with it. This weakened further the ability of Austrian goods to compete and created mounting difficulties on current account. Although some of these exchange rate movements were reversed in the late 1970s by the protracted appreciation of the dollar against the deutsche mark, the current account continues to present a major problem for the Austrian authorities. In reviewing the evidence, Jacques Artus suggests that Austria may be paying a very high price for its exchange rate policy.

Austrian policy makers themselves are a great deal more sanguine, and they have a right to be. Over the years they have shown an ability unmatched elsewhere to pull the right trick at the right time. It is their pragmatism and their willingness to be eclectic that elicits our admiration. In some countries ideology has banished rationality from the policy-making process, while in others labor and capital have fought zero-sum distributional wars. Whether Austrian policy was guided by monetarist or Keynesian precepts is probably less important than its consistent ability to match means to ends and to keep its focus on result rather than appearance.

The Austrian Economy: An Overview

Hans Seidel

The first part of this paper presents some basic facts about the Austrian economy. The second part analyzes how Austria has met the challenges of the 1970s.

Economic Structure and Long-Term Development

Austria is a small country of 7.5 million inhabitants and an area of 40,000 square miles. Geographically, it is situated in the heart of Europe. Politically, it lies next to the iron curtain: Austria shares nearly one-half of its borders with Communist countries.

In 1980 Austria had a per capita income of $10,600, which is approximately the average income in the industrial countries (according to the International Monetary Fund [IMF]). The income level is below that of the most advanced countries, such as Switzerland, Sweden, or Germany, but is definitely higher than in Italy or Great Britain. Austria's position in the income league of the industrial countries is not spectacular at first glance. It is rather impressive, however, when judged in a broader historical view.

The Republic of Austria, which was founded after the breakdown of the Austro-Hungarian monarchy in 1918, was not considered economically viable and in fact was not viable. In the 1920s the economy could only be kept running with the aid of foreign loans. The big depression of the 1930s had severe consequences: one-third of the labor force was unemployed, and gross investment fell short of depreciation. The process of industrialization, which had begun in Austria rather late in the nineteenth century, was interrupted for more than three decades. There was no self-sustained growth to pave the way for a mass consumption society. Even in the peak years between the two world wars, the level of prewar real income was not reached.

After World War II, for the second time within one generation, Austria had to begin from scratch. Although difficult, the country's

7

economic reconstruction—supported by generous economic aid from the United States—was extremely successful. In the first half of the 1950s the usual postwar problems were solved. Inflation was stopped, and the foreign balance of payments was restored without cutting real income. The State Treaty of 1955 reestablished Austrian sovereignty. Nevertheless, the Austrian economy was still lagging considerably behind most of the industrial nations. Income per capita was one-third lower than in the European Economic Community (EEC), and one-fourth lower than in the Organization for Economic Cooperation and Development (OECD)–Europe. It took another two and a half decades before Austria was well established in the middle income group of the industrial nations.

The sustained process of rapid growth in the postwar era was characterized by certain structural features. Austria is a country with a high rate of investment. In 1972 more than 30 percent of the gross domestic product (GDP) was invested in fixed assets. There has been some decline since that investment peak, but the capital stock of the Austrian economy is still growing at a satisfactory rate. For decades investment was given a high priority in Austria, individually and socially. Entrepreneurs hoped to maintain international competitiveness by investing more per employee than their competitors. The trade unions accepted tax concessions made to entrepreneurs as long as additional sums of money were invested by the entrepreneurs. Investment, it was believed, did not destroy, but created, jobs. Unlike investment in fixed assets, expenditures for research and development (R & D) in Austria had been rather low for a long time—and still are lower than in the highly developed small countries. This can be explained partly by the structure of Austrian industry. More R & D is clearly needed, however, to facilitate the real adjustments needed after the second oil price surge.

The labor supply is changing very slowly in Austria. A decline in the labor force of 0.8 percent per annum in the 1960s was followed by an increase of 0.6 percent in the 1970s. Fluctuations in the demand for labor are to some degree cushioned by changes in the number of foreign workers. In 1980, 6.3 percent of all wage and salary earners were foreigners. Given the slow changes in the total supply of labor, the increased demand for labor in some sectors of the economy had to be met by sectoral shifts in the distribution of employment. Fourastier's law of sector shares as a function of income per capita let the share of agriculture in total employment shrink from over 26 percent in 1956, the year after the State Treaty, to 9 percent in 1980. The labor share of the secondary sector reached a peak of 43 percent in 1973 and has been declining since (it was 40 percent in 1980). Nearly 51 percent of the total labor force is employed in the tertiary sector, compared with less than one-third twenty-five years ago. In manufacturing, the share of the heavy industries and the traditional consumer goods industries was reduced, though the leading industries of the first industrial revolution—steel and textiles—still have a larger share and the technical industries have a smaller share than in countries in a comparable economic position.

A small country with limited natural resources, Austria has always been highly dependent on foreign trade. Economic interactions with foreign countries were intensified enormously in past decades. In 1980 Austria's exports of goods and services amounted to 39 percent of GDP, and the share of imports was 41 percent. Two decades ago the corresponding shares were 25 percent and 25 percent, respectively. The growing foreign trade made economies of scale possible and provided comparative advantages in producing goods and services, but made the Austrian economy vulnerable to external shocks. Growth through trade was made possible by the removal of trade barriers. Import quotas were abolished. Free trade areas (no tariffs) were first created in the European Free Trade Association (EFTA) and later in the EEC. Tariff reductions were negotiated within the General Agreement on Tariffs and Trade (GATT). These steps not only stimulated exports, but also opened the domestic market to foreign products. For the first time in its history the Austrian economy is fully exposed to internatonal competition abroad and at home.

Austria usually has a deficit in its balance of trade and, mainly because of tourism, a surplus in its balance of services. The country is a leader in international tourism. Net receipts from tourism add almost 6 percent to GDP (and in some regions, such as Tyrol, as much as 25 percent). Austria managed to maintain its share of international tourism in the 1970s despite stiffening competition from new tourist areas abroad.

The commodity composition of foreign trade has changed completely. Twenty-five years ago Austria's export structure was not very different from that of a developing country. More than 70 percent of total exports consisted of commodities in SITC groups 2 and 5, mainly timber, iron and steel, and paper. Since that time, the commodity structure has shifted more to finished and more sophisticated goods such as machines and electrical appliances. At the same time, the share of industrial products in total imports has increased. In the mid-1950s more than half of Austria's total imports were complementary goods, such as food, energy, and raw materials, that could not be produced domestically in sufficient quantities. In 1972 the share of these products in total imports was less than one quarter. Even with a high energy bill, Austria spent less than 30 percent of its total imports for these commodities in 1980. The sharp increase in the imports of manufactured goods reflects the growing international division of labor resulting from European integration. Austria is exporting manufactured goods in order to buy foreign manufactured goods. The commodity composition and the removal of trade barriers favor trade with Western Europe. Seventy percent of Austria's total trade is with OECD-Europe, and only 12 percent is with Eastern Europe, formerly the most important trading partner of Austria.

Public ownership in the enterprise sector is more widespread in Austria than in other industrial countries of the West. Public utilities are run by central or local governments. The large theaters are state enterprises. After World War II approximately one-fifth of the Austrian manufacturing industry (excluding small business) and two leading banks were nationalized. Nationalization, however, had no ideological basis, but was a simple device to integrate these enterprises, which were formerly German property, into the Austrian economy. Nationalized industries are subject to the same rules as private industries, and they depend heavily on export markets. The nationalized iron and steel industry is not subsidized in Austria, though its competitors in the EEC depend on government support.

Taxes are relatively high in Austria. In 1981, total taxes and social security contributions were 41.3 percent of GDP, compared with 38 percent in OECD-Europe; but Austria, as in many other respects, avoids taking extreme positions. Thus its tax burden is lower than that in the Benelux or Scandinavian countries (Sweden leads, with 54 percent), and in the 1970s it increased less than in many other countries.

Even a short description of the Austrian economy would be incomplete without mentioning the social partnership. The main economic interest groups—labor, business, and agriculture—have strong centralized organizations, partly on a legal and partly on a voluntary basis. Since World War II these organizations have been working together to solve problems through compromise. They developed an institutional framework for cooperation, notably the so-called Parity Commission for Prices and Wages. One result of this cooperation is social peace: there are practically no strikes in Austria. As will be shown in the second part of this paper, Austria could achieve a better trade-off between unemployment and inflation than most other countries.

Adjusting to Oil Price Shocks in the 1970s

Since World War II, Austria's economic performance has twice gained international attention. This happened first in the 1950s, when Austria's postwar economy was transformed into a rapidly growing peaceful economy. (Austria's economic performance in this period was as impressive as Germany's.) Then, in the 1970s, Austria met the challenge of two oil price shocks quite successfully.

Of course, the Austrian economy could not avoid a significant slowdown in growth in the 1970s. Between 1973 and 1980 real GDP grew at an annual average rate of 3.3 percent. This was only half as high as in the five years before 1973, but it still was one percentage point higher than in the rest of OECD-Europe. Compared with the period from 1955 to 1973, economic growth after 1973 was almost two percentage points lower. Thus, the pattern of postwar economic growth in Austria could be described as follows. A period of fast growth in the 1950s was terminated by years of structural adjustment in the early 1960s. Economic growth in Austria, at this time, was slower than in Western Europe (see figure 1). At the end of the 1960s there was a new worldwide economic upswing. Austria soon regained its position, already attained in the 1950s, as one of the fastest-growing countries. Austria held this position even in the difficult years following the first oil price shock.

Despite the slowdown in economic growth, employment in the 1970s in Austria increased by 400,000 people or by 200,000 since 1974. Thus, of course, the growth in labor productivity was depressed. Productivity per employee, however, grew at an annual rate of 3 percent in the period 1973–1980, which was still higher than in many other countries. The increase in employment was sufficient to absorb the growing labor supply. Maintenance of full employment was supported by reducing the numbers of so-called guest workers, and by reduced labor migration from the agricultural sector to the secondary and tertiary sectors. Since 1974 the annual rate of unemployment has never exceeded 2 percent, but in 1981 it will do so. With average unemployment rates of more than 5 percent in the 1950s, 3 percent in the 1960s, and less than 2 percent in the 1970s, Austria was one of the few countries with decreasing unemployment in the long run.

Inflation accelerated in the 1970s, but it never exceeded 10 percent (see figure 2). It reached its peak in 1974, 9.5 percent. In the following years the inflation rate was reduced, step by step, and reached 3½ percent in 1978 and 1979. In 1980, as a result of the second oil price shock, inflation accelerated again and reached 6½ percent. In the 1970s, inflation was lower only in Switzerland and Germany. Probably the most outstanding characteristic of Austria's economic performance in the 1970s was the combination of full employment and low inflation rates. The so-called misery index, the inflation and unemployment rates added together, generally stayed below 10 percent, with a low of 6 percent.

FIGURE 1

GROSS NATIONAL PRODUCT AND INDUSTRIAL PRODUCTION COMPARISONS

Indexes 1973 = 100

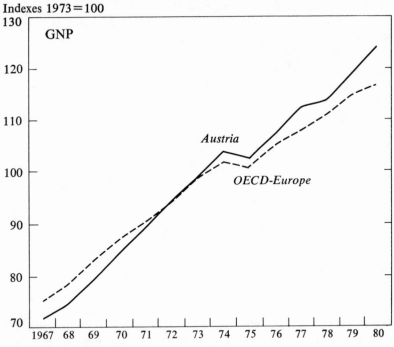

GNP

Indexes 1973 = 100

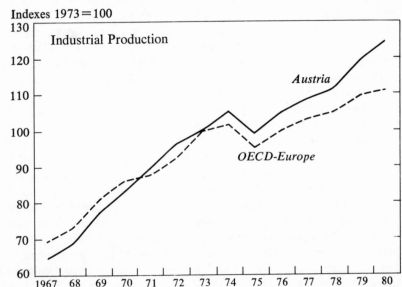

Industrial Production

SOURCE: Austrian Ministry of Finance.

FIGURE 2

PRICES: INTERNATIONAL COMPARISON

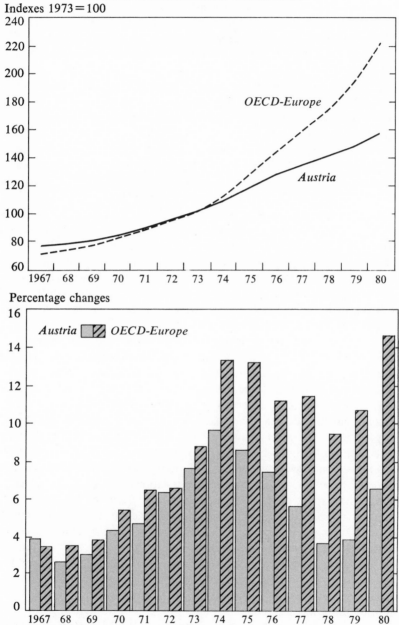

SOURCE: Austrian Ministry of Finance.

13

The development of Austria's foreign trade balance has not been as satisfactory as developments in production, employment, and inflation. The current account of the Austrian economy, which was balanced until 1973, turned negative during the two oil shocks. If we add the relatively high statistical discrepancy to the current balance, we find that it amounted to 2 percent of GDP on average between 1976 and 1980.

The deterioration of the current balance was not a consequence of insufficient exports. Exports of goods were growing faster than the developed countries' average. Austria's share in the exports of OECD countries rose from 1.3 percent in 1970 to 1.5 percent in 1980. The reason for the negative current account can be found instead in the large increase in imports, which was partly a result of increased oil prices and partly a result of the fast growth of the domestic economy.

Macroeconomic Policy. The performance of the Austrian economy is the result of many factors—structural features, the behavior of economic agents, and so on. Clearly, however, economic policy, especially macroeconomic policy, played a decisive role. Some important aspects of Austrian economic policy will be discussed in detail elsewhere. Now we will turn to providing an overall view of the policy mix that Austria used in the 1970s, the philosophy upon which this policy stance was based, and the results it produced.

The Austrian policy mix in the 1970s (some modifications in recent times will be discussed later) was based on the idea that the oil shocks led to cost inflation and demand deflation. Therefore, two different problems had to be solved at the same time. First, cost push had to be reduced in order to keep inflation within tolerable limits. Second, effective demand had to be kept at a level compatible with full employment. In splitting the problem into two parts, it was assumed that cost push could be tackled by means other than a refusal to finance cost increases. A combination of an exchange rate policy and an incomes policy was used as an anti-inflationary device. In order to bridge the gap in effective demand resulting from the low absorption capacity of some of the major oil-exporting countries, budget deficits were recommended, provided that the balance-of-payments deficit on current account, which may arise from such a policy, should not get out of hand. Monetary policy, in this context, played a more or less passive role. It had to finance the level of nominal income that was determined by the other instruments, at interest rates preventing yield-induced outflows of capital.

The Austrian policy mix of the 1970s is occasionally called Austro-Keynesianism. The arguments for this policy relied very heavily on the post-Keynesian concept of a fixed-price and flexible-quantity economy, in which prices do not clear the markets instantly, while output smoothly responds to changes in demand. This model describes fairly well the price- and wage-setting behavior of the Austrian economy, centered in the Parity Commission of Prices and Wages. It lost some explanatory power, though, with the growing internationalization of major markets in the 1970s. The Austrian version, however, differs from most Keynesian views insofar as price stability and a hard currency were given high priority and were regarded as a condition for a permanently high level of employment.

The Austrian concept was developed more through experience than by design. (Some would even argue that when it was applied consciously, it did not work properly because circumstances had changed.) To understand the basic ideas, it is necessary to take a closer look at the main policy instruments.

In the 1970s, when dirty floating began, exchange rate policy in Austria was supposed to stabilize the value of the Austrian schilling (AS) in terms of foreign currencies that were thought to be hard currencies. In practice, that meant that the AS was tied to the deutsche mark (DM). In 1980 one AS bought only ½ percent fewer DM than ten years earlier. At the beginning of the 1970s, this policy seemed to be almost self-evident. Austria had a strong external account, and many experts believed the AS was undervalued. Moreover, the growing European Integration (a free trade agreement with the EEC that came into effect in 1972) favored the idea of a regional currency union on an informal basis (Austria never joined the European Monetary System).

Still, it was not until the mid-1970s that exchange rate policy was explicitly used a means of stabilizing the price level. This change of view was supported by some empirical observations and some theoretical thinking. The hard currency policy reduced considerably the amount of imported inflation, especially in 1974, when U.S. dollar prices of many raw materials and of energy exploded. Import prices rose far less than in countries having weak currencies. Furthermore, it was expected that the hard currency policy would reduce inflation of domestic origin.

In the mid-1970s, many European countries decided to fix monetary targets in order to reduce inflationary expectations. The Austrian economy did not adopt this technique (for good reasons, I believe). Instead of money supply, the exchange rate was chosen as a target. (The Swiss economy is a good example for possible conflicts between monetary and exchange rate targets.) By fixing the exchange rate, it was believed that domestically determined prices and costs would adjust to external conditions.

15

The hope for a smooth adjustment process was partly based on the so-called Scandinavian model of price determination, though it had been shown that the basic equations of this model did not fit too well. Moreover, it was thought that an incomes policy would be compatible with the model. Particular attention was given to wage determination in the sheltered sector of the economy, assuming that workers in the exposed sector would respond to changing world market conditions if they could be certain that workers in the sheltered sector would stay in line.

Many experts questioned the sense of the hard currency policy. For some time Austrian authorities found it hard to convince international organizations that a devaluation of the AS was not indicated. As a matter of fact, until 1977 the hard currency policy failed to work wonders on the development of domestic cost components. Between 1973 and 1977, the nominal effective exchange rate (trade-weighted) rose by one quarter. Since unit wage costs rose nearly as much in Austria as abroad, the AS appreciated in real terms by more than 20 percent (see figure 3).

As a consequence, profits in the exposed sector of the Austrian economy—especially in manufacturing and foreign travel—shrank considerably. It was not until 1978 that wage policy accepted the rules laid down by the hard currency policy. The rate of increase in negotiated wages was nearly halved between 1977 and 1978 and remained at this low level in 1979, even though oil prices began to climb again. Cost competitiveness improved (the real rate of exchange declined, though the weakness of the U.S. dollar continued). At the same time, the fall in the inflation rate accelerated. The Austrian economy entered the "virtuous" circle of a hard currency policy until the second oil price surge fueled inflation again.

The success of the stabilization policy was quite remarkable. The rate of inflation in Austria fell from 9.5 percent in 1974 to 3.5 percent in the years 1978 and 1979. Thus inflation was reduced to the average levels of the 1950s and 1960s. The reduction of the rate of inflation by six percentage points took place without even a temporary increase in the rate of unemployment. The loss of international cost competitiveness was only temporary.

Reducing inflationary expectations at socially acceptable costs remains a big and as yet unsolved worldwide problem. Thus it is understandable that the Austrian performance was noticed by international experts and policy makers, many of whom have expressed different opinions concerning it. Those who do not believe in an incomes policy, like the Federal Reserve's Paul Volcker, praise the hard currency policy that

16

FIGURE 3
Effective Schilling Exchange Rate, 1967–1980

Indexes 1967 = 100

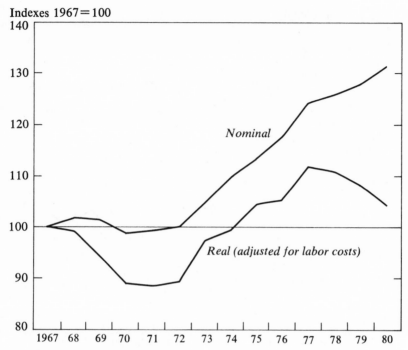

Source: Austrian Ministry of Finance.

forced export industries to rationalize and stand up to high wage demands. Others simply state that trade unions in Austria are more sensible than those elsewhere. Sufficient empirical evidence is hard to obtain because the Austrian system of incomes policy consists of a durable relationship between the so-called social partners, without rigid price-wage controls or quantitative wage guidelines. Thus it is not possible to make comparisons between policy-on periods and policy-off periods which would shed some light on the functioning of the incomes policy. Perhaps the whole discussion about informal incomes policy is purely semantic. What seems important is simply this: the Austrian stabilization policy did not try to improve the trade-off between inflation and unemployment by weakening the trade unions and making the labor market more competitive. On the contrary, it used the power of a centralized system of labor representation to introduce general economic reasoning into the process of wage determination.

17

FIGURE 4

Budget and Current Account Balance, 1967–1980

As a percent of GDP

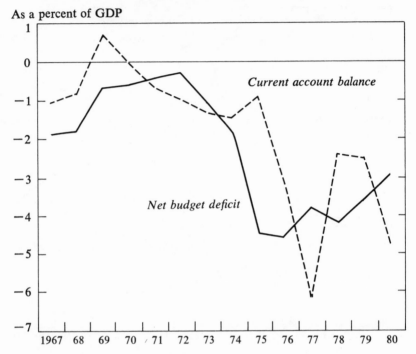

SOURCE: Austrian Ministry of Finance.

Budgetary policy, according to the previous distinction between price and output effects, was primarily supposed to influence the level and structure of employment and output in a Keynesian way. Judging by the results, there was nothing spectacular about budgetary policy, though it was much debated in parliament and in the press. High budget deficits were a common feature of most industrial countries in the years after 1974. Deficit spending was practiced in Austria, however, with more faith in the beneficial effects of such a policy than elsewhere. In 1975 the budget deficit (net of debt repayment) jumped to 4.5 percent of GDP (see figure 4). Deficits were accepted before the years of recession (1958 and 1967), but strong efforts were made afterward to balance the budget again. This time, deficit spending was deliberately continued in 1976, thereby opening a gap between expenditures and receipts that proved hard to close. The acceptance of a medium-term budget deficit could be defended with some arguments. If, it was argued, the bad conditions of the world economy did not allow export-led growth, then, for a certain period, it would be reasonable to stimulate domestic demand and accept the current account deficit resulting from such a full employment strategy. Stimulating domestic demand was thought to be primarily a task of budgetary policy because the enterprise sector suffered from unused capacity and tried to adjust its capital stock to the slower rate of growth. The budget deficit was thought to be temporary. It was hoped that within a reasonable period the world economy would resume a high rate of growth and/or the international competitiveness of the Austrian economy would improve, thereby making budgetary deficits superfluous. There was no detailed discussion of the relation between fiscal and monetary policy. The emphasis on budgetary policy, however, could be defended on the grounds that the desired employment level had to be compatible with an interest rate that prevented the outflow of capital.

A rethinking of budgetary policy began toward the end of the 1970s, partly because the growing national debt increased budgetary and financial problems, but mainly because the continuing deficit in the current account made it necessary to shift the emphasis of employment policy toward strategies that improved export performance. Substantial efforts to reduce the budget deficit, however, were not made before the second oil price surge was well under way. Since 1979 the net deficit has been reduced to below 3 percent of GDP.

Thus, the Austrian economy did meet the challenge of the first oil shock quite efficiently. There were weak points, of course, notably the deficit in the budget and in the balance of payments. Appropriate measures were taken, however, and most Austrians believed that a new equilibrium could be reached within a reasonable time. Unfortunately, in 1979 the second oil price surge interrupted the adjustment process and proved to be more harmful than was anticipated.

At first it was thought that the new problem was limited and could be handled quite easily. The rise in oil prices was regarded as primarily cost-push inflation without serious deflationary effects. (For a long time the OECD secretariat believed that the recession following the second oil price surge would be mild and a recovery would be well under way in the first half of 1981—which proved to be a dangerous miscalculation.) Given these expectations in the fall of 1979, a new cost stabilization program was launched. The AS was appreciated marginally against the DM in order to dampen the rise in import costs; a cheap-money policy aimed to reduce capital costs; and trade unions were asked to pursue a cautious wage policy. Some optimists (including me) hoped that the inflation rate would increase temporarily by no more than one percentage point and that most of the usual ratchet effects could be avoided.

Unfortunately, the cost-stabilizing program was bound to fail in significant respects, given the conditions of the world economy. The sharp rise of the U.S. dollar in foreign exchange markets allowed the effective rate of exchange of the AS to fall (in nominal terms and even more so in real terms) and worsened the terms of trade. Moreover, a loss in real income resulting from the deterioration of the terms of trade added to the difficulties.

Attempts to keep capital costs low were bound to fail because of rising U.S. interest rates. The rate of interest reached a postwar high. In real terms, interest rates were far higher than the expected medium-term rate of growth of production, causing no small concern among those who believe that in a dynamic equilibrium the two rates should be equal. In the middle of 1981, Austria had a prime rate of over 13 percent; bond yields exceeded 11 percent, and the money market rate was 12 percent. The high cost of borrowing made budget deficits and deficits in the current account expensive, though until now Austria had been able to borrow from relatively cheap sources. (In the past, the interest rates paid on the national debt were lower than the rate of increase of nominal GDP. If the present relationship between these two rates continues, and assuming a net budget deficit of 3 percent of GDP, interest payments on the national debt will exceed the net deficit within several years.)

High interest rates and the rising dollar increased cost pressures and reduced effective demand, thereby adding to stagflation. This is not to accuse the United States of "beggar-thy-neighbor" competition in high interest rates (as the Joint Economic Committee did in its 1981 report). Nor can I say whether the present policy stance will lead the United States out of stagflation—but there is no doubt that the adjustment process is much harder than it would have been otherwise.

The slight recession, which started in the course of 1980, deepened in 1981, contrary to expectations. Basic industries such as iron and steel, which still figure heavily in Austrian industry, face severe problems. Although the recession is unexpectedly deep, budgetary policy continues to be slightly restrictive. There is still full employment (the rate of unemployment in 1981 will not exceed 2.4 percent), but in many cases only defensive employment strategies prevent layoffs. The most promising feature of the present situation is the cautious wage policy—that is, workers are accepting real wage cuts. Therefore, it will be possible to keep the inflation rate below 7 percent, and international cost competitiveness will improve.

It is beyond the scope of this paper to develop a full-fledged strategy for the future. Top priority will be given to full employment—there is no question of that. There will be some tentative actions, however, before a new concept emerges. Such a concept will most likely try to avoid the trap of macroeconomic management by microeconomic devices, thereby promoting real adjustments to changing world conditions.

Commentary

Jacob S. Dreyer

The present discussion, like other discussions devoted to Austrian economic performance, has been replete with praise for the undeniable achievements of Austrian economic policy makers. For non-Austrians engaged in analysis, evaluation, and formulation of economic policy, the main practical advantage of participating in discussions about Austria's economy lies in the opportunity to better understand which factors and policies account for Austria's success and, even more importantly, to assess whether they can be transplanted and emulated in the socio-political and economic environments of their own countries with similarly beneficial results.

The paper by Hans Seidel (and that by Helmut Frisch) provides a good overview of rationales for, and the methods of, implementation of macroeconomic policies in Austria. My comments would be directed, therefore, at parts that I find deficient in explaining the underpinnings of Austrian macroeconomic policy or in evaluating its results.

The first observation (which is related to comments made elsewhere by Tom Willett and Michele Fratianni) concerns the Austrian version of the Scandinavian model (AVSM). I think we must be clear about the fact that the AVSM, or for that matter any other version of the Scandinavian model, is not a general equilibrium model, *not* even a fully developed behavioral model. It is enough to examine the manner in which prices are determined: the world price level is naturally determined outside Austria, but "Austrian" variables are also determined outside the model. One can ask what determines the relative shares of the exposed and sheltered sectors of the economy. What determines the adjusted unemployment rate? What determines the expected rate of inflation in the exposed sector? What are the determinants of rates of growth of labor productivity in the exposed and sheltered sectors, respectively? In other words, without passing a judgment on the conceptual bases underlying models of the Scandinavian type and abstracting from Seidel's acknowledgment that the statistical fit of AVSM, never exceedingly good, has further deteriorated in recent years, one has to conclude that AVSM may at best serve as a useful formula for computing the overall rate of inflation. As far as I can see, by no means can AVSM be used to evaluate the effectiveness of alternative policies on the rate of inflation, level of unemployment, or on any other macroeconomic target.

Fortunately, Seidel is quite explicit about the view of the world shaping Austrian economic policy as well as about its overriding objective. Briefly stated, this view is that of a fixed-price and flexible-quantity economy and the overriding policy objective is that of full employment.

I shall refrain from commenting on the extent of price rigidity in the Austrian economy, especially in comparison with that in other countries. I cannot help noticing with satisfaction, however, that, unlike economists, pragmatic economic agents in Austria do not view price rigidity as an immutable law of nature. As Seidel notes, "hard currency policy . . . forced export industries . . . to stand up to high wage demands" and "workers are accepting real wage cuts." Be that as it may, however, if the world is indeed a Keynesian one and low unemployment is an overriding policy objective, what instruments were employed to achieve the remarkable Austrian record of low inflation and low unemployment rates?

No doubt, high net budget deficits since the first oil shock (as reflected in more than a two-and-a-half times increase in the debt/gross domestic product [GDP] ratio between 1974 and 1980) have helped in countering the effects of oil-price-induced deflationary pressures. Yet similar fiscal policies have been conducted in other OECD countries with not nearly the same beneficial results. Also, there is no doubt that perennial and not infrequently very substantial (unadjusted*) current account deficits have exerted downward pressure on prices through augmented aggregate supply of goods and services. Clearly, the relatively small absolute size of the Austrian economy permitted foreign borrowing relative to GDP that would be unthinkable on a permanent basis by large OECD countries. In addition, however, in contradistinction to many *smaller* countries, Austria has had no trouble in attracting foreign capital, primarily as a result of its sound economic management.

According to Seidel, the two main pillars of such sound management in Austria are the durability of the social compact and the implementation of monetary policy. I have brief comments on both of these aspects of economic management in Austria.

Justifiable pride colors pronouncements of Austrian officials on the subject of social consensus in their country, especially against the back-

---

* I confess my reluctance to acquiesce in the apparent practice by my Austrian friends to add statistical discrepancy to the current rather than the capital account.

ground of essentially confrontational labor-management relations in many other industrial nations. One can almost hear a remote echo of the Hapsberg era: *bella gerant alii, tu felix Austria nube*—let other [countries] fight, [while] happy Austria shall marry. There can be no doubt that the roots of the enduring success of the social partnership in the 1970s are to be found in the history and sociology of the Austrian society. Yet there are other countries in Western Europe, similar in size, equally homogeneous ethnically, religiously, and culturally, equally cohesive socially, whose repeated attempts at forging a durable social consensus failed rather miserably.

In my judgment, the institution of social partnership, used so skill-fully to achieve full employment, owes much of its success to very favorable demographic factors in Austria, in marked contrast to the situation in most other Western European countries.

If we look at the period since the first oil shock—the period during which the Austrian economic performance has been demonstrably superior to that of the OECD average—a few interesting facts emerge. First, according to statistics of the International Monetary Fund (IMF), since 1973 there has been virtually no population growth in Austria. While happy Austria shall marry, she shall not necessarily breed! Most reveal-ing is the labor market. Between 1973 and 1980 the total labor force (employed plus unemployed) increased by 108,000 people, which cor-responds to a rate of increase of less than 0.5 percent per year—much less than in virtually all other OECD countries. During the same period, the rate of unemployment went up from 1.6 percent to about 2 percent. Simultaneously, however, the number of foreign workers declined by 52,000. Had these people remained in Austria, the number of unem-ployed in 1980 would have been some 105,000 instead of 53,200 (as reported by Seidel), which means that the rate of unemployment would have gone to some 4 percent—it would have been two and a half times as high as the rate in 1973.

Although I am not about to pass a judgment on Austrian policy toward the so-called guest workers, the fact is that there *was* a consider-able quantity adjustment in the Austrian labor market which made the policy goal of low unemployment much easier to achieve than would be the case in a country which, by circumstances or by choice, cannot induce a contraction of its labor force.

I think that these demographic trends and conditions in the labor market go a long way toward explaining past Austrian successes not only in maintaining low rates of unemployment but, more generally, in assuring the sturdiness of the edifice of social partnership; and I regret that these issues were given virtually no attention in an otherwise comprehensive paper by Seidel.

Turning to the second pillar of Austrian economic management—monetary policy—I must admit that I am somewhat baffled by the description of this policy given by Seidel and other authors. Seidel states unambiguously that, "Instead of money supply, the exchange rate was chosen as a target." This would be quite straightforward were it not for other statements by Seidel and later by other authors. Seidel states that "Monetary policy, in this context [of recommended budget deficits subject to limitations on the size of the resulting current account deficits], played a more or less passive role. It had to finance the level of nominal income that was determined by the other instruments, at interest rates preventing yield-induced outflows of capital."

It seems to me that jointly these statements assign too many targets to the monetary instrument. Surely, this would not be unusual. After all, the Federal Reserve System was trying for a number of years to set targets for monetary aggregates, fix the Federal funds rate, and influence the dollar exchange rate, all at the same time. As we all know, however, the results were not exactly glorious.

Obviously, all these more or less rigid targets—the exchange rate, nominal interest rates, aggregate credit, capital imports—cannot be set independently. What is not clear to me is whether, in effect, we are talking about principal and subordinate targets or targets subject to constraints. I would also find it beneficial to learn more precisely what particular instruments are used to achieve those targets and what are the peculiarities of Austria's financial structure, if any, that make simultaneous attainment of these multiple targets possible.

Austrian Monetary and Exchange Rate Policies

Stephan Koren

Monetary and exchange rate policies play a crucial role in the discussion and conduct of a country's overall economic policy. They are important issues not only in economic policy narrowly conceived, but in politics in general. For a small country like Austria, developments taking place beyond its frontiers are of great moment, for they influence the economic conditions within which its own policies and strategies must be set.

Before examining contemporary policy issues, and the "hard currency strategy" in particular, it may be useful to review the economic and social dynamics of the last three and a half decades, beginning with the post–World War II chaos of complete dissolution of the structures and the order that are necessary for the life of society. To overcome this situation was the greatest and most complex challenge a generation might be faced with—a generation weakened not only by war but also by national and international doubts about its viability in the wake of the collapse of the multinational state.

It is therefore important to recall the forces that triggered and molded the strong dynamics of Austria's postwar development. For the people of that time, the economic, political, and social quality of life today would have been unthinkable; the anticipation of such a development would have been dismissed as a mere utopia. Political and economic energies were concentrated on the most urgent problems and on objectives that were therefore short term. Yet they represented a tremendous challenge to the people and to the creative power of politics.

In examining the economic and monetary developments that followed, we can divide this period, during which Austria emerged as a modern industrialized state, into three distinct phases, in each of which the targets and character of economic events were determined by the most urgent problems then prevailing. The first phase, immediately after the war, was essentially a struggle for survival. Policy, such as it was,

26

was a far cry from economic policy in a modern sense. The same can be said of the monetary sector, where we had not the slightest idea about the amount of money in circulation—and the legal tender was still the reichsmark.

The schilling currency was reintroduced at the end of 1945, while money circulation was drastically limited. When the first budget was drawn up, the largest expense item was the costs of the occupying powers. The scarcity of goods made rationing and price controls necessary. At that time, however, these were a matter of course and did not give rise to regulatory controversy. Similarly, nationalization in industry, energy, and banking was a question of expediency rather than one of principle. The exchange rate between the dollar and the Austrian schilling (AS) was fixed at US$1 = AS10, a rate based on the regulated domestic prices; and foreign payments were of course entirely controlled.

This period of pragmatic improvisation ended in 1947. It was succeeded by a period of reconstruction lasting from 1948 to 1962, which began with two crucial events. One was the announcement of the Marshall Plan, which sparked the later economic dynamics, and the other was an attempt to reorganize the Austrian monetary system in order to reduce the large gap between money supply and the volume of goods. This attempt to stop inflation through drastic monetary means was less successful, and the money supply was soon out of control again.

During this second postwar phase, the country's productive potential was rebuilt with the extensive aid of the United States; the course to be followed by the state-owned industrial enterprises and the power industry was determined; and priority was given to the repair of war damage to infrastructure and housing. During the first years of this phase, however, monetary policy was unable to rein in the money supply, and inflation rates consequently soared. The high inflation not only discouraged a revival of the propensity to save and thus the building up of a domestic capital market, but also thwarted all attempts to restore the balance of payments at the given exchange rate. In spite of various wage and price agreements, attempts to solve the problem of inflation failed because of conflicts of opinion between the political powers about how such a solution should be found: one side was in favor of increased controls, the other in favor of a freer market. Even within the two large political groups there were conflicting opinions.

In 1951 economic policy underwent fundamental changes when a sweeping restrictive program was introduced, employing for the first time a number of tools available for monetary and economic policies. This economic change was due to various pressures. One of these came from the grass roots—that is to say, from the Austrian population, which had had enough of inflation and all its consequences. Another came from abroad, when the United States considerably cut back its foreign aid program. Without drastic government measures this would have led very quickly to unsolvable balance-of-payments problems.

The success of the restrictive measures was stunning. Inflation was soon brought to a halt, and by 1952 the price level had actually declined. Industrial growth began to stagnate, however, and employment decreased by 3 percent. But in 1953 a surprisingly strong boom set in, exports in particular exceeding all expectations.

In succeeding years the Austrian economy entered a period of growth and liberalization. From an external monetary view, this resulted above all in the final fixing of parities and in uniform exchange rates for the schilling (US$1 = AS26). This development gained additional momentum through the conclusion in 1955 of the Austrian State Treaty, which restored Austria's freedom and eased the pressure exerted on its people by uncertainty over the future of the country. It also seems important that from that time on there existed considerably greater consensus on fundamental economic questions among the major parties and groups. This situation changed little after 1966, the year when the coalition government broke up over budgetary issues. The breakup resulted in prematurely held parliamentary elections, in which the Austrian People's party gained an absolute majority. They were not going it alone in economic matters, however, and within the framework of the social partnership there were joint attempts to find solutions.

With the 1970s, a new economic period began worldwide and thus also in Austria, gradually changing the conditions that for many years had been regarded as a safe basis for economic decisions. Several decades of affluence and growth had slowly generated various problems. The patterns, attitudes, and macroeconomic magnitudes we had been used to were no longer valid. Various economies began to develop in different directions, while worldwide economic tensions increased. The countries that supply oil and raw materials recognized—and took advantage of—the economic and political power of their monopoly.

A significant economic event was the breakdown of the system of Bretton Woods in 1971, which despite some rescue efforts has proved to be final, just as the soaring energy prices of 1973 created a problem that we have been faced with to a smaller or a larger extent ever since. Much has been said about 1973 and its repercussions. But what is certain is that the world has not drawn the necessary conclusions. During the following years, much too little notice was taken of the totally changed situation of the world economy.

At that time Austria also was faced with great difficulties. The public authorities followed Keynes's theory of deficit spending in their attempt to compensate for the deflationary potential and to slow down increases in consumer prices. The Austrian budget deficit increased dramatically, reaching rates of 4 percent of GNP and higher. Incomes policy, however, did not take this development into account, so that in a time of so-called zero growth wages went up considerably. The result was a strong deterioration of Austria's competitiveness in international markets, aggravating the current account problem also from the export side.

In autumn 1977 a package of economic measures was introduced, after the fundamental lines to be followed had been discussed. The primary question was whether to settle the current account problem by means of an exchange rate adjustment with all its consequences or to continue the exchange rate policy that was being pursued and to restore payments balance by other measures. The decision taken at that time was to continue the so-called hard currency policy, which was increasingly becoming the centerpiece of Austrian monetary considerations. The need to reduce Austria's current account deficit, however, led in 1977 to extensive monetary, budgetary, and incomes policy measures, which were designed to rein in the growth of domestic demand. It would go beyond the purpose of this paper to give a detailed account of the steps taken, but I will mention some major steps aimed at maintaining the hard currency policy as part of the overall stabilization effort.

As early as the beginning of 1977, when it became clear that the current account deficit was structural, the Austrian National Bank declared that it would not automatically and fully replace (by refinancing) the outflow of central bank money into foreign trade. Interest rates for central bank credits were increased rather sharply for that time, and refinancing was made dependent on the observance of a fixed percentage of credit growth (1.1 percent a month). The central bank also hoped to reduce consumer credits in favor of investment credits because of the high proportion of imports for private consumption. Toward the end of the year, the growth rate for consumer credits was cut by one-half, that is, to 0.55 percent a month, while the central bank gradually increased expansive open-market operations that served export or investment financing in order to improve the current account balance. The government also tried to ease the budgetary strain by introducing a third value-added tax rate of 30 percent for luxury consumer goods (the "luxury tax").

With such attempts to restore the balance in foreign trade, those responsible for economic policy had a dual strategy in mind. On the one hand, they had to take restrictive measures to reduce the current account deficit despite economic recession. On the other hand, they had to initiate or enhance the restructuring of the economy to promote exports and reduce imports.

Strikingly positive effects of the measures taken were evident in the following year, 1978. At 0.5 percent, economic growth was moderate in real terms, but there was practically no unemployment. This situation is typical of Austria: even in periods of weak economic growth, labor market pressure remains lower than in other countries. The low unemployment permitted the pursuit of a moderate wage policy. Apart from the wage claims for 1975–1976, the trade unions' policy conformed to economic developments. Since in 1978 consumption dropped by the surprisingly high amount of about 3 percent, the current account deficit was dramatically reduced. The deficit, adjusted for statistical discrepancies, amounted to AS28.9 billion in 1977 but to only AS6.2 billion in 1978.

In 1979 the course of events was entirely different. International market conditions were determined by the so-called second oil price shock at the beginning of that year. It caused a substantial increase in international interest rates, which led to anticipation that another recession would begin in the second half of 1979 at the latest. Austria, still attempting to stabilize the domestic price level through a hard currency policy (which helped to check the prices of imported goods), had to cope with interest rates as its main problem. With the slackening of economic activity expected internationally, as well as for structural reasons and in the interest of stabilization, the monetary authorities wanted to maintain low interest rates as long as they could. In the first quarter of 1979, even the refinancing rates were reduced. In other words, the Austrian National Bank tried to "dive through" the international interest wave. It worked for a few months only, particularly since economic activities did not slacken, or slackened rather slowly, and interest rates remained accordingly high. Comparatively low capital imports enhanced differences between domestic and foreign interest rates that made foreign investments look profitable for several reasons. Finally, the adverse current account balance led to a marked liquidity squeeze.

Toward the end of 1979 the low-interest policy came under increased pressure. It was no longer possible to keep interest rates low, swimming against the tide of high interest rates worldwide. Therefore the experiment had to be abandoned after the loss of more than one-third of Austrian exchange holdings. It is understandable that a central bank should become increasingly concerned as its foreign exchange losses begin to mount. That matters did not take a tragic turn for Austria was due to the fact that these developments resolved, more or less automatically, the problem of excessive capital imports of the previous year.

30

In other words, the low-interest-rate policy was given up at a time when, despite the considerable outflow of foreign exchange reserves, things were still far from a point of no return. The central bank increased its refinancing rates substantially and thus influenced domestic interest rates in general.

I conclude with some remarks about the monetary situation of recent times and aspects of how to deal with it. Unlike the central banks of other Western countries (particularly the United States, Great Britain, and Switzerland), the Austrian National Bank pursues a policy geared not to money supply but to money demand. No attempts are made to control the target figures of economic growth and employment by regulating the circulation of money—it is rather the money supply that is adjusted to demand.

A decisive factor in the demand for money is the increase or decrease in incomes as determined by the economic and social partners and by the federal government's fiscal policy. The central bank influences incomes indirectly through the fixing of the exchange rate: through import price increases and subsequent consumer price rises, devaluations lead to reductions in real income; revaluations have a price-curbing effect, that is to say, with a given nominal income, they increase real income.[1] The exchange rate of the Austrian schilling is thus deliberately employed as an instrument of overall stabilization policy. The intention is to keep imported inflation to a minimum by permanent nominal appreciations of the schilling relative to the currencies of Austria's most important trading partners. This was particularly important immediately after the final collapse of the system of fixed exchange rates and the raw material boom that followed the first oil price shock of 1973. Especially during a phase when prices in various countries developed differently to an increasing extent, the exchange rate played an important stabilizing role. This deliberate nominal revaluation of the schilling, which was pursued until the dollar rate started to soar at the end of 1980 and particularly between 1973 and 1977, was based on the following reasoning.

Price expectations can be reduced by curbing import prices. This leads to lower nominal wage settlements, which justify the appreciation in retrospect. The economy is finally stabilized at low levels of unemployment and of inflation ("virtuous circle"). The alternative would be a mutual building up of imported and domestic inflation that must lead to expectations of devaluation and to permanent effective depreciations of the currency ("vicious circle").[2] A devaluation strategy is particularly risky for a small country like Austria, since the impact of exchange rate changes on domestic prices (the "pass-through effect") is relatively vigorous. The principle that the hard currency policy should be main-

31

tained despite Austria's structural current account deficit is also recognized by the social partners.[3]

In practice, this concept was interpreted as pegging the schilling to the deutsche mark without following fully the deutsche mark's erratic movements against the U.S. dollar. In 1978, for instance, the value of the deutsche mark rose by 15.7 percent in relation to the dollar, that of the schilling by 13.9 percent. The subsequent devaluation of the deutsche mark against the dollar was also not entirely followed by the schilling. The fluctuations of the schilling–deutsche mark exchange rate are, however, negligible. Pegging the schilling to the deutsche mark avoids the costs of covering foreign exchange risks in trade with the Federal Republic of Germany. The stability of the schilling–deutsche mark exchange rate has contributed considerably to the growth of trade and capital flows between Austria and West Germany.[4] The small fluctuation of the schilling in relation to the deutsche mark also corresponds to the "optimum currency area" hypothesis, according to which the welfare costs of freely floating exchange rates are considerably heavier in a comparatively highly integrated economic area than when closed economic blocs are concerned.[5]

Austria's growing integration into European markets for goods and capital has significantly cut down the autonomy of its economic policy. The pegging of the exchange rate of the schilling to the deutsche mark implies in the longer term a far-reaching adoption on Austria's part of the targets that West Germany sets for its own economic policy. Economic growth, unemployment, the price level, the budget deficit, and the balance on current account cannot develop differently in the long run without forcing adjustments in the exchange rate. Although Austria, in spite of having a faster-growing economy than West Germany, has maintained a relatively stable schilling–deutsche mark rate since 1980, the price that had to be paid was a loss of price competitiveness and growing foreign indebtedness.[6]

If the policy objective is exchange rate stability while the current account deficit is—at least over the medium term—taken for granted, the liquidity outflow through the balance on current account has to be compensated for by capital imports. On the other hand, no outflows of capital in search of profits must take place that, in addition to the current account deficit, signify a reduction in monetary reserves and thus a curbing of the intervention potential of monetary policy. The exchange rate target, therefore, implies that Austrian interest rates cannot differ to any considerable extent from those abroad (above all, in West Germany). That German interest rates have become a yardstick for Austria was noticed when, toward the end of 1979, Austria tried not to follow the international policy of high interest rates because of the costs involved and the cyclical policy pursued. The loss in monetary reserves due to outflows of capital in search of profits was estimated at AS14 billion (40 percent of the foreign exchange and currency holdings at the end of 1979). Because of transaction costs and slight daily fluctuations of the deutsche mark rate, not every interest rate differential triggers off corresponding capital flows; over a period of time, however, the connection is conspicuous. According to the portfolio selection theory, as elaborated by Tobin and Markowitz, a change in the interest rate differential would have to result in corresponding capital flows.[7]

Thus, from the monetary point of view, the Austrian interest rate becomes an intermediate target. Whether it corresponds to the overall foreign trade and payments situation is shown by the change in monetary reserves. If interest rates are too low, outflows of capital take place (reducing monetary reserves); if interest rates are too high, additional capital is imported (increasing monetary reserves). The Austrian National Bank influences interest rates not directly, but indirectly through the liquidity of credit institutions. In line with this concept of an adaptive money supply policy, the demand for central bank money is met. The major indicators employed to establish the demand for central bank money are the current account deficit adjusted for statistical errors and omissions, the increase in note and coin circulation, and the increase in the required minimum reserve.

Notes

1. The effect of exchange rate changes on the overall economy depends, above all, on the behavior of those affected as well as on institutional and structural factors. The growth of nominal wages in the wake of a depreciation, for example, may be higher than the increase in the price level of the economy as a whole. Real income growth in the export industry could trigger off a multiplier effect in other branches of economic activity, which would lead to price increases. On the impact of exchange rate adjustments, see F. Schebeck, H. Suppanz, and G. Tichy, *Der Einfluss von Wechselkursänderungen auf Aussenhandel und Preise* (Vienna: Projekt des Jubiläumsfonds der Österreichischen Nationalbank, 1979).

2. That the virtuous circle is more successful than the vicious circle also appears to have been confirmed by empirical investigations. "The depreciations surveyed were on average less efficient than the appreciations. This probably reflects the fact that it is more difficult to share out real income reductions than real income increases." William A. Allen, "Exchange Rates and Balance of Payments Adjustment: General Principles and Some Recent Experiences," Bank for International Settlements Working Papers, July 1980, p. 36.

3. "The principle of the hard currency policy should be adhered to in the future as well." Beirat für Wirtschafts-und Sozialfragen, "Kurz-und Mittelfristige Fragen der Zahlungsbilanzentwicklung" (Vienna, 1978), p. 42. See also the modified report relating to the deutsche mark in Beirat für Wirtschafts-und Sozial-

fragen, "Bericht zur Zahlungsbilanz 1980," p. 7: "Thus, the envisaged strengthening of price competitiveness might be obtained within the framework of the traditional hard currency policy" (translated by author).

4. In 1980 some 30.8 percent of Austrian exports went to West Germany, and 40.8 percent of imports came from that country; 26.7 percent of Austrian exports were paid for in deutsche marks and 52.7 percent in schillings; and 37.1 percent of imports were paid for in deutsche marks and 24.5 percent in schillings.

5. See Ronald I. McKinnon, *Money in International Exchange* (New York: Oxford University Press, 1979), p. 195.

6. During the period 1973 to 1977, the real effective exchange rate of the schilling indicates a marked deterioration of price competitiveness, whether consumer prices or labor costs are used. It has thus far not been possible to eliminate this deterioration fully. Given that the rate of inflation in Austria is higher than that in West Germany, a bilateral appreciation in real terms against the deutsche mark of 16.2 percent occurred between 1973 and July 1981. The reduced price competitiveness, certain structural weaknesses of the Austrian economy, the growth differential, and the deterioration of the terms of trade have led to a marked expansion of foreign indebtedness. Liabilities less foreign assets amounted to AS65 billion by the end of 1980.

7. See Zoran Hodjera, "International Short-term Capital Movements: A Survey of Theory and Empirical Analysis," *IMF Staff Papers,* vol. 20 (November 1973), p. 700. See, inter alia, Peter Szopo, "Die Bedeutung des österreichischen Kapitalmarktes als internationaler Finanzplatz," *Quartalshefte der Girozentrale,* no. 1 (1981), pp. 39ff.

Commentary

Jacques R. Artus

I will focus my comments on what Stephan Koren and others have called the hard currency policy of Austria. The expression "hard currency policy" is of course somewhat of a misnomer. What the Austrian authorities have really done over the past ten years is to peg the Austrian schilling to the deutsche mark, as is obvious from a perusal of the data on nominal exchange rates presented in figure 1. When the deutsche mark is a hard currency, the schilling is effectively a hard currency. When the deutsche mark is a soft currency, as it has been over the past two years, the schilling is also a soft currency.

Pegging the schilling to the deutsche mark has obvious advantages for Austria. It allows Austria to benefit from the advantages of an optimum currency zone, since West Germany is by far its main trading partner. It also allows Austria to maintain a severe external constraint on domestic prices and wages, since West Germany has a relatively low inflation rate.

There is, however, a basic condition for the success of such an exchange rate policy: that the rate of increase of costs of production in Austria be sufficiently low to ensure external equilibrium. I will argue that this condition has not been fulfilled and that, as a result, Austria is paying a high cost for its exchange rate policy.

The roots of the failure of Austria's exchange rate policy are to be found mainly in developments during the 1971–1975 period. During that period, West Germany allowed the deutsche mark to rise sharply against other major currencies. The Austrian schilling, being for practical purposes pegged to the deutsche mark, went up with it. Since Austria experienced a larger increase in costs of production than West Germany from 1971 to 1975, Austria lost competitiveness in relation both to West Germany and to other countries. The data shown in table 1 indicate that the decline of cost competitiveness over the 1971–1975

The views presented in these comments are those of the author and not necessarily those of the International Monetary Fund.

TABLE 1
INDEXES OF COMPETITIVENESS IN MANUFACTURING
(1971 = 100)

	Normalized Unit Labor Cost in Local Currency[a]			Exchange Rate		Relative Normalized Unit Labor Cost Adjusted for Exchange Rate Changes	
	Austria	West Germany	Other countries[b]	Deutsche marks per schilling	Other currencies per schilling[b]	Austria relative to West Germany	Austria relative to other countries[b]
1971	100.0	100.0	100.0	100.0	100.0	100.0	100.0
1972	107.6	105.3	106.8	98.7	100.8	100.9	101.6
1973	116.8	112.9	118.1	97.7	112.0	101.1	110.8
1974	128.3	122.6	135.4	99.2	121.3	103.8	114.9
1975	149.7	131.9	156.3	101.1	127.0	114.7	121.6
1976	147.8	133.1	164.1	100.4	134.1	111.5	120.8
1977	157.2	138.9	180.4	100.5	143.9	113.7	125.4
1978	162.0	145.3	193.5	99.0	149.1	110.4	124.8
1979	160.9	149.2	205.9	98.1	155.5	105.8	121.5
1980	167.8	160.4	231.1	100.5	159.5	105.1	115.8

a. The normalized unit labor costs are intended to abstract from the cyclical swings in conventionally measured productivity that often distort the actual unit labor cost series.
b. "Other countries" include the United States, Canada, Japan, Belgium, Denmark, France, Italy, the Netherlands, Norway, Sweden, Switzerland, and the United Kingdom.
SOURCE: International Monetary Fund Data Bank.

FIGURE 1

EXCHANGE RATE DEVELOPMENTS, 1971–1980

(Indexes 1971 = 100)

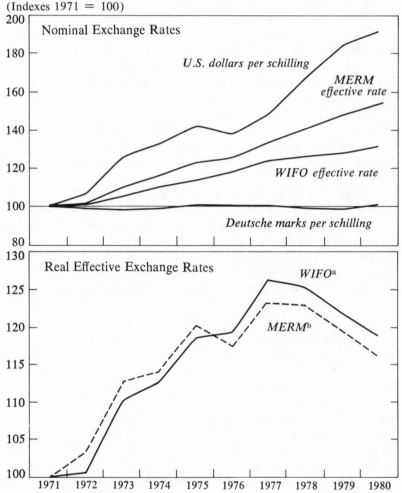

NOTE: WIFO = Austrian Institute for Economic Research; MERM = Multilateral Exchange Rate Model.

a. The figure for 1980 is estimated.

b. As presented by relative unit labor costs, in U.S. dollar terms.

SOURCES: Austrian Institute for Economic Research, *Monatsberichte;* and International Monetary Fund, *International Financial Statistics.*

period was about 15 percent in relation to West Germany and 22 percent in relation to other countries. These declines were never made up during the second half of the 1970s. Furthermore, West Germany had a large

37

excess of competitiveness in 1971, which had been accumulated during the fixed exchange rate period of the 1950s and 1960s, while Austria did not, or at least not to the same extent.

The result of these exchange rate developments was the emergence of a fairly sizable current account deficit in 1976 and its persistence since then (see figure 2). The deficit was particularly large in 1977, when it exceeded 6 percent of gross domestic product (GDP), in part because of rapid growth of domestic demand. It fell to about 2 percent of GDP in 1978 because of a fall in domestic demand. It increased again in 1980 with the rise in oil prices, and it is projected at about 4 percent of GDP in 1981. Even making allowance for the existence of a systematic positive residual in the balance of payments of Austria that by now amounts to 1 to 2 percent of GDP, this deficit seems to me to be too large.

Of even more importance to the future of the Austrian economy is the effect of the decline of cost competitiveness on the growth of the industrial sector. Although percise data are not available, it seems that the rate of return in the industrial sector declined significantly during the 1970s, in particular during the period of rapid exchange rate appreciation. Although domestic costs did not rise rapidly except in 1975, they rose too rapidly given the marked appreciation of the exchange rate. Such a conclusion can be drawn, for example, from the comparison between the evolution of export unit values and unit labor costs in manufacturing shown in figure 3. As a result, investment in industry was weak during the 1970s. The authorities have instituted various programs aimed at promoting industrial investment by granting direct subsidies, tax advantages, or special financing facilities. Unfortunately most of the subsidies have been received by the declining and inefficient sectors, such as steel, textiles, and paper. As a result, most of the growth in the economy has come from the tertiary sector, as shown in figure 3. In particular, Austria's economy and balance of payments have come to depend more and more on German tourists.

No doubt the economic situation of Austria is not as bad as that of other countries, such as Belgium and Denmark, that have also pegged their exchange rates to the deutsche mark; but this is not much of a consolation. It is also doubtful that the period of grace given to Austria by the decline in value of the deutsche mark against other major currencies during the past two years will last very long. Already, by September 1981, the deutsche mark had regained some of its strength. What, then, should be done? Obviously, there are two solutions: one is to implement a different exchange rate policy, and the other is to achieve a lower rate of increase of costs of production.

We are told that a different exchange rate policy would be incon-

FIGURE 2

MAJOR DETERMINANTS OF THE BALANCE ON CURRENT ACCOUNT, 1971–1980

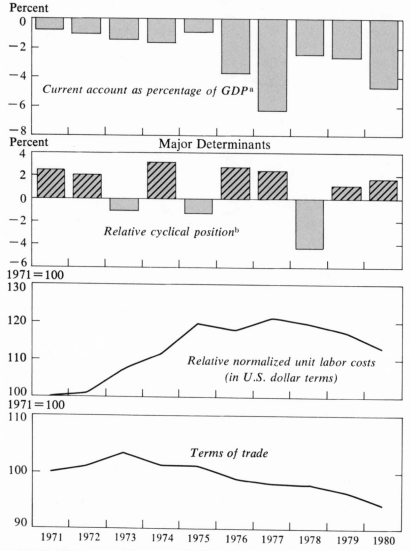

a. Unadjusted balance excluding errors and omissions.

b. The difference between the real growth rates for thirteen industrial countries and for Austria of total domestic demand, including stockbuilding, measured on a weighted basis. A minus figure indicates a relatively lower growth of domestic demand in Austria.

SOURCES: Austrian Institute for Economic Research, *Monatsberichte;* and International Monetary Fund, *International Financial Statistics.*

39

FIGURE 3

Distribution of Employment and Income, 1971–1980

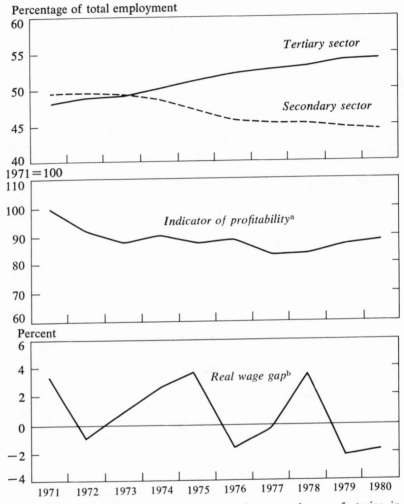

a. Ratio between export unit values and unit labor costs in manufacturing in Austria, in local currency.
b. Increase in real wages adjusted for change in productivity and in terms of trade.
Sources: Austrian Institute for Economic Research, and International Monetary Fund, *International Financial Statistics*.

sistent with Austrian incomes policy. If this means that it is not acceptable because it would lead to a lower increase or even a fall in the real wage rate, the argument must be rejected. Such a lower increase or fall is unavoidable if adjustment is to take place. To reject such an outcome is therefore equivalent to rejecting adjustment. This cannot be done forever. If the present exchange rate policy is to be continued, it has to be on the grounds that employees are more likely to accept a lower increase or a fall in their real wage rate for the sake of safeguarding the exchange rate between the Austrian schilling and the deutsche mark than for the sake of safeguarding the growth potential of the Austrian economy. That is possible, but not obvious.

If the exchange rate policy is to remain the same, the basic question remains: How can the Austrian economy regain some of its lost competitiveness? This can be done only if the rate of increase of costs of production in Austria falls below the rate of increase in Germany. This question raises the issue of the adequacy of the monetary and fiscal policies followed by the Austrian authorities. I will leave it to other participants in this conference to discuss this issue.

Macroeconomic Adjustment in Small Open Economies

Helmut Frisch

Introduction

This chapter examines stabilization policy in Austria for the decade 1970–1980. The analysis is based on the so-called Scandinavian model, with particular reference to its Austrian version. This model has not only played a prominent role in theoretical discussions, but has also strongly influenced the way Austrian policy makers have viewed the economic process of the period.

The first section explains the theoretical foundations of the Austrian stabilization policy. The second section examines the objectives and problems of the activist fiscal policy pursued in Austria, while the third section looks at the role of exchange rate policy and its relationship to the underlying Scandinavian model.

The Austrian Version of the Scandinavian Model

Austria, a small open economy, is connected with the world economy through its "exposed" sector. The exposed sector (E-sector) comprises export industries and those firms that produce for the domestic market but are open to international competition. This includes the greater part of manufacturing and large parts of the trade and services sector. On the other hand, construction, agriculture, and public services, as well as smaller parts of manufacturing and general services, belong to the "sheltered" sector (S-sector) of the economy. Roughly one-third of value added in Austria is produced in the E-sector and two-thirds in the S-sector.

To explain the rate of inflation in Austria, we use a "Phillips-curve-augmented" version of the Scandinavian model following the lines of work by Lars Calmfors, Helmut Frisch, and Assar Lindbeck.[1] The model departs from the original Scandinavian model by introducing a

Phillips relation into the E-sector of the economy.[2] The following six equations make up a generalized version of the Scandinavian model.

Direct international price dependency of the E-sector:

$$\dot{p}_E = \dot{p}_w \tag{1}$$

where the rate of inflation in the E-sector equals the world rate of inflation (prices measured in domestic currency).

Phillips curve:

$$\dot{w}_E = A\lambda_E - B\left(\frac{U - V}{N}\right) + C\dot{p}^*_E \tag{2}$$

where the rate of increase of nominal wages, $\dot{w}_E$, is explained by λ_E, the rate of increase of labor productivity in the E-sector; $(U - V)/N$, excess demand on the labor market, where V = the number of vacancies, U the number of persons unemployed, and N the number of persons employed; and $\dot{p}^*_E$, the rate of expected inflation in the E-sector.

Wage spillover hypothesis:

$$\dot{w}_E = \dot{w}_S \tag{3}$$

where the rate of wage increase in the exposed sector acts as a wage leader.

Markup pricing in the S-sector:

$$\dot{p}_S = \dot{w}_S - \lambda_S \tag{4}$$

where the rate of inflation in the S-sector is the difference between the rate of increase in nominal wages and the rate of increase in labor productivity, λ_S.

Definition of the rate of inflation:

$$\dot{p} = \alpha_S\,\dot{p}_S + \alpha_E\,\dot{p}_E\,;\alpha_S + \alpha_E = 1 \tag{5}$$

A solution of the system, equations (1) through (5), is the following reduced-form equation:

$$\dot{p} = (1 - \alpha_S)\,\dot{p}_w - \alpha_S B\left(\frac{U - V}{N}\right) + \alpha_S C\dot{p}^*_E + \alpha_S(A\,\lambda_E - \lambda_S) \tag{6}$$

This model is approximated by the following estimations in equations (7) through (11), showing empirical results for Austria for the period 1966 to 1979. (Ordinary least squares are used, and the numbers in parentheses are standard deviations of the coefficients.) The resulting reduced-form equation (12) is computed.

$$\dot{p}_E = \quad 0.926 + 0.434\ \dot{p}_w + 0.310\dot{p}_{w-1} \tag{7}$$
$$(0.883)\ (0.143)\qquad (0.142)$$
$$R^2 = 0.61 \qquad SE = 1.88 \qquad DW = 2.26$$

$$\dot{w}_E = \quad 7.803 + 0.385\ \dot{p}_E + 0.379\ \dot{p}_{E-1}$$
$$(1.825)\ (0.179)\qquad (0.179)$$
$$+0.197\lambda_{E-1} -2.89\ (\frac{U - V}{N}) \tag{8}$$
$$(0.212)\qquad (0.60)$$
$$R^2 = 0.83 \qquad SE = 1.62 \qquad DW = 1.57$$

$$\dot{p}_S = \quad 1.242 + 0.558\ (\dot{w}_S - \lambda_S) + 0.116\ (\dot{w}_S - \lambda_S)_{-1} \tag{9}$$
$$(1.051)\ (0.105)\qquad\qquad (0.112)$$
$$R^2 = 0.75 \qquad SE = 1.41 \qquad DW = 1.67$$

$$\dot{p} = \quad -0.149 + 0.350\ \dot{p}_E + 0.68\ \dot{p}_S \tag{10}$$
$$(0.102)\ (0.0014)\quad (0.016)$$
$$R^2 = 0.99 \qquad SE = 0.15 \qquad DW = 2.31$$

$$\dot{w}_S = \quad 2.731 + 0.465\ \dot{w}_E + 0.211\ \dot{w}_{E-1} \tag{11}$$
$$(1.241)\ (0.124)\qquad (0.121)$$
$$R^2 = 0.75 \qquad SE = 1.24 \qquad DW = 2.71$$

$$\dot{p} = \quad 4.91 + 0.437\ \dot{p}_w + 0.061\ \lambda_E - 0.458\ \lambda_S$$
$$- 0.895\ (\frac{U - V}{N}) \tag{12}$$

Equation (7) links inflation in the E-sector and the international rate of inflation $\dot{p}_W$ (a weighted average of the Austrian export and import price index) with a reasonably good fit. In the long run, with $\dot{p}_w = \dot{p}_{w-1}$, approximately 75 percent of the rate of inflation in the E-sector is explained by the exogenous change in world prices. Equation (8) is an estimated Phillips curve. According to the results, the rate of growth of money wages, $\dot{w}_E$, can be explained with two variables: demand pressure on the labor market and the expected rate of inflation. The demand pressure variable is highly significant: the coefficient is 2.9. It tells us that a difference of 1 percent between the rate of unemployment and the rate of vacancies will change the rate of increase of money wages by about 3 percent. The following are the actual values of the excess-demand variable $(U - V)/N$:

1971	1972	1973	1974	1975	1976	1977	1978	1979
−0.2	−0.5	−0.9	−0.6	0.8	0.9	0.7	1.1	0.9

In the boom phase (1973), excess demand contributed $2.9 \times 0.9 = 2.7$ percent to the increase in nominal wages; in 1979 it dampened the wage increase by the same amount. The inconveniently large constant in the

Phillips relation might be attributed to the construction of the excess-demand variable $(U - V)/N$, which is scattered around zero.

The expected rate of inflation is presumed to be generated by an adaptive expectations mechanism. For a steady-state situation, we can argue that the coefficient for the expected rate of inflation is 0.76, meaning that in a steady state 0.76 of the expected rate of inflation is reflected in the actual wage increase in the E-sector. The contribution of labor productivity is small and statistically not significant.

Equation (9) shows that it would be a mistake to reject in the S-sector the hypothesis that unit labor costs explain price developments. The sum of the coefficients is smaller than one, that is, 0.68. This implies that the profit share drops when unit labor costs rise in the S-sector. The constant term is statistically insignificant. The spillover equation (11) shows that in the long run about 67 percent of the growth of nominal wages in the S-sector can be explained by the wage increase in the E-sector, but there also exists an autonomous component of about 2.7 percent per year.

Equation (12) is a reduced-form equation computed from the estimated system. We will discuss equation (12) in the context of the following variables:

Average annual values of the exogenous variables (1965–1979)

$\dot{p}_w$	λ_E	λ_S	$\dfrac{U - V}{N}$
4.09	4.9	2.7	0.56

The contribution of the exogenous variables to the average annual rate of inflation, or rate of change in consumer prices (1965–1979)

Constant	$\dot{p}_w$	λ_E	λ_S	$\dfrac{U - V}{N}$
4.908	1.782	0.297	−1.236	−0.5

Predicted average annual rate of inflation ($\dot{\hat{p}}$) as compared with actual average change in consumer prices ($\dot{p}$), 1965–1979

$\dot{\hat{p}}$	$\dot{p}$
5.25	5.2

According to the preceding figures we offer the following explanation for the rate of inflation in Austria.

1. The direct influence of the international rate of inflation is expressed by the coefficient of transmission in equation (12) with 0.437.

FIGURE 1

TIME PATH OF THE EXCESS-DEMAND VARIABLE, 1966–1980

$(U-V)/N$

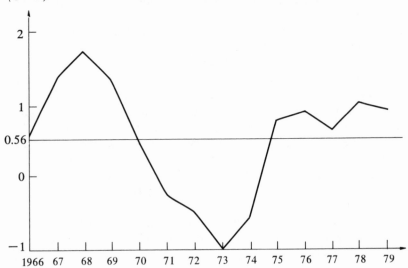

It can be seen that, for the period 1965–1979, an average 1.7 percentage points of the 5.2 percent inflation rate is explained by imported inflation.

2. The rate of growth of labor productivity in the E-sector, λ_E, influences the rate of inflation positively, whereas that of the S-sector has a considerable dampening influence (-1.23 percentage points) on the domestic rate of inflation. The development of labor productivity in both sectors is consistent with the a priori expected effect.

3. The overall demand component is approximated by demand pressure on the labor market, $(U - V)/N$. Figure 1 portrays the time path of the excess-demand variable and shows it to coincide with the business cycle. The variable is scattered between 1.7 percent (maximum) and 0.9 percent (minimum). Thus, it contributes to fluctuations of the domestic rate of inflation between -1.5 and 0.8 percentage points around a trend value determined by labor productivity and the world rate of inflation.

4. The Austrian situation is presented graphically in figure 2 for the two regimes, the periods 1966–1974 and 1975–1979. The line AU determines the inflation margin (the underlying rate of inflation of a small open economy) according to the Aukrust equation: $\dot{p} = \dot{p}_w + \alpha_S(\lambda_E - \lambda_S)$.[3] For Austria for the periods under observation this yields:

$$1966\text{–}1974 \quad \dot{p} = 4.53 + 2/3\,(5.21 - 3.39) = 5.74$$
$$1975\text{–}1979 \quad \dot{p} = 3.30 + 2/3\,(4.28 - 1.41) = 5.21$$

FIGURE 2
INFLATION RATE DETERMINANTS

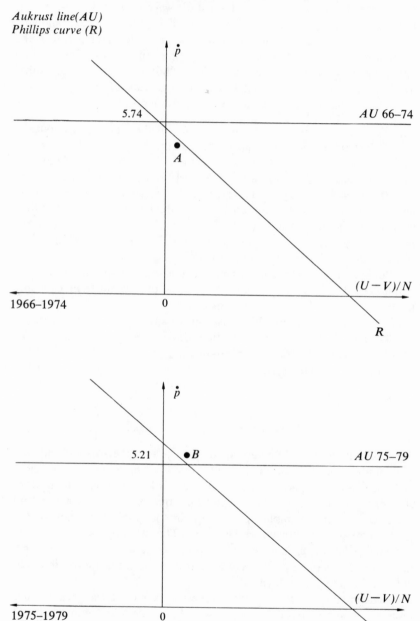

Aukrust line(AU)
Phillips curve (R)

A point on the Aukrust line (AU line) implies that prices and unit labor costs in the E-sector increase at the same constant rate and that the relationship between the profit share and the wage share remains constant. Furthermore, international competitiveness does not change. Combining the Aukrust equation AU and the Phillips relation R enables us to make the following interpretation of the intersection of the curves. The inflation margin is determined exogenously. The Phillips curve, on the other hand, shows the level of excess demand ($=$ rate of unemployment) which generates the required rate of an adjustment-inflation.

We can now consider the performance of the Austrian economy in the context of the Scandinavian model for the periods 1966–1974 and 1975–1979. In the period 1975–1979, the rate of domestic inflation lies above but near the inflation margin defined by the Aukrust line. Therefore the profit share in the E-sector tended to decrease in this period and, in addition, under fixed exchange rates the international competitiveness of the E-sector deteriorated. The rate of growth of money wages has overtaken the rate $\lambda_E + \dot{p}_E$. In the period 1966–1974, the domestic rate of inflation lay on the average below the inflation margin and near the Phillips curve. Thus, in this period the share of profit per unit of output and the international competitiveness of the Austrian economy increased.

The real sector of the Austrian economy benefited from the acceleration of international inflation during 1970–1974, as it was possible to reduce the rate of unemployment to a level below that of the previous period. The average value of $(U - V)/N$ was:

1966–1970	1.12
1971–1975	−0.28
1976–1979	0.9

An acceleration in world inflation, $\dot{p}_w$, shifted both the Aukrust equation (the inflation margin) and the Phillips curve upward. Since the coefficient of transmission, or 0.437 in equation (12), is less than one, the upward shift of the Phillips curve was smaller than that of the Aukrust line, and the new intersection implies a decrease in the rate of unemployment. The situation is portrayed in figure 3. The starting point is A, the crossing point of $\dot{p}_0$ and R_0. After an acceleration of international inflation, the economy will be at position B, with more imported inflation but less unemployment.

The inflationary transmission process in Austria in the period under discussion can be interpreted as follows. An acceleration of international inflation raises first the profit share in the E-sector and thus induces an increase in production and employment. In the labor market, excess

FIGURE 3

THE IMPACT OF AN ACCELERATION IN WORLD INFLATION

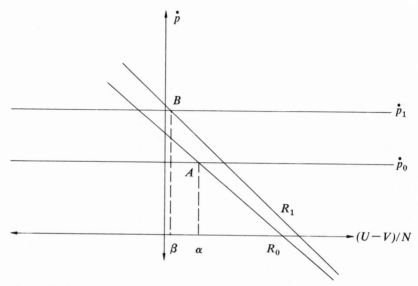

demand develops $(U - V)/N < 0$, whereby (through the Phillips relation) the rate of unemployment falls and money wages rise. A rise in
prices in the E-sector that is stronger than the rise in unit labor costs will
improve the current external account. A surplus in the balance of payments will lead to an increase in the monetary base, thereby increasing
the rate of money supply. On the other hand, if the rise in unit labor
costs overtakes the price rise in the E-sector, the current external account
will deteriorate. Under the condition of a neutral monetary policy,
aggregate demand will shrink and unemployment will develop on the
labor market.

Fiscal Policy

During the 1960s and 1970s, Austrian policy makers tried to conduct
an activist countercyclical fiscal policy according to which public households would withdraw purchasing power from the economy through
budgetary surpluses in the boom period. Given the experience in this
period, can Austrian fiscal policy be labeled "anticyclical"? This is a
rather important question since budget surpluses and deficits will, to a
certain extent, be generated automatically through the fluctuations of
economic activity, and these automatic or induced changes should be
distinguished from discretionary changes in fiscal policy. The actual

FIGURE 4
FULL EMPLOYMENT BUDGET, 1960–1981

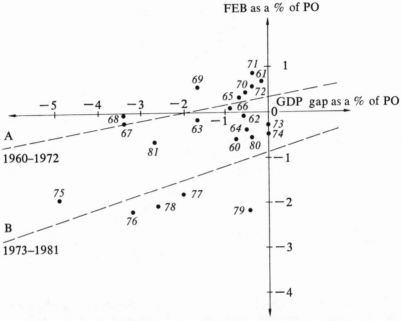

budget does not reveal to what extent the balance arose because of discretionary measures by the government or as an induced result of economic fluctuations. In order to evaluate the effects of the budget, we use the concept of the full employment budget (FEB). Actual expenditures are thereby compared with fictitious tax revenues at the level of full capacity utilization (full employment).[4] In figure 4 we plot on the abscissa the GDP gap, that is, the difference between actual output (gross domestic product) and potential output (PO), in percent of PO. On the ordinate we plot the FEB in percent of PO. The points scattered in this diagram can be explained by two regression lines, one indicating a more restrictive regime of fiscal policy (line A, period 1965–1972), the other a more expansive regime (line B, period 1973–1979).

In the subperiod 1970–1972, the GDP gap was less than 1 percent of the government-generated surpluses in the FEB. The policy was clearly countercyclical in the sense of dampening aggregate demand. Consider the subperiod 1973–1975. In 1973 and 1974 the economy remained in a strong expansionary position (the points lie exactly on the PO line). The fiscal stimulus, however, was procyclical because the FEBs are negative. In the recession year 1975 and following years (1976, 1977, 1978), with underutilization of capacity, the budget deficits exhibit unambiguously expansive effects although they could not entirely compensate for the strong economic downturn. In 1978 and 1980 economic activity recovered rapidly and actual output again approached PO. In these two years the federal budget was clearly procyclical. If we consider the last decade, fiscal policy was anticyclical seven times (1970, 1971, 1972, 1975, 1976, 1977, and 1978) and procyclical four times (1973, 1974, 1979, and 1980).

The expansive effect of the budget deficit is based upon the operation of the multipliers. The multiplier effect in an open economy is essentially characterized by two parameters: the marginal propensity to consume, c, and the marginal propensity to import, h. The multiplier has been estimated for 1975 (in nominal terms) under the assumption that $c = 0.88$, $h = 0.3$, and $t = 0.2$. The quantity t can be called the marginal tax rate. The multiplier is $1/[1 - c(1 - t) + h] = 1.67$.

Because the marginal propensity to import increased after 1975 to about $h = 0.6$, the multiplier declined to about 1.1 in 1980. An additional schilling spent and financed through a budget deficit creates only 1.1 schilling additional domestic income. Imports represent a leakage from the domestic spending stream and imply that a growing part of public expenditure flows abroad. Furthermore, the multiplier is a real rather than a nominal concept. Because of the high inflation rate of 1975 and 1976, the real effect of the multiplier was further dampened. One can say, therefore, that the multiplier lost its effectiveness with the transition of the 1975 recession to a period of recovery in 1976 and 1977. The reduction of the multiplier effect, insofar as it can be explained by the increased propensity to import, was aided by the Austrian hard currency policy as well as by the fact that in this period the most important trading partners of Austria developed a less activist countercyclical policy (for example, West Germany) or even aggravated the recession (for example, Switzerland).

The other side of the coin of the activist countercyclical fiscal policy is the growth of national debt. The financial debt of the Austrian federal government relative to gross national product (GNP) corresponds to the average of the OECD countries; it has, however, increased rapidly in recent years in the wake of deficit spending. Total national debt was about 11 percent of GNP in 1971–1972; it rose in 1980 to about 27 percent of GNP. The large increase in the deficit which occurred in 1975 was generally considered as necessary to offset the cyclical contraction of domestic demand and exports. Economic activity recovered rapidly in the following years without leading to a significant reduction in the budget deficit. There is, however, a shift in government priorities from unconditional support for fiscal demand toward an official goal of reducing the federal deficit to 2.5 percent of GNP (it amounted to 4.4 percent in 1975) in the medium run.

TABLE 1

FINANCIAL DEBT OF THE AUSTRIAN FEDERAL GOVERNMENT
(AS billion)

Year	Total	Domestic		Foreign		Total as Percent of GDP
		Amount	Percent of total	Amount	Percent of total	
1971	46.8	34.7	74	12.1	26	11.4
1972	49.9	39.6	79.3	10.3	20.7	10.6
1973	56.3	47.2	84.0	9.0	16.0	10.6
1974	61.4	47.9	77.9	13.5	22.1	10.0
1975	100.4	68.3	68.1	32.1	31.9	15.3
1976	133.8	98.8	73.9	35.0	26.1	18.5
1977	164.6	117.2	71.2	47.2	28.8	20.8
1978	199.2	139.1	69.9	60.0	30.1	23.8
1979	230.9	167.2	72.4	63.7	27.6	25.3
1980	261.4	189.6	72.2	71.8	27.8	26.7

SOURCE: OECD *Economic Surveys, Austria, 1981*, p. 28.

The actual practice of Austrian national debt policy consists of financing about one-quarter of the budget deficit by foreign credit and three-quarters on the domestic capital market. Table 1 shows that at the end of 1980 the total financial debt in Austrian schillings (AS) amounted to AS261.4 billion, with a domestic share of AS189.6 billion or 72 percent and a foreign share of AS72 billion or 28 percent. To resort to foreign capital markets means that, on the one hand, Austria is continuously exposed to international credit rating. Credit in foreign currency, on the other hand, supports the Austrian hard currency policy since it balances out the losses in international reserves resulting from the frequent external account deficits. In the long run, a high national debt has the unfortunate effect of reducing the possibilities for stabilization policy, although it was stabilization policy that created the national debt in the first place.

Exchange Rate Policy

Exchange rate policy has played a central role in Austrian stabilization policy. After the breakdown of the Bretton Woods system, the Austrian National Bank decided to pursue an index-oriented exchange rate policy. An export-weighted average of the "snake" currencies and the Swiss franc was used as a yardstick for exchange market interventions. From the middle of 1976 on, the schilling was de facto linked solely to

TABLE 2

DEVELOPMENT OF THE EFFECTIVE EXCHANGE RATE
OF THE AUSTRIAN SCHILLING
(1970 = 100)

Year	Effective Exchange Rate	Percent Change	Real Exchange Rate	Percent Change
1975	115.1	2.9	109.6	1.0
1976	119.5	3.8	113.1	3.1
1977	126.1	5.5	116.7	3.1
1978	127.2	0.9	115.5	−1.1
1979	128.9	1.3	113.1	−2.1
1980	132.7	2.9	112.5	−0.5

SOURCE: Austrian Institute for Economic Research.

the deutsche mark.[5] This linkage of the exchange rate to the deutsche mark has had considerable consequences. Since the deutsche mark floated continually upward during the period 1970–1977, this specific construction of a hard currency policy meant an effective appreciation of the schilling of about 26 percent (see table 2).

If the exchange rate appreciates exactly to the extent of the differential between the international rate of inflation, $\dot{p}^*$, and the domestic rate of inflation, $\dot{p}$, there are no real effects. In percentage rates we have $\dot{w} = \dot{p}^* - \dot{p}$, where $\dot{w}$ is the change in the exchange rate. If the rise in the effective (= nominal) exchange rate exceeds the inflation differential ($\dot{w} > \dot{p}^* - \dot{p}$), a real revaluation has taken place. If, on the other hand, the effective exchange rate increases, but increases less than the domestic rate of inflation falls short of the international rate ($\dot{w} < \dot{p}^* - \dot{p}$), there has been a real devaluation.[6]

Although the index of the effective exchange rate moved up during the period 1970–1979, there was a devaluation in real terms in 1978 and 1979. The appreciation of the effective exchange rate was smaller than the difference between the foreign rate of inflation and the domestic rate of inflation.

$\dot{w} =$ percent change in the effective exchange rate		$\dot{p}^* - \dot{p} =$ percent difference in the rates of inflation	
1978	0.9	1978	2.0
1979	1.3	1979	3.4
1980	2.9	1980	3.4

The objective of the Austrian hard currency policy—to keep the schilling in relatively stable relation to the strong currencies of its main trading partners and especially to the deutsche mark—seems to fit the stabilization policy of the Scandinavian model. H. Handler has collected the following arguments favoring the hard currency policy that might reflect the perceptions of Austrian policy makers.[7]

1. Pegging the schilling to the currency of an important trading partner with a higher degree of price stability than Austria will import stability.

2. A small open economy is a price taker in the world market. Prices in foreign currency are therefore assumed to be given. The hard currency policy therefore will squeeze profits in the E-sector and motivate firms to resist excessive wage claims by trade unions. This will reduce inflationary pressures in the whole economy.

3. The hard currency policy is likely to create a climate of monetary stability, thus breaking inflationary expectations and facilitating incomes policy.

4. The profit squeeze in the E-sector as a result of the appreciating schilling will change the production structure and induce entrepreneurs to raise productivity. This will in turn improve the long-run competitive position of the E-sector.

5. Empirical experience in other countries (the United Kingdom, Italy) shows that a weak currency policy, that is, a purposely downward floating of the exchange rate, very easily can become a vicious circle. Devaluation produces more inflation, inflation induces offsetting movements in money wages, the higher wage costs lead to further devaluations, etc.

6. From econometric estimations of price elasticities it cannot be expected that a devaluation of the schilling would significantly reduce the share of imports or increase exports.

The dominant argument for the hard currency policy seems to be based on the vicious circle hypothesis. Following an exogenous depreciation, the vicious economy will suffer a consecutive process of self-reinforcing inflation and depreciation. The process will end with a new equilibrium position where prices and exchange rates are higher than those in a nonvicious economy that has flexible prices and a controlled money supply. The avoidance of this vicious circle seems to be a prerequisite to implementing an incomes policy, one of the basic concepts of Austrian economic policy.

Notes

1. See L. Calmfors, "Inflation in Sweden," in L. B. Krause and W. S. Salant, eds., *Worldwide Inflation* (Washington, D.C.: The Brookings Institution, 1977), pp. 493-537; H. Frisch, "The Scandinavian Model of Inflation: A Generalization and Empirical Evidence," *Atlantic Economic Journal,* vol. 5 (December 1977); and A. Lindbeck, ed., *Inflation and Employment in Open Economies* (Amsterdam: North-Holland Publishing Co., 1979).

2. See O. Aukrust, "PRIM I: A Model of the Price and Income Distribution Mechanism of an Open Economy," *Artikler fra Statistik Sentralbyra,* vol. 35 (1970), and "Inflation in the Open Economy: The Norwegian Model," in Krause and Salant, eds., *Worldwide Inflation,* pp. 107-153.

3. The original Aukrust model is set out in the following six equations (the variables have the same meaning as in the text):

$$\dot{p}_E = \dot{p}_w \tag{1}$$

$$\dot{w}_E = \dot{p}_E + \lambda_E \tag{2}$$

$$\dot{w}_E = \dot{w}_S \tag{3}$$

$$\dot{p}_S = \dot{w}_S - \lambda_S \tag{4}$$

$$\dot{p} = \alpha_S \dot{p}_S + (1 - \alpha_S)\dot{p}_E \tag{5}$$

$$\dot{p} = \dot{p}_w + \alpha_S(\lambda_E - \lambda_S) \tag{6}$$

The difference between the original Aukrust model and the Austrian version of the Scandinavian model is shown in equation (2). While Aukrust uses the long-run assumption that the rate of change of money wages in the E-sector is explained by λ_E, the rate of increase in labor productivity, and $\dot{p}_w$, the world rate of inflation, a Phillips relationship is used in this paper to explain the rate of change of money wages.

The message of the Aukrust equation (6) is as follows: If the domestic rate of inflation develops according to equation (6) and implicitly wages increase according to equation (2), the international competitive situation of a small open economy will not deteriorate and the distribution of income between the profit share and the wage share in the E-sector remains constant. The Aukrust equation determines a quasi-equilibrium inflation margin.

4. See A. Guger, "Der Vollbeschäftigungssaldo als Instrument zur Beurteilung der konjunkturellen Wirkungen der Budgetpolitik des Bundes," *Wirtschaft und Gesellschaft,* vol. 4, no. 4 (1978).

5. See H. Kienzl, "Währungspolitik in Konjunktur und Krise," *Wirtschaft und Gesellschaft,* vol. 4, no. 2 (1978).

6. See H. Seidel, "Der effektive Wechselkurs des Schilling," *Monatsberichte* des Österreichischen Instituts für Wirtschaftsforschung, vol. 51 (August 1978), and H. Dorn, "Wechselkurspolitik ohne feste Spielregeln: Österreichs Hartwährungspolitik 1971-1979," *Wirtschaftspolitische Blätter,* vol. 26, no. 6 (1979).

7. See H. Handler, "The Exchange Rate as an Intermediate Target of Stabilization Policy in Austria," *Kredit und Kapital,* Supplement, no. 6 (1980), pp. 382-400, and Kienzl, "Währungspolitik in Konjunktur und Krise."

Commentary

Thomas D. Willett

We are indebted to Helmut Frisch for presenting very clearly the Austrian version of the Scandinavian model and for estimating it for the Austrian economy. It is apparent from the discussion that this type of model was the foundation for some of the thought about economic policy making in Austria over the past decade. It is thus important not only to deal with the theoretical model, but also to evaluate the empirical parameters, particularly as they relate to the hard currency option and to the larger question of the exchange rate regime. No single set of econometric estimates, however carefully undertaken, is likely to give us definitive answers, but Frisch's efforts are a useful beginning and certainly remind us to focus on the empirical aspects of the issues under discussion.

The basic thrust of my arguments will be that, contrary to the assumptions in Stephan Koren's paper and in several others as well, it does not seem at all clear that the hard currency policy is justified for the Austrian economy by the empirical evidence available so far. From the basic theory of optimum currency areas, it would be very difficult for us to know a priori whether Austria should follow a fixed-rate policy or not.

This approach stresses that the appropriateness of fixed exchange rates cannot be usefully debated in the abstract; it focuses on the factors influencing the choice of exchange rate regime for particular economies under particular circumstances.[1] It argues that large economies will typically be better candidates for flexible rates and small ones for fixed rates. It is fairly clear that countries like the United States and Germany fall into the large category and Liechtenstein into the small. The position of a country like Austria, however, is quite open to question.

For a large, relatively closed economy like the United States, exchange rate variations are an efficient instrument for balance-of-payments adjustments. As one moves to smaller, more open economies, the balance of advantages and disadvantages is altered. The cost of demand management as a method of correcting balance-of-payments disequilibrium tends to fall. Likewise, the effectiveness of exchange rate adjustments tends to fall because of the increased strength of the feedback effects on domestic wages and prices.

Examining the empirical evidence that Frisch has presented and bearing in mind certain criticisms that can be raised about that empirical work, we are left with an open question: has Austria moved so far from the advantages of exchange rate adjustments that a policy of quasi-permanent pegging to the deutsche mark is economically justified?

The basic idea of the Scandinavian model is that the small open economy is essentially driven by the international sector. Those who believe that this model has a great deal of empirical applicability also tend to argue for fixed exchange rates. I contend, however, that this argument does not necessarily follow, because one must distinguish between the role of exchange rates in insulating an economy from world developments and their role in promoting active adjustment. Even if the linkages were so strong between the international and the domestic sector that using exchange rates to alter the relative prices of traded and nontraded goods was only slightly effective, exchange rate adjustment still could offer protection from inflationary pressures in the world economy. The nominal exchange rate could be used to hold the real rate roughly constant, thereby neutralizing the effects of world inflation or deflation.

We know that exchange rates cannot perfectly insulate even a large closed economy like that of the United States. Moreover, in light of the many recent real structural changes, capital flows, and so forth, equilibrium real exchange rates move about, often considerably. But for an open economy these arguments do not necessarily undercut the usefulness of exchange rate flexibility. As we have seen from the numbers presented by Frisch and in Jacques Artus's figures, both nominal and real exchange rates for the schilling have fluctuated substantially over the past decade. World prices, as denominated in Austrian schillings, have been influenced not only by the world rate of inflation, but also very heavily by exchange rate movements.

With this insulation argument as a caveat, what do Frisch's estimates tell us about demand management versus exchange rate variability as instruments to correct balance-of-payments disequilibrium? First, we have estimates of a Phillips curve that indicate the cost of using demand management for balance of payments instead of domestic purposes. In evaluating the results we need to keep in mind the various possible problems, such as the formation of expectations and changes in policy regimes, that may generate unstable coefficients and other econometric

57

difficulties.[2] The Phillips curve coefficient suggests a trade-off of 1 percent unemployment for a little less than 1 percent inflation. This is somewhat contrary to the expectations one might obtain from optimum currency arguments that the smaller and more open the economy, the more favorable the short-run trade-off. Frisch's estimates place Austria approximately in the middle of major industrial countries. According to a recent survey of such estimates by Marian Bond,[3] we may conclude that Frisch's results place Austria below West Germany and France, where the trade-off is roughly a 2 percent price reduction for 1 percent more unemployment for a year. This is just slightly below estimates for Japan and Canada, which run just slightly over 1 percent, but higher than those for Sweden, the United States, and the United Kingdom.

What about the evidence of the effectiveness of exchange rate adjustments? In a tiny open economy there will of course be such strong feedbacks from the international sector that exchange rate changes will not be able to alter relative prices. This notion of strong feedbacks underlies the Scandinavian model. Frisch's estimates, however, suggest that there is a good deal of importance to the domestic sector as well.

Consider the effect of a change in world prices on domestic prices as given in equation (12). This is a somewhat long-run elasticity, measuring all of the feedbacks from the exchange rate to export prices, to wages in the export sector, to wages in the domestic sector, with all of this feeding back onto cost. Professor Frisch calculates a value of 0.437 for the whole price level, including the export sector. Calculating the effect on the price level in the domestic sector yields a value of 0.375. Thus, even in a markup price model that tends to assume passive monetary accommodation, some 60 percent of an exchange rate change is translated into a change in the relative price of traded and domestic goods. Though smaller than in the United States, the relative price effect is still considerable, suggesting a potentially important role for exchange rate adjustment in Austria.

Given this conclusion, we must ask whether trade elasticities are high enough to make devaluation effective. We have referred to opinions that trade elasticities may be too low. Although I do not know the evidence directly, the aforementioned study by Bond suggests that for Austria the average estimate for the sum of the elasticities for export and import demand is 2.25. This is well above the critical values necessary for devaluation to improve the trade balance and puts Austria in the upper range of country estimates. The results for Austria are virtually identical to those for Switzerland and somewhat higher than those for Canada, Germany, and Italy, all of which have a sum of approximately 2. This suggests that devaluation may be an effective instrument for Austria.

This result also suggests a caveat about Frisch's concern over the decline in the Keynesian budget multiplier caused by a substantial increase in the Austrian marginal propensity to import. Noting an increase in the share of imports in GNP substantial enough to raise the marginal propensity to import from 0.3 to 0.6 since 1975, he calculates a drop in the Keynesian multiplier from about 1.7 to about 1.1. I suspect that this overstates considerably the actual increase in the import propensity, because a fair proportion of that increase in imports is probably attributable to a price effect brought about by a loss of competitiveness.

In examining the empirical relationships, I have suggested that any work in this area is subject to many caveats. My guess is that the work of Frisch rather overstates the role of the international sector in determining domestic wages and prices. He has, to begin with, estimated only one model instead of comparing the statistical powers of several alternative models. Moreover, the model he estimates is based on the assumption that the major channels of causation run from the international to the domestic sectors. I suspect considerable multicollinearity among many of his variables. If one looked instead at some of the more traditional hypotheses, they would also provide some fairly good statistical results. Such comparisons should be made in order to come to grips with the extent to which the domestic sector may drive the international sector. It would be useful, for example, to examine the influence of expectations about domestic inflation in addition to the expectations about world inflation dealt with in Frisch's expectations-augmented Phillips curve. Similarly, in addition to showing linkages that run from export wages to domestic wages, as they do for Frisch, it would be useful to test for causality running the other way.

These considerations are of particular importance in the interpretation of one very counterintuitive result from the Scandinavian model—namely, the conclusion that a higher rate of productivity growth in the export sector raises the domestic rate of inflation. This result is due to the one-way causation going from export wages to domestic wages. It is not a very strong result; the estimated coefficient has the right sign for the Scandinavian model but is not statistically significant. This is an area requiring further research, particularly with regard to the possibility of two-way causation.

Let me conclude with a final point regarding the hard currency policy. It has been suggested several times that Austria needs to keep the exchange rate fixed because it will otherwise slide into a vicious circle. There is certainly validity to some of the concerns over vicious circles, but I think they often tend to be greatly overstated. We know that monetary validation is required to generate an ongoing vicious circle.[4] It is also possible that the unpegging of the exchange rate and subsequent depreciation can adversely affect expectations and thereby worsen short-run trade-offs between inflation and unemployment. Still, arguments that use the British and Italian experiences to suggest that letting go of the exchange rate leads into a vicious circle are severely misleading.

I am not even sure that these arguments are correct for those countries. I certainly think that the enviable record of price performance in Austria substantially reduces the dangers. The role of the social partnership in this connection is crucial. Moreover, it is not clear to me why the nominal exchange rate between Austria and Germany, as important as it is, should be the dominant force in that relationship as compared with overall trade-weighted exchange rates and real rates as well. Exchange rate adjustments are not costless, yet I do not believe that the evidence presented so far establishes a strong case for a pegged rate with the deutsche mark as an essential part of sound economic strategy for Austria.

Notes

1. See, for example, Edward Tower and Thomas D. Willett, *The Theory of Optimum Currency Areas and Exchange Rate Flexibility,* Princeton Special Papers in International Finance, 1976, and references cited there.

2. My suggestion is to try a few alternative specifications and alternative time periods and see how stable the results are. A policy regime may have been stable enough that one would find little coefficient instability. Work I have done recently suggests substantial instability in the estimates for the United States using standard open-economy, Phillips curve models. See Charles Pigott, John Rutledge, and Thomas D. Willett, "Some Difficulties in Estimating the Inflationary Effects of Exchange Rate Changes," in R. J. Sweeney and T. D. Willett, eds., *Studies on Exchange Rate Flexibility* (Washington, D.C.: American Enterprise Institute, forthcoming).

3. Marian E. Bond, "Exchange Rates, Inflation, and Vicious Circles," *IMF Staff Papers,* vol. 27 (December 1980), pp. 679-711.

4. I have discussed these questions at some length in my *Floating Exchange Rates and International Monetary Reform* (Washington, D.C.: American Enterprise Institute, 1977), pp. 57-67, and in T. D. Willett and M. Wolf, "Vicious Circle Hypotheses about the Macroeconomic Effects of Exchange Rate Movements: Some Conceptual Distinctions," in Sweeney and Willett, *Exchange Rate Flexibility.*

Austria's Economic Development after the Two World Wars: A Mirror Picture of the World Economy

Gottfried Haberler

Economic Prosperity after World War II

For Austria, as for the whole Western world, the thirty years after the end of World War II was a period of almost unprecedented growth and prosperity. In Austria the situation at the end of the war was grim or even desperate. In 1946, for which we have the first comprehensive statistical figures, GNP (gross national product) was less than two-thirds of the level of 1937, the last year of the first Austrian Republic, which was impoverished at that time by the depression and the disruptive economic pressures applied by Nazi Germany prior to the occupation in 1938. Physical destruction from air raids and ground fighting was extensive, and the eastern part of the country, industrially the most highly developed, came under Russian occupation. Russia laid claim to what was called "German property," comprising substantial parts of the industrial plant located in the Russian zone of occupation. But despite these handicaps, reconstruction began without delay. Immediate American economic aid, followed after 1947 by the Marshall Plan, was decisive.[1] In 1949 real GNP, the broadest measure of economic performance, exceeded the 1937 level, and a year later the 1929 level was surpassed.

Growth continued at a high rate until 1974, when Austria felt the world recession of 1973–1975. There was a short pause, and some difficulties have been experienced in the last two years. I shall later come back to this most recent period. But let me say at once that in my

This is a revised and expanded version of a talk given before the Austrian Society, Minneapolis, Minn., May 1979.

61

opinion these recent difficulties have been comparatively minor and do not change the judgment that the whole period, including the last two or three years, has been a period of great prosperity.

There has been much talk of the German and Japanese economic miracles. But there is also an Austrian economic miracle. The Austrians are aware of it. In self-mockery they often scoff at the German economic success. That is not a miracle, they say, because the Germans work so hard. The Austrian economic recovery is the real miracle. Actually, there is no such thing as a free lunch and no economic miracle without hard work and, we may add, without political stability and reasonably good policies—and Austria is no exception.

The upshot is that the Austrians never had it so good; their standard of living is higher than it ever was. Every conceivable symptom of affluence tells the same story. For example, in 1948 there were about 34,400 passenger cars on the roads (a little more than in 1937). In 1977 the number was 1,465,250. The figures for tractors are 11,700 in 1948 and 308,000 in 1977. Let me mention two figures from the financial area. When I visited Austria for the first time after the war in 1948, I could get 50 schillings for the dollar in the black market. Today there is no black market, and you get less than 14 schillings for the dollar. Starting from scratch, the Austrian National Bank has been able to accumulate an international reserve of gold (valued at the official rate) and foreign exchange of over $4 billion (January 1979), about the same as Belgium and more than Sweden.

Economic Development during the Interwar Period

The favorable economic—and political—development after World War II is in sharp contrast to what happened after World War I. Although the physical destruction of the First World War was much less severe than that of the Second, economic recovery was much slower and the whole interwar period of twenty years was a most unsatisfactory one from both the economic and the political point of view. There was first a short but very disruptive period of hyperinflation, from 1920 to 1922. Inflation was abruptly stopped in 1922 under the supervision and with the financial help of the League of Nations. The Austrian crown was replaced by the new schilling—14,000 old crowns for one schilling. (In Germany the hyperinflation went faster and further. When in 1923 the old mark was replaced by a new mark, the ratio of conversion was four *trillion* old marks for one new mark!)

After 1922 the Austrian economy adjusted to the new environment until it was hit by the Great Depression, which started in 1929 and engulfed the whole Western world, shaking it to its very foundation.

Let me first very briefly sketch the international background and then discuss the specific Austrian developments.

In the 1920s, after the short but severe so-called first postwar depression of 1920–1921, the U.S. and world economy recovered quickly. Currencies were stabilized and the gold standard was restored. Because the price level remained stable from 1921 to 1929, many economists spoke of a new era; the business cycle had finally been tamed if not conquered. The Great Depression, which started in the summer of 1929 in the United States, came as a rude awakening and as a great surprise, and was at first not recognized for what it was. It was a great disaster, not only economically but also politically. It gave a great boost to Soviet Russia, which proved to be immune to the depression. The catastrophic slump shook confidence in the viability of the free market, capitalist economic system. It is no exaggeration to say that Hitler probably would not have come to power and that the Second World War might have been avoided if Germany had not experienced over 30 percent unemployment.

In the United States the first phase of the Great Depression was followed by a lengthy cyclical expansion (1933–1937), but in mid-1937, long before full employment was reached, the United States was hit by another short but extremely vicious slump. The U.S. economy did not reach full employment before the outbreak of the Second World War in 1939, which was preceded by heavy armament spending.

Many other countries, including the Scandinavian countries, Australia, and Nazi Germany, recovered earlier and faster than the United States from the depression. But the world economy as a whole was still in poor shape in 1939.

So much for the international background. Now to the specific Austrian developments.

As mentioned earlier, the physical destruction of World War I was less severe than that of World War II. But there was the trauma of the dismemberment of the Austro-Hungarian empire. The new Austria, the German Austria (Deutsch-Österreich) as it was called, had been the center and Vienna the capital of the ancient, economically well-balanced Habsburg empire, one of the five major European powers. It was not easy to adjust from the status of a *Grossmacht* (major power) of 60 million inhabitants to that of a *Kleinstaat* (small state) of 6 million.[2]

The economic viability of the new state was widely questioned, and Vienna, a city of 2 million in a country of 6 million, was regarded as an economic liability. This led to a strong popular movement for joining Germany ("Anschluss") which was, however, opposed by the victorious powers, especially by France. A clause forbidding the Anschluss was inserted in the Austrian peace treaty of St. Germain.

The doubts concerning the economic viability of a small independent Austria proved to be unfounded. The country made good progress and by 1928 or so the pre-war standard of living was exceeded. Needless to add, the post–World War II experience conclusively demonstrates the economic and political viability of Austria. Vienna proved to be an economic asset and not a liability. I might mention in passing that during the whole interwar period, including the bad years immediately after the war and the depression years after 1929, Vienna was one of the world's leading intellectual centers. World-famous schools, Freud's psychoanalysis, Carnap-Schlick's logical positivism, the Austrian School of Economics, centered on the famous private seminar of Ludwig von Mises, and Hans Kelsen's "Reine Rechtslehre" (Pure Theory of Law), flourished and spread around the world. Vienna was the home of two of the world's most famous twentieth century analytical philosophers, Karl Popper and Ludwig Wittgenstein, of the famous critic, satirist, and poet Karl Kraus and of the great philosophical synthesizer Felix Kaufmann, whose work bridged the gap between phenomenology and logical positivism and covered the methodology of mathematics and the natural sciences on the one hand and that of the social sciences on the other.[3]

But the economic situation deteriorated rapidly after the onset of the Great Depression in 1929. In 1931 Austria and Germany proposed a customs union. France objected violently on the ground that a customs union would jeopardize Austria's political independence and thus violate the peace treaty. French financial pressures on Austria and Germany forced the two countries to abandon their plan of a customs union. Moreover, withdrawals of French credits triggered the collapse of Austria's largest bank, the Credit Anstalt, which was already in a badly overextended condition. The breakdown of the Credit Anstalt, in turn, started a chain reaction of financial crises, the breakdown of the German and Italian banking systems, and in September of the crisis year 1931 Britain was forced to take the historic step of abandoning the gold standard and letting the pound depreciate. The Austrian schilling was devalued in 1932, with beneficial effects on trade and on the general economic position. But these initial benefits were progressively eroded when in the next few years many countries devalued their currencies, Czechoslovakia, Belgium, France, Italy, and the United States among them. In 1936 Switzerland devalued the franc. Austria should have grasped this opportunity to devalue again in good company, but did not dare for political reasons.

In the meantime Hitler had come to power and Nazi Germany exerted increasing political and economic pressures on Austria. Thus in 1935 a heavy blow was struck at the important Austrian tourist industry by the imposition of a tax of 1,000 marks on each German tourist going to Austria.

I will now discuss briefly the political developments. In this area, too, there is a sharp contrast between the post-World War II years and the interwar period.

Political Developments

The whole interwar period was marked by a sharp antagonism between the two major parties: the conservative Christian-Social, Catholic party on the right and the Social Democrats on the left. There was a small third, at first mildly German-nationalist, anti-clerical party which later became the nucleus of the rising national-socialist (Nazi) movement. The poisoning antagonism of the two leading parties led to violent clashes. Each party built up its own paramilitary forces. Both parties were anti-Nazi. But when the Nazi movement in Austria became strong after Hitler's takeover in Germany, the anti-Nazi forces failed to unite. Early in 1934 an impasse developed in parliament and the government of Chancellor Dollfuss crushed the socialist opposition by force. Many socialist leaders went into exile in Czechoslovakia and France. Later in 1934 Dollfuss was murdered in an attempted Nazi coup d'état. The putsch did not succeed, because Hitler was not yet ready to intervene openly and Mussolini backed up the authoritarian Austrian regime. Dollfuss's successor, Dr. Kurt Schuschnigg, carried on the struggle for Austrian independence. The economic and political situation deteriorated. In 1938, after Mussolini became engaged in the Abyssinian conquest, he withdrew his support of Austria and allied himself with Hitler. Schuschnigg was forced to capitulate. This was the end of the first Austrian republic.

After World War II the political development was entirely different. The Austrians had learned their lesson. With Russian occupation of the eastern part of the country and Communist regimes established north, east, and south, Austria could not afford the luxury of internal strife. The two main parties of the interwar period, the Christian-Social party (renamed the Austrian People's party) and the Socialist party, reconstituted themselves, and a democratic two-party system has functioned smoothly and efficiently since 1945.

After the death of Stalin in March 1953 Russian policy became more conciliatory, and in May 1955 a "State Treaty" (not a peace treaty, because Austria was not considered to have participated in the war) was signed in Vienna, terminating the four-power occupation and establishing Austrian sovereignty and permanent neutrality.

The Austrian contrast of political stability and peace after 1945, and instability, civil strife, and violence in the interwar period mirrors a similar improvement in Western Europe at large. The rapprochement and friendship between France and Germany is the most important and conspicuous manifestation of the changed atmosphere. Active American participation in world affairs after World War II, in contrast to withdrawal into isolation after World War I, surely was a decisive contributing factor. Unwittingly and unintentionally, Soviet Russia, too, contributed to Western European cooperation and harmony by aggressive moves and intermittent saber rattlings, often at critical points. External threats helped to speed up the movement toward European integration.

Economic Success 1945-1973—Economic Failure 1919-1939

Why was the performance of the Austrian economy after World War II so enormously better than after World War I? Specific Austrian reasons are maintenance of political stability, absence of civil strife, and avoidance of serious policy mistakes that were made in the 1930s—such as severe monetary deflation and the refusal to devalue a clearly overvalued schilling, which caused heavy unemployment.[4] That American aid was massive and of paramount importance has already been mentioned.

However, even the best policies during the interwar period could not have completely offset the adverse impact on Austria of the great world depression or prevented Hitler's takeover. Therefore, the really important questions are, *first,* why in the United States and in the Western world at large the economic performance was so much better in the thirty years after World War II than in the twenty years of the interwar period, and, *second,* whether the period of prosperity has not come to an end. Have we not paid too high a price in terms of inflation for rapid growth? Was the vaunted prosperity not merely an inflationary bubble that is just about to burst with disastrous consequences? There are quite a few people, some economists among them, who give an affirmative answer to the second question. Some speak of a new crisis of capitalism, others of a new severe depression or a Kondratieff downswing.

With the benefit of hindsight, a straightforward answer can be given to the first question: The period of 1945–1973 was so much more successful economically than the period of 1919–1939 because deflation was avoided. To put it differently, the depression of the 1930s became so bad because of gross monetary mismanagement on the national and international level. In the United States in the early 1930s the Federal Reserve, through acts of commission and omission, permitted the quantity of money to contract by about 30 percent. Just consider what that means. Today, economists are scared stiff when the money supply fails to rise for a few months by the targeted amount; then, in the early 1930s, it was allowed to shrink by a third over a protracted period.

Equally severe deflation occurred in other countries, notably in Germany. The British economy was already depressed in the 1920s because the government had committed the capital mistake of returning after the war to the gold standard at the prewar parity of $4.86 to the pound. Immediately after the war the pound had depreciated by about 20 percent and was gradually pushed up to the prewar level, thus putting the economy under deflationary pressure.[5]

Internationally, deflation was propagated from country to country by countries that independently depreciated their currencies in a beggar-thy-neighbor fashion—the British pound in 1931, the U.S. dollar in 1933–1934, the French and Swiss franc in 1936, and so on. Each devaluation alleviated the depression in the depreciating country, but inflicted deflationary shocks on other countries, which then tried to protect themselves by import restrictions. These horrendous mistakes were avoided in the post-1945 period under the aegis of the International Monetary Fund (IMF) and the General Agreement on Tariffs and Trade (GATT).

This is what has become known as the monetarist interpretation of what went wrong in the 1930s.[6] Is there a Keynesian alternative?

Austro-Keynesianism or Austro-Monetarism. In Austria, as in the United States, Britain, and other countries, the superior performance of the economy in the post–World War II period in comparison with the interwar period has been attributed to the application of a Keynesian policy and does not fit into the monetarist scenario. The same is supposed to be true of the rapid recovery of the Austrian economy after Hitler's takeover of Austria in April 1938.

I cite two examples: In his important book, quoted above, Felix Butschek argues that the explosive economic development of Austria (after the Nazi takeover) in the last three quarters of 1938 and first three quarters of 1939, which expressed itself in a real GNP growth of 12.8 percent and 13.3 percent (annual rate), respectively, can be regarded as a confirmation of the efficacy of the Keynesian policy prescription, but "lends no support to the monetarist explanation."[7]

Werner Neudeck, in a paper entitled "Mises and the Austrian Academic Tradition," speaks of the "triumph of Keynesianism in Austria" that started with the Nazi takeover in 1938.[8]

It is, however, possible to give a convincing monetarist explanation of the Austrian development. First, monetarists are right to give a monetary explanation of the exceptional severity of the Great Depression of the 1930s. It was monetary deflation that "turned a retreat into a rout," to use Schumpeter's colorful phrase; in other words, it turned what might have been a severe cyclical recession into a disastrous depression. As we have seen in the United States, the Federal Reserve, by acts of commission and omission, permitted the quantity of money to shrink by 30 percent. Under fixed exchange rates (the gold standard) the U.S. depression was bound to spread to the rest of the world, including Austria. Several countries, Australia and the Scandinavian countries among them, managed by monetary expansion and devaluation of their currencies to extricate themselves from the deflationary spiral long before the U.S. economy turned upward again, but Austria clung to a grossly overvalued schilling to the end of the first republic, in 1938.

Second, it is true that the enormous economic success of the Hitler regime can be called a triumph of Keynesianism because government deficit spending was an essential ingredient.[9] Monetarists, too, however, recommend government deficit spending in a deep depression with mass unemployment, because it is better to inject money directly into the income stream through government deficit spending than to rely entirely on monetary policy. In a deflationary milieu when people expect prices to decline further, even a zero nominal interest rate may take a long time and require a large monetary expansion to turn the economy around. Thus a large pool of liquidity would be created, which would in turn create inflationary pressure in the subsequent upswing.

Keynesians and monetarists can agree on how to get out of a deep depression, but the monetarists would point out that without previous gross monetary mismanagement there would not have been a deep depression at all.

Third, in 1952 Austria went through a short but relatively severe recession, which can be characterized as a painful but healthy stabilization crisis. The following figures quoted by Koren[10] show the rapidity and magnitude of the change. From 1949 to 1950 the wholesale price index jumped by 32.5 percent and the consumer price index by 18 percent. From 1950 to 1951 the increases were 34.3 percent and 27 percent, respectively. A sharp reduction of American aid forced the Austrian government to take strong measures to stop inflation. Bank credit was sharply restricted, and the discount rate was raised from 3.5 percent to 6 percent. Monetary restraint was supported by fiscal measures to cut the budget deficit. Public expenditures were reduced, taxes were increased, and the prices of public services (railroad fares, postal rates, and so forth) were raised. An essential feature of the stabilization policy was a devaluation of the schilling brought about by abolishing the system of multiple exchange rates. All this fits the monetarist scenario.

Koren calls the success of the stabilization amazing. From 1951 to 1952 the inflation rate, as measured by the two indexes, dropped to 11.1 percent and 18 percent, respectively. From 1952 to 1953 wholesale prices declined by 5.6 percent and consumer prices declined by 5.4 percent. "True, in 1952 the growth of industrial production came to a halt and employment even declined by 3 percent." In 1953 an astonishingly vigorous upswing of economic activity started.[11] Unsurprisingly, the upswing brought about an increase of 4.5 percent in wholesale prices and 3.7 percent in consumer prices, but inflation did not get out of hand.

All this fits well into a monetarist framework and shows that what Keynes called the "classical medicine" still worked wonders. It must be stressed, however, that unlike the Federal Reserve and the German Bundesbank, the Austrian National Bank does *not* pursue a policy of setting money growth targets. Such a policy would be inconsistent, as we shall see, with the exchange rate policy that keeps the schilling pegged to the German mark.

The World Economic Malaise of the 1970s and 1980s: The End of the Keynesian Era?

Before describing the development of the Austrian economy since the stabilization crisis or recession of 1952–1953, the world economic background, with special reference to the U.S. economy, must be sketched briefly.

The 1950s and 1960s were the heyday of Keynesianism. They also saw rapid growth and moderate inflation, though the price trend was unmistakably upward. Many economists thought the business cycle had been banished, or at least tamed, to a tolerable level by skillful "demand management" and "fine tuning," (that is to say, by manipulating government expenditures and taxes to offset fluctuation in the private economy).

It did not work out that way. Rising inflation and the severe recession of 1973–1975 caused a change from euphoria and optimism to various shades of gloom and pessimism. The business cycle, declared dead several times before, is very much alive.

Many economists and policy makers regard the first oil shock, the quadrupling of crude oil prices in 1973, as the cause of the change in outlook. Actually, the oil shock was preceded by a highly inflationary commodity boom, which was superimposed on an inflationary groundswell. In the United States the 1973–1975 recession was the sixth in

69

the postwar period. Each successive upswing of the business cycle started from a higher level of inflation, though it is still true that during recessions the rate of inflation declines. Thus in the 1973–1975 recession, the U.S. inflation rate was 12½ percent in 1974, and it was brought under 5 percent in 1976. Inflation rose again, however, and reached the two-digit level late in 1978. It remained there despite the short recession of 1980. It then came down in the eighth postwar recession, which began in July 1981.

The current recession is severe and comparable to the 1973–1975 recession. Moreover, all postwar recessions have been inflationary in the sense that the price level has increased, although at a decreasing rate, whereas in earlier (classical) recessions prices used to decline. In other words, inflation has taken the nasty form of stagflation, the combination of inflation and high or even rising unemployment. It must be stressed that the current decline in economic activity is still a recession, not a real depression. (By depression we mean a slump like that of the Great Depression of the 1930s or earlier ones.) In the 1930s unemployment rose to 25 percent; in the current recession it rose to 10 percent.[12]

In the United States inflation has sharply declined in the current recession. During the first quarter of 1982 the consumer price index was practically flat. But this may be a temporary lull. The so-called underlying or core inflation, as measured by the rise in the level of nominal wages or unit labor costs, is still unacceptably high.

The 1981–1982 recession and the preceding wave of high inflation were truly international in scope. Even Germany and Switzerland experienced inflation of 6.6 percent and 8 percent, respectively, which is high by their standards; in Germany unemployment reached 8 percent in January and February 1982. The international character of the current recession is highlighted by the fact that in 1981 the value of world merchandise trade declined for the first time since 1958—by 1 percent from 1980. This decline was preceded in 1980 by a 20 percent increase over 1979.[13]

There was much turmoil in the foreign exchange markets. The dollar slumped badly until October 1979, when the Federal Reserve, under the new chairman, Paul Volcker, dramatically reversed operating procedure and tightened monetary policy. Since then the dollar has strengthened, having been buoyed by record high interest rates in the United States and the expectation that the Reagan administration would push the fight against inflation. The dollar reached its high point in August 1981 and has declined somewhat since then. Record large budget deficits have kept interest rates high even in the recession and have cast some doubts on the future.

The Austrian Economy since 1952

How does the Austrian economy fit into this global scenario?

We have seen that it recovered quickly from the stabilization crisis of 1952. Since then—especially after the signing of the State Treaty in 1955, which lifted the four-power occupation—the performance of the Austrian economy (as measured by the growth rate of real GNP, inflation, and unemployment) has been one of the best in the entire OECD area.

Austria did not escape the world recession of 1973–1975, but the recession was much milder there than in the United States and most other industrial countries. The growth of real GNP declined, but in only one year, 1975, was it slightly negative. As in the United States and elsewhere, the recession was preceded by rising inflation. As in the United States, inflation in Austria reached its peak in 1974 (9.5 percent for consumer prices), but declined in the following years and never reached two digits. Unemployment rose slightly—from 1.5 percent in 1974 to 2 percent in 1975.[14]

The recession of 1981–1982 had a stronger impact. It caused a decline in real GNP growth to 0.1 percent in 1981, but unemployment increased to its highest level so far, 5.4 percent in January 1982 and 5.1 percent in February. Throughout Austria's postwar period unemployment has been very low by U.S. or even German standards—well below 3 percent most of the time until the end of 1981.

This is a remarkable performance, all the more so because the Austrian schilling has since 1973 been pegged de facto to the high-flying German mark, which implied a sharp appreciation of the schilling against the dollar up until 1980 and the many currencies that are pegged to the dollar.

How was that possible? I start with a discussion of the exchange rate policy.

For a small country like Austria with a population conscious of the inflation rate and exchange rate, it is desirable to have a confidence-inspiring anchor for the currency. The currency of Germany, Austria's most important trade partner by far, emerged as the obvious choice.

Since the mark appreciated against the dollar, the schilling, too, had to appreciate against it along with the many other currencies pegged to it. Thus in 1972 the rate was 23.12 schillings per dollar. In 1980 it was 12.94, and since then it has fluctuated between 15 and 17. The schilling has become a very hard currency, along with the mark, yen, and Swiss franc.

71

The hard currency policy was an essential ingredient of the anti-inflationary policy. It will be recalled that in Austria, as in the United States and elsewhere, inflation reached a high point (9.5 percent) in 1974. Pegging to the mark required that the Austrian inflation rate parallel that of Germany. Appreciation against the dollar helped to reduce the Austrian inflation, because the schilling price of many imports was reduced. Following the first oil shock, for example, the crude oil price in dollars remained stable for a few years and declined in schillings.

The hard currency policy in a broad sense has achieved its purpose. The inflation rate has been sharply reduced since 1974, to approximately the German level. The low point was 3.6 percent in 1978 and 1979. Since then, partly because of the oil shock, it has gone up again, as it has in Germany, to about 6.5 percent. Switzerland is the only country that for several years had practically zero inflation, but since 1979 Swiss prices have risen.

There remain several important questions: What are the implications of the hard currency policy of disinflation for monetary policy, for growth, and for employment?

The success of the hard currency policy of disinflation required a sufficiently tight monetary policy. Thus restrictions were placed on bank lending. A comparison of the Austrian approach with that of Germany and Switzerland is instructive: the Bundesbank and Swiss National Bank set money growth targets and let the exchange rate adjust; but Austria, for good reasons, set the exchange rate and adjusted monetary policy. As mentioned earlier, this does not mean that Austria followed Keynesian rather than monetarist prescription. Essentially the Bundesbank provides the monetarist basis for Austrian policy.

In regard to growth, the hard currency policy of disinflation has inevitably led to a slowdown. The rate of growth of real GNP, which sharply increased immediately after the recession—to over 6 percent in the second half of 1976 and to over 5 percent in the first half of 1977—declined to about 2 percent in the second half of 1977 and to 0.4 percent in 1978.

We have seen that unemployment has remained remarkably low, even in years of declining GNP growth. How was that possible?

In Austria full employment has been a prime objective. Many measures have been employed to create and preserve jobs. Austria's large public sector provides plenty of opportunities to maintain the work force in slack periods at the expense of the public treasury. Foreign investments in Austria have been subsidized by generous tax breaks. Some protectionist measures have been applied in the form of selective imposition of value-added taxes on imports.

A major factor in holding down labor cost of output and in preserving jobs has been the restraint and moderation of the labor unions. This is often referred to as "incomes policy" and "social partnership." The broad lines of wage policy are set by a tripartite commission composed of representatives of employers, employees, and the government. Thus the growth of union and other wage rates has sharply declined from the high rates of the inflationary period. The index of "the workers' net wage in collective agreements," which in 1975 rose by 19.1 percent, has declined to an average rise of 6.7 percent in 1978. The monthly earnings of all employees in industries exhibited a decline in annual growth from 15.9 percent in 1975 to 7.6 percent in 1977 and a further drop in the first ten months of 1978.[15]

To repeat, the overall performance of the Austrian economy has been excellent. There is, however, a dark cloud in the otherwise clear sky—large budget deficits and large current account deficits financed mainly by public sector borrowing abroad have rapidly grown in recent years. The budget deficits grew from schilling 1.7 billion and 1.4 billion in 1971 and 1972 to around schilling 30 billion in each year since 1975. That is from less than 1 percent to 3 or 4.5 percent of GDP. The current account deficit was $35 billion in 1977, $9 billion in 1978, $14 billion in 1979, $21 billion in 1980, and $22 billion in 1981. Also, according to recent reports, Austria has accumulated claims on Eastern bloc countries of about $6 billion. These claims are the result of financing exports to Eastern European countries to create or preserve jobs in the export industries. If jobs have to be created by investing public funds, it would be better to invest in Austria instead of accumulating claims on Eastern bloc countries.[16]

This obviously cannot go on indefinitely. The current account deficit, which recently has been running at about 4 percent of GDP, must be eliminated or at least sharply reduced. The problem is manageable, but requires some belt tightening. This means that, since exports have to be increased and/or imports reduced, small temporary reductions in domestic consumption or investment will be unavoidable because it is unlikely that output can quickly be increased sufficiently.

Given the successful experience of Austria with its postwar economy, one would expect that a prudent solution to this problem will be found—a solution that will reestablish equilibrium and place the country, once again, on a sustainable growth path.

Notes

1. Stephan Koren, in an authoritative study, describes the desperate situation of the Austrian economy at the end of the war: "Only thanks to American economic aid was it possible to extricate the economy quickly and efficiently

from this desperate situation. The necessary resources for the development of electric power and basic industries could be obtained from counterpart funds of American supplies. Without this source of capital, the reconstruction and expansion of the heavy industry would not have been possible." Stephan Koren, "Die Industrialisierung Österreichs—Vom Protektionismus zur Integration," in Wilhelm Weber, ed., Österreichs Wirtschaftsstruktur: Gestern-heute-morgen (Berlin, 1961), pp. 248-49.

2. On the economic and political problems of the transition, see the excellent study by K. W. Rothschild, "Wurzeln und Triebkräfte der Entwicklung der Österreichischen Wirtschaftsstruktur," in Weber, Österreichs Wirtschaftsstruktur, pp. 51-75.

3. On Karl Kraus and his influence on Wittgenstein, see Allan Janik and Stephen Toulmin, Wittgenstein's Vienna (New York: Simon and Schuster, 1973). On Mises's private seminars, see "Ludwig von Mises—Seine Ideen und Seine Wirkung," Wirtschaftspolitische Blätter (1981).

4. In 1937 the unemployment rate in Austria was 21.7 percent. See Felix Butschek, Die Österreichische Wirtschaft 1938 bis 1945, Institut für Wirtschaftsforschung, Stuttgart, 1978, p. 115.

In his important study Butschek mentions another factor that contributed to rapid growth in the postwar period—namely, the heavy investment in industrial plant and equipment that was made after the Nazi takeover in 1938 and 1939. During the war Austria became a sort of air raid shelter for German industry because Austria was less exposed to Allied bombing raids than Germany. In the last phase of the war, however, the comparative immunity from bombing disappeared. After the war some of the German-built works, especially in steel and aluminum, could be restored to full production with American aid. This constituted a significant addition to the Austrian capital stock. I doubt, however, that it could have offset more than a small fraction of the overall loss of capital caused by bombing, ground fighting, Russian takeover of German property, and failure during the war to maintain intact the capital stock of industries not essential for the war effort.

5. In his famous pamphlet The Economic Consequences of Mr. Churchill (London, 1925, republished in Essays in Persuasion, several editions), Keynes had correctly predicted the depressive consequences of the revaluation for which Winston Churchill was responsible as Chancellor of the Exchequer. The full story of the British return to gold in 1925 has been told only recently after hitherto secret official papers have become available. See D. E. Moggridge, British Monetary Policy, 1924-1931: The Norman Conquest of $4.86 (Cambridge, 1972). The subtitle is an allusion to Montague Norman, the powerful governor of the Bank of England, who was to a large extent responsible for the return to gold at the prewar parity of $4.86. The new material tends to exonerate Churchill. In a remarkable "most secret" memorandum addressed to his advisers before the decision to return to gold at the old parity was made, Churchill had asked all the relevant questions, but he received wrong or misleading answers from his advisers.

6. See the "truly great book" (Sir Roy Harrod's words) A Monetary History of the United States 1867-1960, by Milton Friedman and Anna Jacobson Schwartz, (Princeton, N.J., 1963), especially the "magnificent" (Harry G. Johnson's word) chapter 7, "The Great Contraction 1929-33," available separately as a paperback. See also Gottfried Haberler, The World Economy, Money, and the Great Depression, 1919-1939, American Enterprise Institute (Washington, D.C., 1976), and Gottfried Haberler, "The Great Depression of the 1930s: Can It Happen Again?" in The Business Cycle and Public Policy, 1920-80, A Compendium of Papers Submitted to the Joint Economic Committee, Congress of the United States, November 28, 1980, available as American Enterprise Institute Reprint No. 118, Washington, D.C., 1980. It is interesting that Schumpeter, who was not a

monetarist, attributes the exceptional severity of the depression to the deflation caused by the collapse of the U.S. banking system in the early 1930s. "It spread paralysis" through the whole economy and "turned retreat into rout." See *Essays of J. A. Schumpeter,* edited by Richard Y. Clemence, Addison-Wesley Press (Cambridge, Mass., 1951), p. 214.

7. Felix Butschek, *Die Österreichische,* "Theoretical Epilogue," pp. 114-20.

8. "Ludwig von Mises—Seine Ideen und Seine Wirkung," *Wirtschaftspolitische Blätter* (Vienna, 1981). The author makes reference to the Austrian literature.

9. For a more detailed analysis of a comparison of the Nazi economic policy with the contemporaneous New Deal policy under Roosevelt, see Haberler, *The World Economy, Money, and the Great Depression,* p. 13. German translation in *Währung und Wirtschaft in Deutschland 1876-1975,* published by the Deutsche Bundesbank (Frankfurt, 1975).

10. See Koren, "Die Industrialisierung Österreichs."

11. Ibid.

12. Moreover, unemployment today in the 1970s and 1980s is different from unemployment in the 1930s. Generous unemployment and welfare benefits not only have sharply reduced the distress of joblessness for the individual worker, but also have created spurious, voluntary unemployment. The recorded unemployment figures contain an unknown but sizable number of people who prefer to be unemployed temporarily. Furthermore, a large part of the unemployment is "structural," not "Keynesian," that is to say, not due to a deficiency of aggregate demand and not curable by Keynesian policies. In the United States, for example, the shockingly high unemployment among black teenagers (close to 40 percent!) is largely due to minimum wage laws and cannot be eliminated by pumping up the economy through monetary expansion. Thus 10 percent unemployment now should be compared with, say, 30 percent in the 1930s.

13. See "International Trade in 1981 and Present Prospects: First Assessment by the GATT Secretariat," *General Agreement on Tariffs and Trade, GATT* (Geneva, 1982). It might be mentioned that in the Great Depression of the 1930s the value of world trade declined by about two-thirds while volume fell by about one-third, the difference reflecting the catastrophic decline of the price level (deflation).

14. Professor K. W. Rothschild believes that the official figures somewhat understate the increase in "genuine" unemployment in the recession. His tentative estimate is that if two corrections are made (one for the departure of foreign workers and the other for different statistical treatment of certain groups of retired people), the "true" unemployment rate for 1975 is raised from 2 percent to 3.2 percent. This correction leaves the Austrian unemployment rate still substantially lower than in all other industrial countries, with the exception of Norway, Sweden, and Switzerland. See K. W. Rothschild, "Zyklisches Verhalten und Niveau der Österreichischen Arbeitslosigkeit: Zwei hypothetische Betrachtungen," in *Zeitschrift für Nationalökonomie,* vol. 37, no. 1-2, 1977, pp. 183-96. Switzerland is a special case because of the large decrease in the number of foreign workers.

15. "Index der Arbeitsnettotariflöhne." See monthly *Bulletin of the Austrian National Bank,* January 1979, p. 59.

16. One is reminded of two statements by Keynes. Years ago Keynes wrote: "To lend vast sums abroad for long periods of time without any redress, if things go wrong, is a crazy construction. . . . If a loan to improve a South American capital is repudiated we have nothing. If a popular housing loan is repudiated, we as a nation, still have the houses." (See J. M. Keynes, *The Nation and the Atheneum,* London, August 1924.) On another occasion he said: "If I owe my bank 50,000 pounds, it is my problem. If I owe 10 million pounds, it becomes the problem of the bank."

Discussion

The discussion focused on three main issues, beginning with the relationships between policy targets and instruments. To Jacob S. Dreyer it seemed that too many variables were assumed to be in the control of the authorities at any one time. Citing several references in the papers by Hans Seidel and by Stephan Koren and Helmut Frisch to exchange rate targets, interest rate targets, and money supply targets, he said that all three could not be taken simultaneously as exogenous. The authors agreed that this was impossible and indicated that the identity of policy targets had shifted in the 1970s as Austrian policy adapted to changes in world monetary conditions. In the second half of the decade, the hard currency policy vis-à-vis Germany made the exchange rate the focus, making interest rates and money supplies endogenous. Koren and Seidel noted, however, that this did not necessarily mean that Austrian interest rates had to match Germany's. Any attempt to create major disparities would lead to reserve movements. Seidel said that credit rationing provided some limited opportunities for uncoupling Austria's financial variables from Germany's.

A second topic was the role of the social partnership in Austria's strong employment performance. Michele Fratianni noted that the Frisch model implied money illusion among workers and suggested that the partnership might contribute to money illusion, thus raising the unemployment-reducing powers of expansionary policies. Fritz Machlup suggested that, given the anxieties in Austria over the vicious circle, performance in the social partnership partly depends on a desire to preserve the schilling's relationship to the deutsche mark. Moving the rate or adopting a managed float might weaken the partnership and thereby its ability to moderate wage movements. Various other details in the specification of the Frisch model also elicited a variety of comments. In regard to the presence of money illusion, Frisch agreed that this creates some difficulties, but he argued that using an exogenous price level as the deflator simplified both the model and the calculations.

In his closing comments, Koren addressed several points raised by Jacques R. Artus. In regard to the reserve of competitiveness in the early 1970s, he noted that when Austria joined the Bretton Woods system in 1952 the schilling was undervalued at 26 to the dollar. As for the current account deficit in 1976, he would argue that rather than the result of the exchange rate policy it was due to an accident in Austrian incomes policy in 1975–1976, which permitted a large rise in real wages. Koren agreed that the current account deficit was becoming too large, but he argued that efforts had already been under way to reverse it when the second oil shock interfered, in 1979. It is the intention of the authorities to use incomes policy rather than exchange rate policy as the main instrument in this battle.

Seidel addressed the question of Austro-Keynesianism, arguing that the top priority given to full employment was a Keynesian characteristic. In regard to instruments, Austrian policy makers were Keynesian, at least until 1979, because they believed that high employment could be achieved with budget deficits and that inflation was mainly cost-push in nature, arising from import price and labor cost movements and from profit markups. Recently, however, they were behaving in non-Keynesian ways, by cutting budgets and raising interest rates in the face of recession.

Seidel indicated his disagreement with most of the points made by Artus. The growth of the service sector, for example, was indeed noteworthy, but he wanted to point out that industrial production in the 1970s grew more rapidly in Austria than in the rest of Western Europe. Similarly, investment is something one needs to worry about, but Seidel claimed that Austria comparably did not look bad. Cost competitiveness depended on the period of observation. There were severe losses from 1971 to 1976 or 1977, but some of those were regained later. In 1981 cost competitiveness equaled its 1967 level. Finally, in regard to structural change, Seidel did not believe that recession was the right way to bring it about. He believed nonprice factors were crucial in shaping Austria's external and internal performance.

Frisch acknowledged, with gratitude, many of the technical points and suggestions made by participants and by Thomas D. Willett in his prepared remarks. As for the appropriateness of the hard currency policy for Austria, he recalled the extended debate in Austria in the mid-1970s and the widespread hope of importing stability by tying the schilling to the deutsche mark. He reiterated the general anxiety over the vicious circle and noted that incomes policy, which depended heavily on compromises between employers and trade unions, could be expected to work only in the absence of excessive exchange rate volatility. Thus the model presented would indeed be consistent with occasional changes in exchange rates but not with flexible rates. The decisions leading to the hard currency policy were considerably influenced by political factors, so he tried to rationalize the given political economy in his model.

Part Two
Microeconomic Issues:
Structure and Performance

Introduction

Sven W. Arndt

The Social Partnership

The close links between microeconomic structure and macroeconomic policy and the possibility of conflict between short- and long-run considerations were suggested quite strongly in the papers and discussion of part one. Austria's remarkable success story is due in no small part to the structure of its institutions and to the characteristics of its social arrangements.

The social partnership, which is described in detail in the chapter by Johann Farnleitner and Erich Schmidt, is unique in western social democracies. Much more than the typical incomes policy, it is an extensive "system of institutionalized cooperation"[1] that touches virtually every aspect of economic policy. Designed initially as a means for employers and trade unions to grapple with postwar inflation through direct negotiations, it has evolved into a mechanism for the resolution of conflicts among the main social groups. For such a system to work, there must be considerable prior consensus on the socioeconomic structure and on the prevailing income distribution. Such a system is also more likely to work successfully in a country in which the public sector and its role in production are large and in which the organizational structure of the private sector is highly centralized.

Interactions between macroeconomic policy and economic structure are ever present. One of the avowed purposes of the hard currency policy, for example, is to support the Austrian version of the social contract. The fixed exchange rate vis-à-vis the Federal Republic and the relative openness of the Austrian economy restrain the exposed sector's freedom of action in matters involving prices and wages. Increases in productivity-adjusted wages beyond those occurring abroad threaten competitiveness if prices are raised or impair profit shares and thus capital formation if they are not. The wage-price moderation achieved by this policy is then presumed to spread to the sheltered sector.

The degree of cooperation and consensus that Austrian labor and capital have been able to muster is remarkable indeed, particularly in comparison with other western social democracies. The principal organ of the social partnership is the Parity, or Joint Commission on Wages and Prices. A Prices Subcommittee oversees prices except those of imports, special categories, and those under the direct control of the public authorities. Its pricing strategy has been to focus on supply conditions and to rely mainly on markups over cost.

The Wages Subcommittee "oversees" the wage bargaining process in which highly centralized negotiations establish base wages that leave substantial room for wage drift. The committee's influence falls mainly on the timing of wage adjustments. It is a process that relies crucially upon the discipline and self-restraint of the trade unions.

Controlled prices and wages must not only be consistent with each other, but must stay within the constraints imposed by the hard currency policy. Price policies focusing on costs tend to inhibit demand-pull inflation; they help control inflationary expectations and reinforce the recognition that money wage increases in excess of productivity growth will raise costs, which form the basis for subsequent price increases. In practice this has meant that Austrian wages have moved less aggressively during economic booms than elsewhere. There has, however, also been a tendency for wage gains to exceed productivity increases during recessions, partly in order to provide Keynesian boosts to demand. Such a countercyclical wage strategy tends to stabilize wages over the business cycle; but to the extent that it does not eliminate the cycle itself, it merely transfers to other variables—including nonwage incomes—the burden of cyclical adjustment.

There were substantial periods during the 1970s when incomes policy failed to stay within the bounds established by the hard currency policy and wage-price movements elsewhere. International competitiveness was lost, the current account moved into substantial deficit, and the conditions were created for a long-run misallocation of resources into the sheltered sector.

In addition to their macroeconomic implications, incomes and other social policies affect the allocation of resources over time and thereby the structural transformation of the economy. There is always the danger that a commitment to full employment will be translated into a determination to preserve existing jobs, even when that is incompatible with considerations of long-run competitiveness. The timely reallocation of capital and labor out of declining industries may thus be retarded, thereby impairing the growth of jobs and living standards over time.

SVEN W. ARNDT

The Labor Market

Labor market policy, indeed resource management in general, is fraught with problems and potential conflicts. In the short run, employment must be provided for workers whose skills and quality are largely given and nowhere is the state more committed to full employment than in Austria. In the long run, however, human capital formation must be fostered and skills nurtured in ways calculated to maintain international competitiveness and to advance living standards.

Felix Butschek chronicles in some detail Austria's remarkable success in achieving and maintaining full employment. We learn from his paper and from Marvin Kosters's discussion that sensible minimum wage policies have helped spare Austria the youth unemployment problems found almost everywhere else. We are also told that similarly sensible approaches to unemployment compensation and job training have preserved incentive structures and thus minimized the adverse employment effects often associated with excessively generous subsidies to the unemployed.

Achievement of full employment objectives was facilitated by the presence in Austria of large numbers of foreign workers. Indeed, the guest workers appear to have carried the major share of adjustment, acting as cyclical shock absorbers in the labor market. To this safety valve must be added the role of the public sector as major employer and its tendency to hoard labor and resist layoffs.

Looking toward the future, Butschek is at once concerned and encouraged. He is optimistic about the adequacy of skilled workers in Austria; indeed, he notes the existence of excess supplies of skilled workers. Still, he is concerned about Austria's ability to generate enough jobs, fearing that shortened workweeks, early retirement, and other such devices may have to be used to raise employment. He therefore appears to be satisfied with the quality of labor, but concerned about the quantity of jobs.

It is not clear to what extent these considerations suggest mismatches peculiar to the labor market or to resource management in general, and to what extent they point to inconsistencies in overall economic policies and strategies. The complexity of the process in Austria, the deep involvement of the state, and the centralized nature of decision making raise many questions about targets, instruments, and criteria and about the channels and linkages along which impulses are transmitted within the structure of the Austrian economy. The answers to these many queries may not be readily forthcoming, in Peter Katzenstein's view, because of the inherent ambiguities in the political economy of Austria.

Industrial Structure and Competitiveness

On the whole, Austrian policy has moved with considerable skill and circumspection. Its accomplishments with respect to macroeconomic stability are especially impressive. Inflation has been modest by international standards; growth has been strong and well above the average for members of the Organization for Economic Cooperation and Development (OECD); unemployment has remained low, even in periods of world recession, and industrial peace has kept losses of national product and wealth to a minimum.

The evidence is more equivocal at the microeconomic level. While it is apparent that profits have been squeezed, especially in the exposed sector, it is not clear whether, and if so how, capital formation has been harmed, partly because the state has intervened with subsidies. The question of adequacy and appropriateness arises mainly in connection with the quality of investment in Austria. Investment strategies, especially those involving projects of large size, may not have been sufficiently forward-looking. Capital formation—both human and physical—is the principal instrument for securing long-term competitiveness and for protecting comparative advantage. While all manner of projects offer short-run relief from unemployment, many do not adequately serve the purposes of long-run competitiveness.

Administering investment subsidies is a tricky business in itself, as the papers by Oskar Grünwald and Karl Vak suggest. Investment subsidies may create employment without upgrading the quality of the productive factors, thereby guaranteeing early obsolescence in a world of rapidly shifting comparative advantage. Moreover, to the extent that such subsidies are capital subsidies, they encourage capital substitution and thus complicate even the short-run achievement of full employment. Often they merely compensate for the investment-inhibiting effects of other policies. In this connection it may be appropriate to ask whether, and if so to what extent, the cost-oriented pricing policy of the social partnership retards the responsiveness of resources to demand shifts.

There has been a tendency to use resources for the preservation of existing jobs, thereby creating the potential for long-run resource misallocation. It is not altogether clear that the manufacturing sector in particular and the Austrian economy in general possess the kind of flexibility and adjustment capacity that will see them through the competitive challenges to come. There has been a tendency toward rapid expansion and labor hoarding in the public sector, and while these may be defended on grounds of short-run employment policy, they do not offer a promising weapon in the international competitive struggle.

The European democracies are faced with potentially explosive situations in many industries. Operations are inefficient in comparative terms; the quality of labor and capital is low relative to their cost; management and trade unions resist pressures to adjust, hoping to push the burden of change onto future generations; mechanisms that would enhance factor quality are inadequate for the task; and the measures adopted tend to be defensive and protectionist rather than forward-looking. Unless important breakthroughs are achieved in public attitudes and official policies, the needed adjustments will not be forthcoming, and the economies will suffer. Here again, Austria would appear to be in relatively good shape. Whereas in some countries deep-seated conflict permeates the relations among social groups, the relative consensus among Austria's social partners and their demonstrated ability to seek solutions through compromise leave the country comparatively well poised in the international competitive struggle.

This raises the question of whether Austria can improve its performance as a magnet for foreign investment. There would appear to be good reasons for investing in Austria. Foremost among them is the relative stability and predictability of the economic environment. Of equal importance is the availability of a disciplined work force. Industrial peace prevails. Together, these factors reduce the risk and uncertainty attached to foreign ventures.

The Austrians appear to have understood that it is not only the thrust of economic policy and the nature of institutional arrangements, but their constancy and reliability that matter. Too often, policy making degenerates into a ceaseless and aimless process of change. Rules, regulations, and policy signals in general are in a perpetual state of flux, their half-lives declining rapidly. In such an unsettled world, planning and investing for the long term are fraught with dangers, and the country that achieves relative stability acquires an important comparative advantage.

Trade and Trade Finance

With the exchange rate fixed and aimed at control of domestic inflation under the hard currency policy, balance in external payments must be pursued by other means. For substantial periods in the 1970s, Austria's current account was in deficit and needed to be financed. Inasmuch as long-term private capital inflows were not always adequate for the task, short-term capital, foreign borrowing by government, and reserve losses played important roles.

A current account deficit may be viewed from two perspectives. At a given exchange rate, prices of tradable goods may be rising faster than world prices, causing the country to lose competitiveness, with home and foreign customers shifting their purchases away from domestic products. Austria's price performance was, as we have already seen, superior in comparison with its non-German trading partners; it was, however, inferior to the German performance. Moreover, the positive competitive effects of its price performance were more than offset by the DM-linked appreciation of the schilling. The total effect was, therefore, a net decline in its competitive position persisting well into the second half of the decade.

Since then, relative unit labor costs, relative consumer prices, and relative export unit values of manufactures have all moved in directions favoring Austria. Indeed, at the very end of the decade, export unit values had returned to their values of 1970 and were continuing to fall; but this improvement is deceptive at least in part because costs have tended to rise relative to prices in the export sector, thereby squeezing profits and possibly inhibiting capital formation. Moreover, inasmuch as the prices of domestic goods have risen substantially relative to those of imports, import penetration has been relatively pronounced.

An alternative, but equally illuminating, perspective on the current account views it as the discrepancy between aggregate output and aggregate absorption. This is the "living beyond one's means" description of a current account deficit, because home absorption exceeds home production. It occurs when the sum of private investment and government expenditure exceeds the sum of private saving and government tax receipts (allowing for net factor earnings from abroad). In dynamic terms it means that faster growth at home than abroad causes imports to expand faster than exports so that the trade balance deteriorates. The trade balance may deteriorate even when growth rates are equal, provided that the income elasticity of demand for imports at home exceeds the average elasticity of a country's trading partners.

While the evidence on relative income elasticities is far from clear-cut, a recent multi-country study by Goldstein, Khan, and Officer[2] shows relatively large cyclical responses of Austria's imports to variations in income. Indeed, it was the relatively high income elasticity of demand for automobiles in Austria that prompted the government to encourage General Motors to open its plant near Vienna.

Notes

1. See Organization for Economic Cooperation and Development, *Economic Surveys: Austria* (Paris, February 1982), pp. 22-30, and *Integrated Social Policy: A Review of the Austrian Experience* (Paris, 1981).

2. See M. Goldstein, M. S. Khan, and L. H. Officer, "Prices of Tradable and Non-Tradable Goods in the Demand for Total Imports," *Review of Economics and Statistics*, vol. 62 (May 1980), pp. 190-99.

The Social Partnership

Johann Farnleitner and Erich Schmidt

Background

The social partnership is a pivotal institution in Austrian society. It is not merely the forum that enables diverse social and economic groups to work out their differences; it embodies the Austrian approach to economic and social problems, which is to seek solutions through compromise and consensus rather than through confrontation.

Austria's history since 1918 has shaped the relations between business and workers that are now manifest in the partnership. In the First Republic, cooperation among interest groups and among political parties was minimal. Then came the chaos of civil war in 1934 and the loss of national independence in 1938. Between 1938 and 1945, Austrians of various backgrounds and of diverse political persuasions were thrown together in confinement where they had many opportunities to contemplate past errors and future prospects. The war was followed by ten years of Allied occupation, a period during which it occasionally proved useful to transfer decision making to the social partnership level in order to avoid intervention by the Allies. The wage-price agreements of those years of reconstruction are an instructive example.

The social partnership has its origin in the cooperation that developed among the major political parties during the long period of coalition government, which lasted from 1945 until 1966. As early as 1947, the four largest economic interest groups, with the support of the government, formed the Economic Commission. In this way, the responsibility for important decisions affecting the economy shifted from the government to the leading interest groups outside Parliament.

Structure of the Social Partnership

The Austrian Constitution stipulates the establishment of various chambers to represent the diverse professional groups. Membership in

87

the various chambers is compulsory. The chambers are empowered by law to represent the interests of their members in public affairs and in contacts with the authorities. Thus, the chambers must be consulted by the government on economic and financial legislation and policy. Their representatives also serve on a large number of advisory boards. The form of the chambers' organization, too, is stipulated by law. Common to all of them is their democratic structure, which requires all positions to be filled through elections.

Austria's independent entrepreneurs are represented in the Federal Economic Chamber, which is composed of six sections for industry, commerce, trade, transport, tourism, and finance, credit, and insurance. Representation is organized at the provincial level, followed by a system of indirect elections for the appointment of officials at the federal level.

The Chambers of Agriculture are based in the provinces, where all officeholders are elected directly by farmers. Representation at the federal level is provided by the Presidential Conference. The Chambers of Labor, also based in the provinces, cover the interests of employees, who are represented at the federal level by a council of the Chambers of Labor. The chambers are autonomous corporations whose positions are filled through direct elections and whose activities are financed by compulsory membership fees.

Unlike the chambers, the Trade Union Federation is based on voluntary membership. It represents employees of private as well as public enterprises. Approximately 60 percent of Austrian employees belong to the federation, although the percentage is considerably higher in industry. The federation has a total membership of about 1,600,000 and is in legal terms a "juridical person," while the unions it incorporates are not. Thus, while a union may negotiate a collective agreement, legally the federation must endorse it. Moreover, it is the federation that decides jurisdictional questions among unions, which are, in the main, organized on an industrial basis. The exception is the Union of Private Employees.

The interest groups are prepared to bear political responsibility and to refrain from adversary representation of their interests—in spite of the actual state of the economy and of society. One of the preeminent goals of these groups is to become involved in day-to-day politics and to bear political responsibility.

The social partnership developed in close relation with the so-called government coalition between the Austrian People's party and the Socialist party from 1945 to 1966. The partnership became more and more important because this coalition was, during the last decade of its existence, characterized by a loss of flexibility. Whenever solutions on the level of the political parties were not obtainable, the task of finding a compromise was shifted to the social partners. The two great political parties became accustomed to this way of handling political and, especially, economic problems. The effectiveness of the partnership did not undergo substantial change in 1966, or, in 1970, when a socialist minority government rose into power, or, thereafter, when power shifted to a one-party socialist government.

Since 1966 the government has limited its role in the partnership, in that the chancellor and the ministers have renounced their right to vote. The government has recognized the advantages of letting the organizations work out problems among themselves. This implies that the responsibility in critical issues of everyday policy, such as the problems of prices and wages, have been largely transferred from the government to the organizations. It is easy to see that under such circumstances, prices and incomes cannot furnish ready slogans for electoral campaigns.

The Instruments of the Social Partnership

Cooperation in the business of the social partnership is voluntary and informal, both sides having until now refused to force this free form of cooperation into regulation by law. The most important organ in this cooperative effort is the Joint Commission for Prices and Wages, established in 1957.[1] The commission, also known as the Parity Commission, has four members from the government and representatives from each of the four interest organizations. The chair is taken by the federal chancellor or by the minister of trade and industry.

The institution is founded on the principle of parity with equal rights for each member regardless of constituency size. Representation of the four organizations also ensures parity between employers and employees and between organizations dominated by the Austrian People's party (Federal Economic Chamber, Presidential Conference of the Chamber of Agriculture) and those dominated by the Socialist party (Chamber of Labor, Trade Union Federation).

In both the Parity Commission and its subcommittees, decisions must be unanimous, and, since the commission has no basis in law, participation is strictly voluntary. In the Parity Commission, the members of the government do not vote; they try—when necessary—to effect a compromise between the social partners.

The commission generally meets once a month and serves as the second and final stage of reference for wage and price matters on which unanimous agreement cannot be reached in the appropriate subcommittee. Every three months the commission undertakes a policy review. Present at these sessions are also the minister of finance, the president

89

and vice-president of the National Bank, and the directors of the Austrian Institute for Economic Research. Before the meetings of the Parity Commission the chief officers of the four organizations and their economic advisers meet to discuss the agenda. These "presidents' discussions" have acquired decisive importance and avert potential strife. Nearly all decisions are arrived at during these discussions.

A significant degree of statesmanship characterizes the work on this level. While the procedures in the subcommittees focus chiefly on technical aspects, the presidents review every issue from a political point of view as well. The presidents try hard to present to the Parity Commission unanimous results instead of controversial positions.

The Prices Subcommittee

The Prices Subcommittee was set up in 1957 and is composed of six members, one from each of the four employers' and workers' organizations, one from the Ministry of Trade and Industry, and one from the Ministry of Finance. It meets up to three times a week (though usually only once) under the chairmanship of the Federal Economic Chamber, which also provides for the secretariat. Applications by individual firms or branches for price increases are submitted by the Federal Economic Chamber; if not approved, the applicants are asked to provide further justification. The Prices Subcommittee can accept an application unanimously, wholly or partly, hold it over, or refer it to the Parity Commission.

One of the agreements among the social partners provides a time limit for dealing with applications: if a question cannot be decided within six weeks, it is referred to the Parity Commission, which has an additional five weeks to decide it. After establishing this provision, however, the partners decided in another agreement not to use it. The reason for this surprising change of rules was the recognition that such a solution would in the long run simply create a system of price-increase notifications that would diminish the influence of the commission.

The Prices Subcommittee oversees the prices of all goods and services, except officially regulated prices and tariffs controlled by the Official Price Commission (set up by the Price Act), import prices, fees charged by professional groups that do not belong to the Federal Economic Chamber, seasonal price variations (fruit, vegetables), most service charges and fashion goods prices, new products, and trade margins (as long as their proportion of the consumer price remains the same). In practice, price control covers mainly trademarked articles, staple commodities, and some standard services. The number of applications handled per year varies from 150 to 350. The subcommittee

90

controls about 20 percent of the articles in the consumer price index shopping basket.

Presentation of proposed price increases to the subcommittee is voluntary, and in practice there is no direct penalty for failing to make a proposal. The deliberations of the subcommittee are based on information provided by the applicant. The subcommittee's prime concern is to ensure that only absolutely unavoidable cost increases be allowed to affect prices and that both the extent and the timing of unavoidable rises are evenly distributed. It also works to keep the price front calm by preventing any group from exploiting a particular market situation.

A longstanding practice of this subcommittee is to pass on to customers and/or consumers any cost increase that can be proved by invoices or collective agreements. But there is one important exception: wage increases based on agreements at the shop level or on individual contracts are regarded as avoidable costs and therefore not accepted as justification for higher prices.

The Prices Subcommittee tries to accept price increases from a given enterprise or branch only once a year, in order to conform to the policy of the Wages Subcommittee, which never permits wage negotiations during the period of validity of an agreement. Only for extraordinary price increases of raw materials and energy has the subcommittee developed a special arrangement for passing on such unavoidable costs. Sometimes price increases have been accepted only under the condition that the trade margin in absolute figures should remain unchanged.

Normally the subcommittee does not deal with questions of profits and losses. During the past few years, however, some cases have arisen in which price increases were demanded and granted on the basis of insufficient profits or extraordinary losses. In any given case, the result of the negotiations depends on various factors, but especially on the technical calculations and the patience, perseverance, and eloquence of the applicants.

The procedure of price determination is voluntary, but there are remarkable sanctions provided in the Price Control Act. If the social partners unanimously inform the minister of trade and industry that a price has been increased, the minister is entitled to fix an economically justified maximum price for a six-month period. Normally, the minister is entitled only to regulate the prices of certain products (for example, milk, milk products, grain, bread, and energy), but since 1975 the minister may also examine the justification for every price increase. In doing this, he must consider only the needs of the enterprise. The minister will never examine the justification of a price increase approved by the social partners. Thus, entrepreneurs prefer to go to the Parity Commission rather than get involved in prolonged and probably politically influenced official price examinations.

The Wages Subcommittee

This committee was set up in 1962 to reduce the workload of the Parity Commission, which had originally controlled wages itself. Its members include representatives of workers and employers (two each from the Federal Economic Chamber and the Trade Union Federation, whose subordinate bodies usually conduct the wage negotiations, and one each from the Chamber of Labor and the Chamber of Agriculture). It meets every fortnight under the alternate chairmanship of the Trade Union Federation and the Federal Economic Chamber.

Control over wages is exercised as follows. A particular trade union informs the Trade Union Federation of its intention to open wage negotiations, and the federation applies to the Wages Subcommittee for its agreement. The channeling of all applications through the Trade Union Federation ensures that proposals for wage increases are co-ordinated in advance, giving the federation the opportunity to determine the date, sequence, and, to a certain degree, the extent of individual claims. Under the direction of the subcommittee, negotiations take place between the professional association of the employers and the trade union concerned.

Although no guidelines exist, some characteristics of the wage-search process can be enumerated. The Trade Union Federation tried in the past to realize an average real increase of wages of 3 percent (so-called Benya formula). Behind this concept was the idea that entrepreneurs should be pushed to high rates of productivity by predictable increases of labor costs. In practice, employers are prepared to take into account the inflation rate of the last year and the actual increase of productivity when considering wage increases. In recent years both sides have agreed to grant above-average wage increases to lower-paid workers.

The outcome of these discussions must be submitted to the subcommittee for its approval. The subcommittee has no influence on the actual content of the agreement worked out—least of all on the extent of the wage rise, although it can postpone its implementation. Finally, it can refer the application to the Parity Commission. This is mandatory if unanimity cannot be reached, or if the application involves a matter of principle or is likely to lead to an application for a price increase.

The agreements, which determine wages and the provision of numerous social benefits, are drawn up and formalized by the appropriate suborganizations of the Federal Economic Chamber and the Trade Union Federation. They are valid for all employees in the particular branch of the economy concerned. The wages set in the collective agreements are minimum rates, and in many firms it is customary to award extra payments. For this reason, many of the agreements provide not only for an increase based on the minimum wage, but also a second, generally lower, increase for the wage actually paid.

The principal role of the Wages Subcommittee is to decide when to approve new wage negotiations, thus influencing the period of validity of collective agreements and helping to ensure a balanced wage policy. The unions accept the procedure as binding; negotiations on new collective agreements are never held without the consent of the Parity Commission.

It may be interesting to know how far relative wages have been affected by the process described above. In his study "Wage Rigidity and the Structure of the Austrian Manufacturing Industry," Wolfgang Pollan found that the evidence seems to favor the cost-adjustment hypothesis over the union-oriented approach.[2] Wage developments in the manufacturing sector do not conform to a uniform pattern, but rather show substantial variations, a result that is not consistent with the claim that one of the main goals of individual unions is the maintenance of customary wage differentials relative to other employee groups.

The Economic and Social Advisory Board

At the end of 1963 the Economic and Social Advisory Board was set up as the third and last permanent subcommittee of the Parity Commission. It reflects the logical extension of the Parity Commission's activities, which had hitherto been confined mainly to wage and price policies. Its creation was partly due to the growing conviction that a broader scientific basis was required for economic policy measures designed to solve the structural problems evident in decreasing growth rates and rising inflation of the first half of the 1960s.

The Economic and Social Advisory Board was given the task of studying economic and social questions in the context of the economy as a whole. Its findings serve as a basis for recommendations to be made by the Parity Commission to the federal government. The advisory board differs from similar institutions abroad because it is both a group of expert advisers and a body for resolving conflicts of interest. It is composed of three advisers from each of the four main employers' and workers' organizations and of two secretary-generals (provided by the council of the Chambers of Labor and the Federal Economic Chamber); the chairmanship rotates twice a year among the four organizations. Its pattern of membership ensures that in pursuing investigations it tries to reconcile differences between the bodies concerned (minority votes are possible, but rare). While this function makes the advisory

93

TABLE 1
INDUSTRIAL DISPUTES IN SELECTED COUNTRIES, 1970–1979

Country	Code	1970	1971	1972	1973
Austria	WI	7,547	2,431	7,096	78,251
	DL	26,616	3,702	15,104	160,138
Belgium	ND	151	184	191	172
	WI	107,670	86,979	66,622	62,281
	DL	1,432,274	1,240,472	354,086	871,872
Denmark	ND	77	31	35	205
	WI	55,585	6,379	7,601	337,100
	DL	102,000	20,600	21,800	3,901,200
France	ND	2,942	4,318	3,464	3,731
	WI	1,079,800	3,234,500	2,721,348	2,245,973
	DL	1,742,175	4,387,781	3,755,343	3,914,598
Germany, Fed. Rep. of	WI	184,269	536,303	22,908	185,010
	DL	93,203	4,483,740	66,045	563,051
Ireland	ND	134	133	131	182
	WI	28,752	43,783	22,274	31,761
	DL	1,007,714	273,770	206,955	206,725
Italy	ND	4,162	5,598	4,765	3,769
	WI	3,721,919	3,891,253	4,405,251	6,132,747
	DL	20,887,459	14,798,589	19,497,143	23,419,286
Netherlands	ND	99	15	31	7
	WI	52,233	35,560	19,548	58,113
	DL	262,810	96,846	134,187	583,783
Norway	ND	15	10	9	12
	WI	3,133	2,519	1,185	2,380
	DL	47,204	9,105	12,402	11,382
Spain	ND	1,547	549	710	731
	WI	440,114	196,665	236,421	303,132
	DL	1,092,364	859,693	586,616	1,081,158
Sweden	ND	134	60	44	48
	WI	26,669	62,919	7,145	4,252
	DL	155,700	839,000	10,507	11,802
Switzerland	ND	3	11	5	—
	WI	320	2,267	526	—
	DL	2,623	7,491	2,002	—
United Kingdom	ND	3,906	2,228	2,497	2,873
	WI	1,800,700	1,178,200	1,734,400	1,527,600
	DL	10,980,000	13,551,000	23,909,000	7,197,000
United States	ND	5,716	5,138	5,010	5,353
	WI	3,305,200	3,279,600	1,713,600	2,250,700
	DL	66,413,800	47,589,100	27,066,400	27,948,400

NOTE: ND: Number of disputes; WI: Workers involved; DL: Working days lost.

TABLE 1 (continued)

1974	1975	1976	1977	1978	1979
7,295	3,783	2,352	43	699	786
7,243	5,512	589	11	10,222	764
235	243	281	220	195	215
55,747	85,801	106,654	65,761	90,813	55,722
580,032	607,809	896,805	664,236	1,002,489	615,484
134	147	204	228	314	218
142,352	59,128	87,224	36,305	59,340	156,589
184,200	100,100	210,300	229,700	128,800	173,000
3,381	3,888	4,348	3,302	3,202	—
1,563,540	1,827,142	2,022,500	1,919,900	704,800	—
3,379,977	3,868,926	5,010,687	3,665,940	2,200,400	—
250,352	35,814	169,312	34,437	487,050	77,326
1,051,290	68,680	533,696	23,681	4,281,284	483,083
219	151	134	175	152	140
43,459	29,124	42,281	33,805	32,558	63,612
551,833	295,716	776,949	442,145	624,266	1,548,322
5,174	3,601	2,706	3,308	2,479	2,000
7,824,397	14,109,732	11,897,819	13,802,955	8,774,193	16,237,444
19,466,714	27,189,142	25,377,571	16,566,143	10,177,033	27,530,428
14	5	11	19	10	30
2,979	268	15,255	35,945	2,548	31,844
6,854	480	13,984	236,090	2,834	306,730
13	22	35	15	14	10
22,149	3,282	21,586	2,429	4,459	2,773
318,433	12,473	137,651	25,049	62,888	7,010
2,009	2,807	3,662	1,194	1,128	2,680
557,318	504,250	2,556,373	2,955,000	3,863,855	5,713,193
1,748,695	1,815,237	12,593,100	16,641,700	11,550,911	18,916,984
85	86	73	35	99	207
17,470	23,631	8,715	13,101	8,319	32,315
57,604	365,507	24,744	87,151	37,135	28,664
3	6	19	9	10	8
299	323	2,395	1,380	1,240	463
2,777	1,733	19,586	4,649	5,317	2,331
2,922	2,282	2,016	2,703	2,471	2,145
1,626,400	808,900	668,000	1,165,800	1,041,500	4,607,800
14,750,000	6,012,000	3,284,000	10,143,000	9,405,000	29,474,000
6,074	5,031	5,648	5,506	4,230	4,780
2,778,100	1,746,000	2,420,000	2,040,100	1,623,600	1,720,100
47,990,900	31,237,000	37,859,900	35,821,800	36,921,500	35,467,300

SOURCE: International Labor Office, *Yearbook of Labor Statistics, 1980* (Geneva, 1980).

95

board's work more difficult, it has the advantage that the board's recommendations can be carried out and indeed usually are carried out by the government. For its practical work the advisory board has set up working parties comprising numerous advisers from government departments, research centers, higher education centers, employers' and workers' organizations, and business enterprises. The Economic and Social Advisory Board's report and recommendations are sent to the presidents of the four main employers' organizations. If approved, they are forwarded through the Parity Commission to the government. The board has worked on medium-term budget forecasts, the stimulation of the capital market, coordination of the construction industry and the progressive reduction of working hours, and the improvement of the current balance.

The activities of the social partners go far beyond the joint commission. Their predominant influence is exerted in the following areas:

• *Agricultural marketing regulations.* These include the Milk Marketing Fund, the Grains Trade Fund, the Wine Marketing Fund, and the Commission for Cattle.

• *Competition laws.* The Cartel Law provides a decisive role for a joint commission for cartel matters; only the chambers are entitled to file complaints to the Cartel Court. The Unfair Competition Act and the Consumer Protection Act contain similar provisions.

Nearly all important acts provide advisory bodies in which the social partners are represented. There are about 200 such bodies.

Criticizing the Social Partnership

Social partnership is not only praised and supported, it is also criticized, primarily within each organization. By conceding a compromise solution, it can run into a conflict with its members who may expect their viewpoint to be pursued more aggressively. Less important, but noteworthy, is the radical-socialist criticism put forward by the Communist party and by the Young Socialists. In their view, social partnership means nothing but the renunciation of the class struggle and loss of the hope to realize Marxist conceptions in society. Also important are the so-called radical-democratic comments critical of the social partnership's lack of publicity, its tendency to anticipate Parliament's decisions, and the prolonged course of development in politics. Constitutionalists contend that social partnership is neither provided for nor formally established in Austria's Constitution. Conservative criticism may also be cited. There are groups that feel insufficiently represented, such as farmers; groups that tend to be incorporated into

strengthened in the years since the onset of general floating in exchange rates.

At present, as the Austrian economy confronts the need to reduce both its current account deficit and its public sector deficit, as well as the need to restructure the composition of domestic expenditure, social partnership is likely to be put to a new test. With the Austrian schilling effectively pegged to the deutsche mark, the requisite improvement in competitiveness will only come about if wage and salary increases can be contained and if, over the medium term, productivity can be increased. In the first instance this will require the moderating influence of social partnership. In the second instance it will have to be instrumental in changing the composition of expenditures in a manner that raises the share of productive investment at the expense of private and public consumption, thereby also increasing the degree of "sustainability" of any given current account deficit. It is in this connection that Farnleitner's remark about social partnership acting as a possible constraint on the financing of investment takes on special significance.[1] Accordingly, it may be worthwhile to analyze—both over the cycle and in an international context—developments in investment relative to GDP on the one hand and developments in enterprise profitability and the composition of investment financing on the other. Finally, Farnleitner and Schmidt, by virtue of their association with the Federal Economic Chamber and the Trade Union Federation, would appear to have access to the records of deliberations in the various commissions and hence would be well placed to evaluate these records. Such an evaluation should offer additional insights into the mechanism of incomes policy in Austria, something I believe has not been done to date, or at least has not been published.

What Farnleitner and Schmidt say about two fundamental aspects of social partnership, its ubiquitousness and the nature of its dispositions, may be complemented by a few general remarks. Austria's social partnership is an intriguing animal, for it appears in many guises. One day we see it as the Parity Commission, the next as the Prices Subcommittee, and the third day as the Wages Subcommittee. Nor is this all, since it is active in other economic and political affairs in which the law assigns it an important role, such as social insurance, agricultural policy, regulation of cartels, and "mandatory" price control under the Price Control Act. Differences in guises apart, the basic nature of the social partnership consists invariably of the same quartet, the three chambers and the Trade Union Federation. Watching this quartet play, the impression of seeing in action a state within the state without a mandate from the electorate is not altogether illusory. Longstanding awareness of potential conflict with the Austrian Constitution—which reserves final and exclusive administrative authority for the particular cabinet minister and not for any commission whose decisions were taken collectively—has no doubt contributed to labeling as voluntary, rather than legally binding, compliance with the decisions in the Parity Commission and the two subcommittees. What function the law assigns to the quartet is strictly "advisory" and does not extend to decision making, though this apparently limited mandate both enhances the quartet's importance and acknowledges it formally. The controls of social partnership are thus voluntary in a largely nominal sense; in effect they may be as binding as the mandatory controls under the Price Control Act.

Notes

1. In his presentation at the conference Farnleitner pointed out that "as far as price control is concerned there is undeniably one disadvantage. Since it is based on the principle of cost control, the enterprises are usually not allowed to exploit a favorable market situation only for the reason to increase profits. This fact is especially important in time of an economic boom, and it may be one of the reasons for the insufficient equity capital of Austrian industry."

Full Employment during Recession

Felix Butschek

The most remarkable feature of Austrian economic development since the downturn of 1974/1975 has been continuing full employment. Although in most Western developed countries unemployment rates began to increase at the beginning of the 1970s—a trend that became even more widespread and pronounced after 1974—unemployment in Austria never exceeded 2.1 percent (1.6 percent of the total labor force). Austria succeeded not only in avoiding unemployment, but moreover was able to achieve continuous growth in employment in contrast, for example, to Switzerland. Only in 1975 did the number of persons gainfully employed stagnate; in all other years it increased. In 1980 employment was 5.7 percent higher than in 1975.

This development is even more remarkable in light of the very unfavorable internal conditions prevailing at the time. Austria not only shared with other countries a decrease in the demand for labor as a result of reduced growth in the gross domestic product (GDP), but also had to contend with the problem of a rapidly growing domestic labor supply. As a result of high birthrates during the 1960s, large cohorts entered the labor force during the mid-1970s. At the same time, low retirement rates prevailed—partly due to the decimation of the working-age population during World War II. Thus the annual labor supply growth rate was calculated to have been slightly higher than 1 percent. (Table 1 compares unemployment rates in Austria in 1974–1980 with those of selected countries of the Organization for Economic Cooperation and Development [OECD].)

In addition to the economic policy preference of the Austrian federal government and its concomitant Austro-Keynesian policies—which will be described later—a variety of factors contributed to this development. Some of these resulted from discretionary policies; others are the result of autonomous forces.

TABLE 1
UNEMPLOYMENT RATES IN SELECTED OECD COUNTRIES, 1974–1980
(percent)

Country	1974	1975	1976	1977	1978	1979	1980
Austria	1.5	2.0	2.0	1.8	2.1	2.0	1.9
Belgium	4.1	6.8	8.6	9.9	10.5	10.9	11.8
Federal Republic of Germany	2.6	4.7	4.6	4.5	4.3	3.8	3.9
Denmark	2.5	6.0	6.1	7.8	7.3	6.0	6.9
Finland	1.7	2.2	4.0	6.1	7.5	6.2	4.9
Great Britain	2.6	3.9	5.3	5.7	5.7	5.4	6.8
Italy	5.4	5.8	6.7	7.1	7.2	7.7	7.5
Netherlands [a]	3.5	5.0	5.3	5.1	5.0	5.0	5.8
Norway	0.6	1.1	1.1	0.9	1.1	1.3	1.1
Sweden	2.0	1.6	1.6	1.8	2.2	2.1	1.9
Japan	1.4	1.9	2.0	2.0	2.2	2.1	2.0
United States	5.6	8.5	7.7	7.0	6.0	5.8	7.1

a. Inclusive of jobless housewives.
SOURCE: OECD; United Nations.

From World War II to the Longest Postwar Boom

Historical analysis does not offer many clues to the specifics of the Austrian labor market of today. The postwar shortage of labor was followed by a tendency toward labor surpluses during the reconstruction period, despite high GDP growth rates. During the "stabilization crisis" of 1952, the unemployment rate shot up to 8 percent. This tendency cannot be ascribed to demographic factors, because during that period the population remained constant and the number of persons of working age decreased. The increase in the labor supply was due, on the one hand, to rising participation rates of women and, on the other, to a rapid shift from self-employment to wage employment. The beginning of the "first Austrian economic miracle" during that period led to an increased absorption of these surpluses and to a balanced labor market.

The early 1960s were marked by structural changes in commodity and labor markets. The size of the working-age population further decreased, but now there were no longer compensating increases in participation rates. Increasing school attendance rates and improvements in the pension system lowered activity rates. The number of domestic wage and salary workers stagnated, since the reduction in the supply of workers due to a smaller labor force was compensated for by the shifting of the self-employed into wage employment. For this reason the lower GDP growth rates of the 1960s did not have any noticeable effect on the situation of the labor market, especially since reductions in statutory work hours and the introduction of a compulsory ninth school year also reduced the supply of labor.

The longest boom of the postwar years, which began in 1968, would have been impeded by labor supply shortages, had not the social partners already agreed at the beginning of the 1960s to give up their restrictive policies toward labor migration and permit a higher number of foreign workers to enter Austria. The rapid buildup of the stock of foreign labor reached its highest level in 1973, with 226,800 foreign workers—that is, 8.7 percent of total wage and salary employment. This foreign addition to the domestic labor force made it possible to increase employment by approximately 2 percent per annum at the beginning of the 1970s, a rate that had not been achieved since the 1950s. At the same time the number of unemployed persons was reduced—due in part to the export of seasonal unemployment. In 1973 unemployment reached its lowest level of 1.2 percent. (Table 2 shows the determinants of the labor supply in Austria for 1946–1980.)

The early 1970s were characterized by the basic changes in labor supply conditions mentioned previously. While the total population declined, the labor force increased. The demographic increase in the working-age population was made even more acute by the fact that the "education explosion" of the early 1970s began to lose force and no more important changes occurred in the area of old-age pensions. Labor force participation rates started to pick up again, however, because of the continuing trend toward female employment. In addition, the trend from self-employment to wage employment continued, if at reduced rates. Thus with an annual average increase in the number of employed of 35,000, or 1.4 percent since 1974, the rapid increase in the supply of labor continued in spite of the recession of 1974/1975 and lower GDP growth rates since then.

Crisis Management

Initially the Austrian government "reacted" to the crisis of 1974 (the oil-price-induced recession) by accepting reduced tax receipts and maintaining expenditures at their planned levels. Later in 1974 government expenditures were even stepped up. Depending on the economic credo of the observer, opinions vary widely as to the success of these fiscal policy measures. In the land of Austro-Keynesianism, high positive effects have usually been attributed to them. Hans Seidel estimated that the first-round effects accounted for between 1 percent and 3 percent

TABLE 2

DETERMINANTS OF THE LABOR SUPPLY IN AUSTRIA, 1946–1980
(average annual change, inclusive of migration)

	1946/1952	1952/1962	1962/1967	1967/1975	1975/1980
Population					
Change (absolute)	−8,600[e]	20,200	38,700	24,600	−2,900
Change (%)	−0.1[e]	0.3	0.5	0.3	−0.0
Population of working age[a]					
Change (absolute)	−34,300[e]	−500	−10,000	9,600	47,400
Change (%)	−0.8[e]	−0.0	−0.2	0.2	1.1
Labor force					
Change (absolute)		9,800	−26,200	11,800	17,300
Change (%)		0.3	−0.8	0.4	0.5
Self-employed[b]					
Change (absolute)[d]		−20,800	−29,300	−21,200	−12,300
Change (%)[d]		−2.1	−3.5	−3.2	−2.4
Supply of wage and salary earners[c]					
Change (absolute)[d]	43,600	30,600	3,100	33,000	29,600
Change (%)[d]	2.2	1.4	0.1	1.3	1.1

a. Males: fifteen to under sixty-five years of age; females: fifteen to under sixty years of age.
b. Self-employed and family workers.
c. Wage and salary earners and unemployed persons.
d. Calculated by means of corrected data.
e. Data are for 1947 to 1952.
SOURCE: Federal Ministry of Social Administration.

of value added.[1] By multiplying the real growth effect of the budget deficit by the annual output elasticity of employment, the effects of these policies on employment can be estimated as between 0.5 percent and 1.5 percent of total employment during the critical phase. They should have been considerable, especially in 1975 and 1977.[2]

Deploying the instruments of an active labor market policy in Austria was of less overall importance, even though quite essential for regional and individual employment problems. Most of these instruments had been developed during times of full employment in accordance with OECD recommendations, mainly for the purpose of improving the allocation and training of labor. Now, however, they were applied to maintain and secure jobs.

Of primary importance were training programs for workers. Thus employees who were laid off from work did not become unemployed. Furthermore, it was assumed that new jobs could more readily be found if workers were better trained. More directly, on-the-job training was subsidized, thus enabling firms to keep excess workers on the payroll, at least temporarily. In several cases of critical relevance, direct subsidies were given. These new instruments at least partly replaced subsidization of short-term work, an established instrument. Attempts at benefit-cost calculations show that in 1975, for example, around 9,000 workers (0.3 percent of wage and salary earners) could be kept employed at a relatively low cost, which amounted to about 0.3 percent of federal budget expenditures (see table 3).

Changes in the Structure of Demand

Austria's discretionary economic and labor market policies were aided by a number of autonomous factors in securing full employment during this critical phase (1974–1980). One of the most important of these factors is the expansion of the country's service sector. At the beginning of the 1970s, employment in the tertiary sector began to rise rapidly. While the manufacturing sector reduced its number of employees after 1973, expansion in the service sector continued and hardly reacted to cyclical patterns. The overall number of wage and salary earners increased by 131,800 between 1974 and 1980; employment in the secondary sector declined by 37,000; and in the service sector employment increased by 179,000. This development can be attributed primarily to the increase in the supply of public services since the beginning of the 1960s, especially in the areas of education and health, but also to the expansion of private services such as trade, banking, insurance, and tax consulting. In addition, several steps to reduce the workweek had a positive effect on service sector employment, given this sector's relatively low productivity. It seems that

TABLE 3

THE NUMBER OF WORKERS IN AUSTRIA AFFECTED BY
LABOR MARKET POLICIES, 1974–1980
(absolute numbers)

	1974	1975	1976	1977	1978	1979	1980
Training programs	2,700	2,500	2,500	2,000	3,200	3,800	1,900
In institutions	2,100	1,600	1,500	1,100	2,500	2,900	1,200
In firms	600	900	1,000	900	700	900	700
Job creation	1,200	1,800	900	1,000	1,300	1,600	1,200
Short-term work	800	4,100	200	40	—	—	500
Apprenticeships	500	500	900	1,400	1,800	2,300	1,900
Total	5,200	8,900	4,500	4,440	6,300	7,700	5,500
As % of wage and salary earners	0.20	0.34	0.17	0.16	0.23	0.28	0.20
Labor market expenditures as a percentage of:							
Gross domestic product	0.08	0.08	0.08	0.07	0.09	0.09	0.06
Federal budget	0.29	0.27	0.25	0.24	0.29	0.28	0.20

SOURCE: Federal Ministry of Social Administration; calculated by Austrian Institute for Economic Research.

the overall expansion in tertiary-sector employment was less the result of a favorable situation in the market for qualified personnel and more the result of the development of demand for services.

The extraordinary increases in service sector employment in Austria are most likely the result of a catch-up process. During the 1950s Austrian economic development was characterized by rapid expansion of industrial output—only later, and then slowly, did the service sector expand.[3] Up to the present time, the rapid increase in service sector employment does not seem to be exaggerated. When the share of the service sector is correlated with per capita GDP and compared with that of other countries, Austria's position is approximately on the average curve.[4] In earlier years Austria was rather below the norm, as was Germany.

On the demand side, the rapid expansion of the service sector supported a long-term development having social origins—namely, female employment. Out of a total rise in employment of 131,800 between 1974 and 1980, 97,300 were women. The favorable situation in the market for female labor prevented female unemployment and also made possible a further increase in the labor force participation rate of middle-aged women even after the recession year of 1974.

Another factor that stimulated the demand for labor can be traced back to the development of labor productivity. Since 1974/1975 nearly all Western industrial countries have experienced sharp declines in labor productivity.[5] Austria was also affected by this phenomenon. Whereas the gross domestic product per hour worked increased at an average annual rate of 4.8 percent between 1967 and 1975, this rate fell to 3.0 percent between 1975 and 1980. This reduction is also a result of the shifting of workers into the low-productivity service sector (this structural effect amounts to about 25 percent during the period investigated), but productivity was also lowered in the secondary sector. Thus after 1975 much more labor had to be employed than before to achieve the same increases in GDP. This development benefited the Austrian labor market, on the one hand, but, on the other hand, imposed an additional burden on enterprises because of the relatively higher labor costs.

In this regard, it might be of interest to mention something about the "climate" of the Austrian economy. The policy of social partnership —as well as a host of historical reasons—makes Austrian entrepreneurs think twice before dismissing workers. This is especially true in the nationalized industries, where maintaining a given level of employment is a major objective. To a lesser degree, the same also holds true for private industry. Such a policy cannot be kept up forever because of the costs of this excess labor, but it certainly helps during short-run fluctuations in employment.

It is impossible to quantify the effects of all demand-stimulating measures separately, since they overlap each other. Expenditures by the Labor Market Administration are budget expenditures, which moreover influence the output elasticity of employment, since in reality they have the same effect as increased spending on civil servants.

Labor Supply Restrictions

Of course, all these demand effects together would not have been sufficient to absorb the growing supply of labor. At the beginning of the critical period, however, Austria possessed a relatively large supply of foreign labor. In 1973 the maximum number of 226,800 was reached, or 8.7 percent of the work force. After that year the number of foreign workers was reduced: by 1980 they numbered 174,700, or 6.3 percent of wage and salary earners. The reduction of employment in manufacturing and the building trades primarily affected foreigners. The reduction in foreign employment was not achieved through layoffs or dismissals. Since a considerable number of foreign workers return (voluntarily) to their home countries every year, the Austrian Labor Market Adminis-

TABLE 4
FOREIGN WORKERS IN AUSTRIA, 1961–1980

Year	Total No. of Foreign Workers	Change from the Previous Year	
		Absolute numbers	Percent
1961	16,200	—	—
1962	17,700	1,500	9.3
1963	21,500	3,800	21.5
1964	26,100	4,600	21.4
1965	37,300	11,200	42.9
1966	51,500	14,200	38.1
1967	66,200	14,700	28.5
1968	67,500	1,300	2.0
1969	87,700	20,200	29.9
1970	111,700	24,000	27.4
1971	150,200	38,500	34.5
1972	187,100	36,800	24.5
1973	226,800	39,700	21.2
1974	222,300	−4,500	−2.0
1975	191,000	−31,300	−14.1
1976	171,700	−19,300	−10.1
1977	188,900	17,200	10.0
1978	176,700	−12,200	−6.4
1979	170,600	−6,100	−3.5
1980	174,700	4,100	2.4

SOURCE: Federal Ministry of Social Administration.

tration reduced foreign employment by restricting the entry of "replacement" labor into Austria. Quite late, and only at a low rate, have Austrian workers taken the jobs of foreigners, especially in construction, metals, and wood products. (Table 4 shows the annual changes in the number of foreigners employed in Austria from 1961 to 1980.)

Overall statutory reductions in working hours that had already been put in place during the years of full employment also helped to alleviate labor market problems. Opinions vary widely as to the effectiveness of working-hour reductions as an instrument of employment policy. For Austria such effects have been established by means of econometric investigations.[6] In 1975 the normal workweek was reduced from forty-two to forty hours, and in 1977 the minimum vacation period was extended from three to four weeks. There is reason to assume that these

TABLE 5
AGE-SPECIFIC UNEMPLOYMENT RATES IN AUSTRIA, 1967–1979

Age Group	1967ᵃ/1975			1975/1979		
	Male	Female	Total	Male	Female	Total
Under 17	0.15	0.77	0.42	0.20	1.15	0.61
18–19	0.32	1.47	0.87	0.61	1.56	1.07
15–19	0.23	1.15	0.66	0.41	1.38	0.85
20–29	0.28	3.63	1.61	0.66	1.93	1.19
30–39	0.24	2.70	1.03	0.58	2.19	1.15
40–49	0.42	1.61	0.86	0.70	2.00	1.17
50–59	0.87	1.78	1.23	1.18	1.94	1.50
60–64	1.20	3.04	1.70	1.15	1.89	1.39
65 and older	1.48	1.85	1.62	0.67	1.19	0.89
Total	0.41	2.44	1.18	0.70	1.92	1.18

a. The data for 1967-1972 are corrected for the number of retirement applications, after April 1, 1974, exclusive of women after maternity leave.

SOURCES: Employed persons as of the end of July (basic census of the Organization of Austrian Social Security Administrations); registered unemployed as of the end of August (Federal Ministry of Social Administration).

measures did have positive effects on the employment situation, especially as 1975 was the first year when there was an ample labor supply after a long period of scarcity.

The Structure of Unemployment

Since unemployment in Austria did not noticeably increase after 1975, no major structural changes in unemployment should be expected. Youth unemployment, for instance, a problem of grave dimensions for many other countries, has never existed in Austria. When the average figures of the boom years 1967–1975 are compared with those of the stagnation phase 1975–1979, it can be seen that age-specific unemployment rates of nearly all age groups exhibited moderate increases (see table 5). The only exceptions are middle-aged women, who were affected by changes (effective 1974) in the rules regarding compensation after maternity leave, and higher age groups, where significant reductions in unemployment rates occurred, indicating discouragement effects, with older workers apparently leaving the labor force entirely.

In many countries an insufficient demand for labor seems to have affected young people disproportionately. This can be explained by the hypothesis that employers hesitate to employ youths whom they would have to pay the same wages as adults, but who have not yet gained any working experience. For this reason the productivity of young people is assumed to be lower, at least in the short run.[7]

In Austria, specific rules are in effect regulating the compensation of young workers. Graduates of compulsory education programs who at age fifteen do not continue school usually enter the so-called dual training system—that is, they become apprentices. This training program seems to be quite efficient. Those who have gone through the program generally perform well even in occupations for which they have not been specifically trained, and rarely have difficulty in finding a job. Apprentices can also be used in firms, and assist in the regular production process after a short period. Moreover, their employment is very attractive to firms since their compensation is only approximately one-fourth of the average wage. Thus even in times when there were high increases in the supply of youth labor, the demand for apprentices always outran the supply.

It seems, however, that the lower overall demand for labor has affected higher age groups. As was mentioned earlier, the reduction in old-age unemployment rates can be interpreted as the result of discouragement. Data show that since 1975 these age groups have indeed left the labor force at a faster rate. If one attempts to estimate the amount of hidden unemployment by means of analyzing labor force participation rates, school attendance rates, and retirement rates, one can find a small number of such unemployed among youths, very few in the female middle ranges, but a considerable number in the higher age groups, especially women. It does seem, however, that in most of these cases people do not leave the labor force, strictly speaking, but move into the public pension scheme. Many of the women qualify for early retirement.[8] Although it is true that in most of these cases active employment is not given up voluntarily, there are no grave social consequences. (Table 6 shows data on hidden unemployment in Austria for males and females from 1974 to 1979.)

The small changes in the number of unemployed persons in Austria did result in specific developments of the flows of unemployed. Whereas in most Western industrial countries the relatively high numbers of unemployed are due to a lengthening of the period during which workers are out of a job, the opposite is true for Austria. Starting in the mid-1970s, a slight increase occurred in the inflow into the ranks of the unemployed, but this was overcompensated for by increasing outflows: the average period of unemployment in Austria fell from 10.2 weeks in 1974 to 8.1 weeks in 1979.[9]

In this context it is also important to note that unemployment compensation in Austria, in contrast to many other countries, is relatively low.

TABLE 6
HIDDEN UNEMPLOYMENT IN AUSTRIA, FOR MALES AND FEMALES, 1974–1979

Age Group	1974	1975	1976	1977	1978	1979
		Males				
15–19		900	1,500		1,600	3,500
20–29						
30–39						
40–49						
50–59	50	300	400	600	1,000	1,700
60–64		3,300	1,400			
65 and older						
Total	50	4,500	3,300	600	2,600	5,200
		Females				
15–19					2,400	
20–29	5,500					3,700
30–39		3,900				4,200
40–49						
50–59				4,200	4,800	16,700
60–64						
65 and older						
Total	5,500	3,900		4,200	7,200	24,600
Total (males and females)	5,550	8,400	3,300	4,800	9,800	29,800
Total (males and females between ages 15 and 49)	5,500	4,800	1,500		4,000	11,400
Rate of hidden unemployment (males and females, 15–49)	0.20	0.18	0.05		0.14	0.40

SOURCE: Author.

It amounts to a maximum of 60 percent of the reference wage up to an upper limit. Thus there is no incentive whatever to prefer unemployment to a—even less qualified—job. In addition, labor exchange offices tend to monitor closely the willingness to work and thus do not regard unemployment compensation as a welfare payment. This practice speeds up the absorption of unemployed persons into existing jobs. This data would

TABLE 7

Growth in the Domestic Labor Force of Austria, 1980–1991

| Year | Growth of Labor Force | |
	Absolute numbers	Percent
1980/81	29,000	1.0
1981/82	31,000	1.1
1982/83	31,700	1.1
1983/84	30,500	1.1
1984/85	29,000	1.0
1985/86	26,600	0.9
1986/87	20,300	0.7
1987/88	18,100	0.6
1988/89	16,000	0.5
1989/90	12,900	0.4
1990/91	8,400	0.3

SOURCE: Austrian Institute for Economic Research.

indicate that Austria's labor market has grown slack since 1975 and that problems have started to appear in certain enterprises and sectors. Still, the total demand for labor has been strong enough to absorb workers who have been laid off elsewhere.

Maintaining Full Employment

The question arises whether it will be possible in the future, as it has been in the past, to maintain full employment in Austria. The Austrian labor force is expected to increase annually more than 1 percent, at least up to 1985 (see table 7). To absorb the extra labor supply, *ceteris paribus*, a GDP growth rate of about 4 percent would be necessary, so large as to seem completely unrealistic. It is therefore imperative to examine the factors that have determined Austrian labor market conditions as to their probable future development. To what extent can these factors be influenced (favorably) by labor market instruments?

First, there is no reason to assume that the trend toward slower productivity growth (down to about 3 percent per annum), which has manifested itself since 1975, will not continue through the 1980s. There is nothing in the available Austrian data that points to the elimination of jobs because of rationalization, as has been reported for Germany in the mass media. It does not seem likely, however, that the extremely low productivity gains of the past years (2.5 percent in 1980; 0 percent in

TABLE 8

Average Annual Changes in Production, Labor Productivity,
and Hours Worked in Austria, 1958–1980
(percent)

	1958/1962	1962/1967	1967/1975	1975/1980
Gross domestic product (GDP) (in constant prices)	4.8	4.4	4.6	4.0
Wage and salary earners	1.5	0.2	1.3[a]	1.1[b]
Working hours	−1.6	−0.4	−1.5	−0.1
Number of hours worked	−0.1	−0.2	−0.2	1.0
GDP/hours worked	4.9	4.6	4.8	3.0

a. Corrected for changes in the status of family workers.
b. Calculated by means of corrected data.
Source: OECD and the Institute for Economic Research.

1981), which point to high rates of hoarding of labor, can last, because in the medium term firms will not be able to bear these cost burdens. (Table 8 shows average annual changes in production, labor productivity, and hours worked in Austria from 1958 to 1980.)

Labor market policies can influence the development of labor supply only to a limited extent; but there have already been some autonomous changes resulting from the changed labor market situation. The older U.S. literature would have expected repercussions in the participation rates of the "secondary labor force" under conditions of longer-lasting underemployment. The more recent international developments have different characteristics, however. In most Western industrial countries no reductions in female participation rates occurred after the 1975 recession with its concomitant rising unemployment. This phenomenon has been explained by changes in the occupational behavior of women, whose labor participation, in contrast to earlier years, has acquired permanent status.[10] This development has been especially noticeable in Austria. The Austrian situation, in addition to exhibiting such long-range trends, is also characterized by reductions in the participation rates of older age groups, a trend that is likely to continue.

In contrast to the female participation rate, male participation rates in the prime age categories fell in Austria, as well as in most other countries (see figure 1). This surprising phenomenon can be interpreted in several ways, many of which do not seem plausible, such as changes in the propensity to work, and so on. Instead, this development seems to be the result of the expansion of the so-called underground or black economy which has been observed recently in most countries.[11] The

FIGURE 1

Trends in Labor Force Participation Rates in Austria, 1961–1979

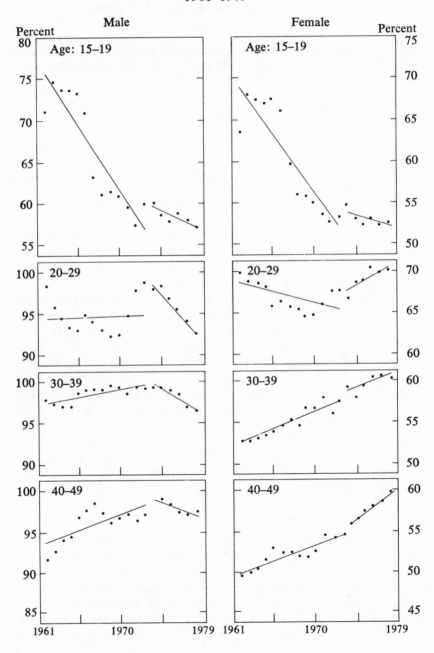

FIGURE 1 (continued)

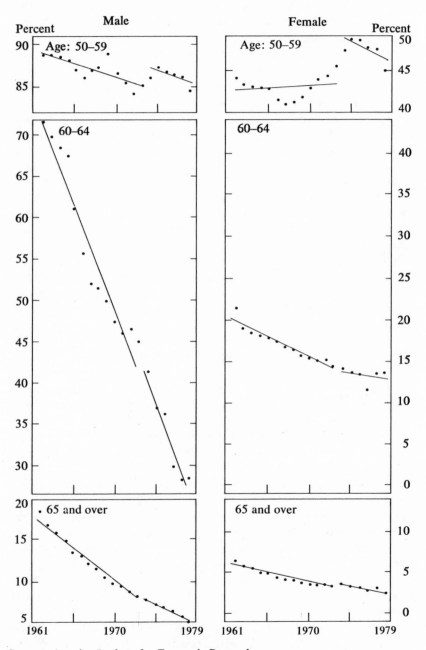

SOURCE: Austrian Institute for Economic Research.

expansion of the black economy does not really solve the problems of labor market policy. On the one hand, it inhibits the increase in registered excess labor supply as long as it absorbs new workers. On the other hand, its production satisfies parts of total final demand. If demand does not expand sufficiently, the black economy will also be adversely affected. If this sector stagnates, it cannot absorb any more labor; if it shrinks, labor might even flow back into the official sectors.

Recent developments in the Austrian labor markets also included a reduction in the shifting from self-employment to wage and salary employment. Although the number of self-employed in agriculture fell on average by 3.6 percent per year between 1968 and 1975, the rate of decrease amounted to only 2.9 percent per year between 1975 and 1980. Similar developments occurred outside of agriculture, where the number of self-employed decreased by 2.3 percent per year between 1968 and 1975 but by only 1 percent between 1975 and 1980. It is not unlikely that this slowdown will continue at an even higher rate in the future and may come to a complete end for self-employed persons outside of agriculture.

Such endogenous developments may ease labor market problems in the future, as in the past, but they will not be able to prevent problems entirely. There are, however, a number of policy options open to the Austrian government that may be used to maintain reasonably full employment.

Formulating Labor Market Policies

The number of foreign workers in Austria can still be substantially reduced. Yet the question is open as to how much longer this can continue, or whether domestic workers can be substituted for foreigners. Foreigners in Austria normally hold unskilled jobs at relatively low pay. It is difficult to estimate the extent to which Austrian workers are prepared to accept such jobs.

In addition, several changes might be made in institutional factors. Compulsory education, for example, might be extended by one year; the period of maternity leave for women after giving birth might also be extended. Considerable effects could result from a general reduction in the pensionable age. The major problem with all these proposals, however, is their considerable cost, which would have to be covered by the federal budget. Given the present budgetary problems of the Austrian government, though, it is highly unlikely that such measures will be adopted.

This leaves the option of again reducing working hours. Such reductions seem to have been quite successful in the past. There is no telling, however, whether this success can be repeated, given the trend toward underemployment and reduced economic growth. If the hoarding of labor is strong and expectations about the future are pessimistic, a reduction in work hours could take place without labor market effects if firms are able to meet their given production volume with their available labor. The reduction in working hours could be completely counteracted by extraordinary increases in the output per man-hour. This would, of course, mainly apply to the secondary sector. It is highly unlikely that the service sectors—especially the public sector—would be heavy hoarders of labor, mainly because of their rigid forms of organization. Thus the service sector might very well show positive effects in terms of new jobs.

The costs of a reduction in working hours, however, are likely to create problems. In the past, reducing the number of hours worked did not lead to a decrease in the compensation of workers—thus firms' costs increased. In the future, if reduced working hours are to remain as an instrument of employment policy, however, they may possibly have to be implemented without financial compensation to workers. Yet many people argue that it is politically impossible to lower wages and salaries —thus reductions in working hours have to be rejected for cost considerations. This line of argument is heard frequently in West Germany, but need not necessarily apply to Austria. It is true that cuts in nominal wages are unlikely; but that should not be the focal point as long as nominal GDP is increasing. For example, if working hours were reduced by one hour per week, or 2.5 percent, without financial compensation, negotiations during each of the two following wage rounds would result in 1 percent less wage increases than would have been expected according to historical experience (based on productivity growth, the rate of inflation, profit performance, and so on). This does not seem unduly harsh. This reasoning leads to the conclusion that for Austria, statutory reductions in working hours should not be rejected completely as an instrument of employment policy.

It is uncertain, however, whether autonomous changes in the labor force and the remaining instruments of labor market policy will be able to maintain full employment in the future in Austria. It is quite probable that some additional economic growth will be necessary during the next three years in order to overcome the critical phase, which will last until 1985.

By the mid-1980s the Austrian labor market will look different from today. During the second half of the decade, the growth of the Austrian labor force will slow down, coming to a halt by 1990. Thus, unless extreme external shocks occur, the employment problem will then become less acute. Of course, the slowdown in the growth of the labor supply is not strong enough to lead to labor shortages in this decade. Even if the economy starts to boom again toward the end of the decade, labor scarcities will be mitigated by increasing labor participation rates in specific sectors, especially for higher age groups. It is also likely that approaching labor shortages would be postponed by a more intense utilization of labor. The growth rate of output per hour, which had dropped to 3 percent after 1975, might rise again to around 5 percent per annum. This expectation is based on the experience of the past few years, when cyclical fluctuations showed up less in changes in the number of persons employed and more in changes in productivity gains.

Structural Changes in the Labor Market

After World War II the conditions affecting the supply of labor in Austria underwent dramatic change. One of the most significant developments was the fact that during this period a large number of the self-employed joined the ranks of wage and salary workers. This happened especially in the agricultural sector, where a very fast rate of growth of labor productivity, in conjunction with slackening demand, resulted in deteriorating income opportunities and created a strong incentive for migration. In 1952, 32.4 percent of the total work force was in agriculture; in 1981, however, agriculture's share amounted to only 9.0 percent. The migration out of agriculture must be understood in a broader sense insofar as a large number of youths coming from agricultural families began their work experience outside this sector. Thus about one-fourth of the total labor force shifted between sectors during this period. This was the reason for the high increase in wage and salary employment which—as has been mentioned previously— had not been anticipated from purely demographic developments. Out-migration from agriculture continued during the following years at the same rate, but has increasingly lost importance because of the dwindling number of people in this sector. During the mid-1960s this development made it necessary for the Austrian labor market authorities to turn to foreign workers.

The massive shifts in the composition of the producing sectors of the Austrian economy led to similarly significant changes in the regional distribution of the population and in this way influenced the supply side of the labor market. These regional shifts were characterized by a permanent process of concentration, depending on the conditions of production. This process, however, developed neither continuously nor evenly. During the 1950s, the concentration process centered on the cities (with the exception of Vienna, whose larger size excludes such effects). During the following decade, it shifted to the suburbs, a process that is still under way. During the 1950s and the 1960s these shifts in the population structure were the result of migratory movements of Austrian workers. During the 1970s, when the out-migration from agriculture had begun to lose its importance, regional changes were mainly caused by the influx of foreign workers, since this type of labor was employed and directed toward the economic centers (cities, suburbs, and environs).

The shifts in labor market conditions in Austria mirrored changes in the conditions of production. Austrian regional policy attempted to counter these movements, with the aim of creating equal income opportunities in all regions of Austria. These intentions were supported by the labor market developments of the early 1960s. During the second half of the 1950s, full employment was achieved in the cities and industrial centers. Toward the end of the decade, severe labor shortages began to appear in those regions. This fact motivated a large number of firms with a relatively simple production program to locate in agricultural areas in order to make use of the existing labor reserves. Many of these establishments were subsidiaries of German parent companies that wanted to locate in Austria in order to bridge tariff barriers between two different economic blocs (the European Economic Community and the European Free Trade Association). Labor reserves in these regions consisted mainly of women who had not yet been employed. Thus additional jobs and income opportunities were created in agricultural areas without changing the regional population distribution.

From the mid-1960s on, the wave of new firms coming into existence began to subside. Since 1975 it has virtually come to an end.[12] For this reason recent attempts to industrialize the agricultural areas have failed completely. These regional problems, however, have to be seen in the context of the size and the geographical dispersion of the total national area of Austria. The major centers are distributed over the country in such a way that nearly all regions—with the exception of a few mountainous areas—are within 100 kilometers' commuting distance of a central region. Thus, until now, regional disparities have been balanced out by either migration or commuting.

The worldwide crisis that has affected the basic industries since the mid-1970s has added a new regional problem: the old industrial areas. Austria possesses a few industrial regions, with historical roots, which were founded in the early days of industrialization. These industries were quite successful in the postwar years and especially during the periods of high growth, but have encountered severe difficulties since 1975. The fact that these industries have been extremely slow in adapting to changes in demand has increased their difficulties. It seems unlikely that this problem can be solved by out-migration from these areas since the inhabitants of these regions have proved to be very immobile,[13] in contrast to the agricultural population, which in the past exhibited a high degree of mobility. It seems possible that these areas might become centers of unemployment in the future, even if the rest of the country achieves full employment again.

The Trend toward More Highly Qualified Labor

Since World War II the occupational structure of the Austrian work force has undergone drastic changes. Changes in demand and technical progress, on the one hand, and improved access to education, on the other hand, led to considerable changes in labor quality. The reduction in agricultural employment as a result of increasing productivity and stagnating demand has already been mentioned elsewhere. Also, productivity increases in manufacturing were responsible for stagnation in the number of occupations. Since services can be rationalized only to a very limited extent—at least until recently—and since growing income increases the demand for services, the number of service employees increased remarkably. The percentage of white-collar workers in total wage and salary employment rose from 20.7 percent in 1951 to 35.5 percent in 1971.

Changes in the structure of production produced a clear trend toward more highly skilled occupations (see table 9). This trend also occurred within individual sectors of the economy. It can be shown by comparing skill levels with the change in the number of individual occupations: that the occupations with the highest skill levels showed the highest growth rates.[14] Even the heavy in-migration of foreign workers with relatively low skills did not change this trend significantly. This trend continued until after 1974, but lower rates of economic growth also slowed down structural change. No basic change is expected in the 1980s for the range of medium skills. Problems for labor market policies occur only when it is a question of whether the available supply of labor will match the expected demand in terms of skills.

Of course, this does not mean that the supply of and demand for skilled labor in each individual occupation have to correspond exactly. Certain skill requirements can be met satisfactorily with basic qualifications and with additional training later. Imbalances will have to appear in these partial markets, however, before any changes can be expected. The experience of the past shows that existing labor market policy instruments should be enough to solve these problems.

TABLE 9
CHANGES IN THE SKILL LEVELS OF OCCUPATIONAL GROUPS IN AUSTRIA, 1951–1971

Occupational Group	Standardized Rates of Change[a]		Percentage of Persons Completing Secondary Education or Apprenticeship (1971)
	1951/1961	1961/1971	
Agriculture	−30.0	−35.8	11.8
Manufacturing	4.2	−4.5	48.0
Sales personnel	35.8	20.6	61.2
Transportation	4.3	12.3	48.4
Service occupations	10.9	10.8	28.4
Technical occupations	32.6	60.8	87.0
Office workers	24.7	25.2	71.8
Health, teaching, cultural occupations	8.0	30.1	80.4

a. The standardized rates of change have been adjusted by the change in total employment. Thus structural changes between two periods can be compared directly.
SOURCE: Austrian Statistical Office, censuses for 1951, 1961, and 1971; author's calculations.

It has been variously suggested that during the coming decade Austria will suffer from an excess supply of skilled workers. This suggestion does not seem to be justified. Even during periods of slow growth this type of labor has always been in heavy demand. Even though the number of skilled workers has steadily increased, at given wages the demand for such workers has always exceeded supply. The share of skilled labor in total employment in manufacturing and the construction sectors has increased in the long run.[15] The scarcity of skilled labor continued in spite of the fact that the high birthrates around the mid-1960s resulted in an increasing number of apprentices toward the end of the 1970s. This number will decrease during the 1980s, for demographic reasons. Thus it can be expected that the supply of skilled labor will grow more slowly during the coming decade.

The Education Explosion

Problems might arise, however, in the area of high-level education. At the beginning of the 1960s the term "education explosion" was coined.

It had a number of meanings. It was supposed to direct attention to the importance of human capital for economic growth. It was maintained that many countries would not be able to meet the demand for university-educated graduates because it was felt that it would be impossible to increase the number of students and graduates quickly enough. Thus it was argued that many countries would suffer heavy losses in terms of forgone economic growth. Social considerations were later added to these economic arguments. According to one of them, a university education should be available to everybody, not just to a relatively small social stratum that perpetuates itself. This formed the basis of the argument that education is a social right, owed every citizen without cost, in which economic considerations are not allowed to be of concern.

These considerations caused all Western industrial states to increase their efforts in the field of education dramatically. The government covered all educational costs; students from lower-income families received stipends; the number of professors and academic personnel increased considerably; and new universities were founded. These efforts increased the number of university graduates considerably within a relatively short period of time, but it now seems that forecasts about the demand for university graduates were too high. Most Western countries soon began to have an excess labor supply in certain fields, which has increased since 1974/1975 because of low economic growth. Similar surpluses also have begun to appear in Austria. It is not expected, however, that imbalances in this labor market segment will lead to unemployment, since university graduates are highly skilled workers who can be used in a number of jobs. It seems likely, though, that some university graduates will not be able to find the kinds of jobs that correspond to their education.

Notes

1. H. Seidel, *Unsere Staatsfinanzen,* Ministry of Finance (Vienna, 1978), p. 76.

2. F. Butschek, *Vollbeschäftigung in der Krise* (Vienna: ORAC, 1971), p. 32.

3. F. Butschek, "Umschichtungen in der Struktur der Erwerbstätigen," *Monatsberichte* des Österreichischen Institutes für Wirtschaftsforschung, no. 2 (1970).

4. H. Kepplinger, *Sektoraler Strukturvergleich zwischen Österreich und der Bundesrepublik Deutschland* (Vienna: ORAC, 1979), pp. 22 ff.

5. E. F. Denison, "Explanations of Productivity Growth," *Survey of Current Business,* U.S. Department of Commerce, no. 8 (1979).

6. For employment in the manufacturing sector the following equation provided the best "explanation."

$$BS = -4.886 + 0.480 Y_{Ind_t} + 0.298 Y_{Ind_{t-1}} - 0.433 AZ_t - 0.372 AZ_{t-1} - 0.231 AZ_{t-2}$$
$$\quad\quad\;\; 11 \quad\quad 13 \quad\quad\;\; 20 \quad\quad\quad 39 \quad\quad\; 42 \quad\quad\; 54$$

$$R^2 = 0.92;\ DW = 1.56$$

where BS = total employment in manufacturing, Y_{Ind} = the value added of manufacturing, and AZ = hours worked. All variables were transformed into annual growth rates. The equation contains the effects of all changes in hours worked —that is, those that result from cyclical fluctuations as well as those that result from reductions in statutory working hours. The latter dominate changes in hours to such an extent, however, that the equation presented can be used to draw interpretations as to the effect of reductions in statutory hours on employment.

The coefficient of the hours variable, lagged two years, is barely significant. If this variable is eliminated, however, the fit of the equation is reduced, and the coefficients of the other two working-hours variables also become insignificant. The lag structure demonstrates the gradual adaptation of effective to statutory working hours.

No equivalent data are available for the total economy. If one attempts to approximate hours worked in the total economy by the hours in manufacturing, the statistical performance of such an equation is similar but worse. Signs and relationships are the same. See Butschek, *Vollbeschäftigung,* p. 80.

7. OECD, *Youth Unemployment* (Paris, 1978), p. 25.

8. F. Butschek, "Versteckte Arbeitslosigkeit in Österreich," *Monatsberichte* des Österreichischen Institutes für Wirtschaftsforschung, no. 7 (1981).

9. G. Biffl, "Analyse der Bewegungen auf dem Arbeitsmarkt," *Monatsberichte* des Österreichischen Institutes für Wirtschaftsforschung, no. 11 (1980).

10. J. Kreps and R. Clark, *Sex, Age and Work* (Baltimore and London: The Johns Hopkins University Press, 1975).

11. Butschek, "Versteckte Arbeitslosigkeit," p. 391.

12. N. Geldner, "Die regionale Dynamik," in H. Seidel and H. Kramer, eds., *Die österreichische Wirtschaft in den achtziger Jahren* (Stuttgart and Vienna: G. Fischer, 1980), p. 199.

13. G. Tichy, "Alte Industriegebiete in der Steiermark—ein weltweites Problem ohne Lösungsansätze," *Berichte zur Raumforschung und Raumplanung* (Vienna and New York: Springer-Verlag, no. 3/1981), p. 22.

14. E. Walterskirchen, "Berufsstruktur 1951 bis 1981," *Monatsberichte* des Österreichischen Institutes für Wirtschaftsforschung, no. 2 (1976), p. 64.

15. E. Walterskirchen, "Berufschancen für Facharbeiter," *Monatsberichte* des Österreichischen Institutes für Wirtschaftsforschung, no. 11 (1976).

Commentary

Marvin H. Kosters

The paper by Felix Butschek has a very provocative title and raises some very interesting issues: full employment during recession—how could it occur?

Since 1974, unemployment rates in Austria are reported to have been in the 2 percent range. During that period, unemployment rates in the United States have been in the 6 to 9 percent range. The rate is now about in the middle of the range, at 7½ percent. The question this raises is: Why the disparity?

Actually, there are two puzzles, I believe. First, why have unemployment rates been so low in Austria? Second, how did they stay so low during a period of recession, during a period in which inflation was falling? I found Butschek's paper very interesting, but I think it goes somewhat further in answering the second of these questions—how was unemployment kept down?—than it does in answering the first—why is it so low in the first place?

Let me begin with comments about the low unemployment rate. First, there are questions concerning the comparability of the data used in constructing unemployment rates for the two countries, the United States and Austria. It should be noted that the Austrian unemployment data are not comparable with ours in terms of their treatment of the self-employed. Austria's unemployment rate would be 1.6 percent rather than 2 percent if the self-employed were simply added to the labor force. But this measure of unemployment would not be comparable to any of several measures of unemployment used in the United States. In many respects the unemployment rate, as it is constructed in Austria, appears to be more similar to our insured unemployment rate than to our household survey data on unemployment. It is this rate that has been in the 6 to 9 percent range in recent years. Our insured employment rate, of course, has been in the 3 to 4 percent rate in the recent past.

124

The hidden unemployment data referred to in Butschek's paper are similar in many respects to our overall unemployment rate, though we also have hidden unemployment data based on concepts that extend well beyond the estimates of hidden unemployment in Austria. So there are very important questions of comparability. The sources of the information and the way the data are put together are quite different in Austria and the United States.

Another element in the low-unemployment picture concerns teen-agers. When we look at the data on Austria, we find that there are essentially no unemployed teen-agers, whereas unemployment among teen-agers in the United States has been high and has been increasing during the postwar period. Even if we had no unemployed teen-agers in the United States, however, our unemployment rate at the present time would still be close to 6 percent—so teen-age unemployment is not the only element in the picture.

One very important consideration in discussing unemployment among teen-agers in the United States is the federal minimum wage. Over the past thirty years or so, the level of that minimum wage has been about half of the average wage in manufacturing, and also the coverage in the economy of that federal minimum wage has been increased over time. If we compare U.S. minimum wage levels with what was reported for apprentices in Austria—about one-fourth of the average wage—the difference between the situation in Austria and that in the United States is quite large. Our average wage in the private nonfarm sector is about $7.00 per hour; one-fourth of that would be a wage of $1.75, instead of the current minimum wage level of $3.35. This is a considerable difference as it applies to young workers, and it raises the question of whether there are comparable wage differentials for different skill levels in Austria for other workers who are not young workers or apprentices. It would be interesting to know whether wage dispersion in Austria is large relative to that in the United States and whether a low-wage segment of the wage distribution for all ages might help to account for low unemployment also among older workers in Austria.

Another element relevant to the low unemployment rate in Austria concerns unemployment compensation. Basically, I think there are at least two factors involved. One is the size of unemployment compensation payments compared with earnings levels. In Austria, unemployment compensation is apparently approximately 60 percent of earnings, subject to an upper limit for high-wage people. In the United States, unemployment compensation payments levels vary among states. In many cases, they are above the 60 percent level, they are not generally subject to limits, and for some special programs, such as trade adjustment assistance, payments at a 70 percent rate are made. In addition, supplementary unemployment benefits are available to some of our workers, such as those in the auto industry. In general, our system seems to be more generous.

Another important issue is whether or not these payments are subject to the income tax. At least in this country, this is an important question. Our unemployment compensation payments are not subject to the personal income tax, except that in the recent past, a change was introduced for joint returns with an adjusted gross income above $25,000. At these higher income levels, unemployment compensation payments are subject to income taxation; at lower levels they are not. This is a particularly important factor for families with more than one earner or with other income sources. The replacement wage needs to be very high in some circumstances for a family to attain higher after-tax income if an unemployed member returned to work than if he were to remain unemployed.

Probably at least as important as payment rates and their treatment is the work requirement test, and apparently this is quite stringently applied in Austria. Apparently, if someone reports himself to be unemployed and seeks payments in Austria, he is very likely to be assigned a job. There is an indirect indication of this stringency in the data on the labor force participation of older male workers aged sixty to sixty-four years old. Their labor force participation shows a decline over the past twenty years, an astounding drop from 70 percent to about 30 percent. My inference from these data and the discussion in Butschek's paper is that if someone reports himself to be unemployed and seeking a job in Austria, he no longer qualifies for pension payments because he is assigned to a job. This is a different unemployment picture than exists in the United States. As a related matter, the figures for hidden unemployment in Austria show a large expansion in that component of unemployment.

With regard to the work requirement, the situation in the United States almost seems to be precisely the reverse of that in Austria. In the United States, to qualify for payments under various programs other than unemployment compensation, a person must report himself as available for work. By reporting himself as unemployed, he qualifies to receive payment. In Austria, as we have already mentioned, if a person applies for payments and thereby declares himself unemployed, he is assigned a job. So much for factors contributing to what seems to have been a very low measure of the Austrian unemployment rate.

Why didn't unemployment in Austria rise from 1975 to 1980 in the face of slackened demand and reduced inflation? There are, of course, various ways of addressing this question. First, let me describe it in demographic terms. From about 1973 or 1974 to about 1979, there was an increase in employment in Austria of approximately 150,000. About 100,000 of the additional employment was accounted for by women, through their increased labor force participation. The other 50,000 can be accounted for approximately as follows. About 50,000 foreign workers were no longer employed, and about 50,000 additional domestic working males were employed. This is a rough way of characterizing what happened. The change in numbers of foreign workers employed is attributable to changes in the flow; essentially, fewer workers were let in as replacements for those leaving in a rotating group of foreign workers. An interesting point is that the unemployment rate for foreign workers seems to have been in the 6 to 9 percent range, much like that in the United States.

Another factor that may be relevant to maintaining low unemployment and one that is discussed in Butschek's paper is an active manpower policy. The emphasis on active manpower policies is quite common in discussions of European labor market policies, and I think Butschek rightly indicates that it was not the main factor that was involved. I thought it would be useful to look at it, however, and compare it with our own manpower policies, which have sometimes not been regarded as very active.

At their peak in this country—which was about 1979—U.S. manpower programs were enormously larger, both as a share of the work force and as a fraction of the gross national product, than those in Austria. I examined U.S. training programs in institutions and firms, direct job-creation programs, short-term work programs, and so on. Certain comparisons can be made. At their peak in Austria, some 0.34 percent of wage and salary employees were in these programs. In 1975 in the United States the comparable figure was almost 4.5 percent, larger by more than a factor of ten. Taking the peak years for each country, in Austria about 0.08 percent of the gross domestic product was spent on these programs, while in the United States 0.62 percent was spent, not quite a factor of ten. So the U.S. programs were enormously larger if I have interpreted the programs and data correctly. In addition, apprentices are included in the Austrian numbers. In our numbers, they are not. Although we do not have a large apprentice system, this underscores the difference in program sizes.

There is another major difference between the Austrian situation and that in the United States. In the Austrian case, the size of the program was cut in half in a year, from 1975 to 1976. Ours was never reduced. It doubled in real terms from about 1973 and 1974 to 1979. It stabilized somewhat after 1974, but it was never reduced, so it did not perform much of the countercyclical function.

Although these comparisons surprised me somewhat, they do not seem to account for the continued low unemployment in Austria. It seems to me that much of the answer must lie in other policies. It has been mentioned that Austrian firms, especially in the nationalized industries, lay off workers reluctantly. It seems to me that this is likely to have been a significant element. There are some indications that employment was maintained and paid for through a combination of all the various price-setting elements in the social partnership arrangements that essentially amount to what I would regard as internal and disguised subsidies that permit workers to be kept on the rolls. This is a viable short-term approach when it is carried out carefully in terms of price increases allowed to account for increased costs of employing what in the British economy have been called "redundant workers," and so on.

The data on productivity provide a hint that this may have occurred. The productivity figures in Butschek's paper are: 4.8 percent from 1967 to 1975, 3 percent from 1975 to 1980, 2.5 percent in 1980, and zero in 1981. It seems to me that these policies, had they been significant—and they seem to have been significant during this period—raise questions about the extent to which redundant workers are being accumulated in the Austrian economy. This raises questions about the possible need to work toward rationalizing the problem in the future. Such adjustments might be quite painful when there is a perceived need for reducing the number of redundant workers.

One difference in labor market developments in Austria and in the United States appears to arise more from how policies are labeled than from actual differences in policies. As I have already noted, worker training and public service employment programs in the United States were not contracted after 1975. Although such programs were contracted in Austria, the pronounced expansion of employment in public services may have more than offset this decline. To some extent, the counterpart of increases in government-supported employment programs in the United States was expanded direct government employment in Austria.

Finally, it seems to me that some puzzling concerns are expressed in Butschek's paper. It is mentioned, for example, that in view of the continued growth of the labor force, it might be necessary to make further cuts in working hours and so on. The author also mentions that 4 percent real growth seems completely unrealistic, even though a growth rate only slightly lower than this occurred during the past decade. I would have thought that the projected labor force increases would help to make possible a fairly strong growth rate. The paper seems to suggest, however, that the need for higher growth is somewhat unfortunate instead of presenting an opportunity and a challenge.

In summary, stabilizing unemployment seems to have been given overriding policy emphasis in Austria during the past five or six years. It seems, however, to have come at a price in terms of productivity, in terms of the possible buildup of redundant workers, and in terms of what is called "hidden unemployment" in this paper, but which in our system would show up as actual unemployment.

Austrian Industrial Structure and Industrial Policy

Oskar Grünwald

The Structure of Austrian Industry

Industrial Growth. Austria is one of the highly developed industrial countries of the world. Mining and manufacturing contribute approximately 30 percent to the gross national product (GNP). Industry employs 630,000 people, which is 22 percent of the total labor force. During the past twenty years, industrial growth generally exceeded the growth of GNP, which confirmed industry in its function as an important pacemaker of the economy. With an increase of 4.7 percent (see table 1) for the period of 1960/1980, the growth of Austria's industrial production exceeded the average growth of industry in countries of the Organization for Economic Cooperation and Development, or OECD (see table 2).

Industry and Small Business. If the figures concerning industry are to be compared with international data, one has to bear in mind that small businesses (*Gewerbe*) in Austria have a significant share of the production of goods which is not included in official industry statistics. The approximately 3,000 largest of these small businesses in the producing sector accounted for 145,000 employees, while the 6,846 industrial establishments had a total of 630,000 employees. These small businesses are relatively important in mechanical engineering, where they contribute 16 percent of total Austrian production. In the automotive industry, including the production of parts and repairs, the share of small businesses is 27 percent; in the fabricated-metals sector it is 35 percent; electrical equipment, 16 percent; and textiles, 5 percent.[1] The figures presented in this study are based on Austrian industry statistics. Thus a direct comparison with international figures is only possible to a certain extent because other countries—perhaps with the exception of Germany—include small businesses in their statistics and Austria does not.

130

TABLE 1

ANNUAL GROWTH OF GNP AND INDUSTRIAL PRODUCTION
IN AUSTRIA, 1960–1980
(percent)

	1960/ 1965	1965/ 1970	1970/ 1975	1975/ 1980	1960/ 1980
GNP	4.3	5.3	3.8	4.0	4.3
Industrial production	4.4	6.3	3.3	4.8	4.7

SOURCE: Austrian government statistics.

The Growth of Productivity. The output of Austrian industry has almost tripled during the past two decades (table 3) without a significant increase in the labor force. The rising volume of production was therefore accompanied by a distinct increase in productivity.

Sectoral Development. An analysis of the sectoral development of Austria's industry shows that the highest growth rates were achieved in the chemical, electrical, wood, pulp and paper, and machinery industries. Foundries and vehicle industries attained smaller growth rates, whereas

TABLE 2

ANNUAL GROWTH OF INDUSTRIAL PRODUCTION IN VARIOUS COUNTRIES,
1960–1980
(percent)

	1960/1965	1965/1970	1970/1975	1975/1980	1960/1980
Austria	4.4	6.3	3.3	4.8	4.7
OECD	6.0	5.8	1.9	4.2	4.5
OECD-Europe	4.7	5.5	1.9	3.1	3.8
Federal Republic of Germany	6.7	5.2	0.4	3.5	3.9
France	5.0	5.8	2.4	3.4	4.1
Italy	6.9	7.0	1.7	5.5	5.2
Norway	6.2	6.1	3.5	0.4	4.0
Sweden	7.3	5.2	2.9	−0.4	3.7
Switzerland	4.7	5.9	−0.6	2.8	3.1
Great Britain	3.2	2.4	0.6	1.4	1.9
United States	6.3	3.7	1.8	4.5	4.1
Canada	7.5	5.0	4.0	3.0	4.8

SOURCE: OECD.

TABLE 3
GROWTH OF PRODUCTIVITY AND EMPLOYMENT IN AUSTRIA, 1960–1980
(percent)

	1960/1970	1970/1980	1960/1980
Industrial production	76	49	163
Industrial work force	2.8	0.1	2.9

SOURCE: Austrian government statistics.

the mining sector remained stagnant (see table 4). The different growth rates resulted in a considerable change in the sectoral pattern during the past twenty years. The share of basic industries declined sharply, and that of traditional consumer goods also decreased. The chemical industry, however, and investment goods and technical products enlarged their positions (table 5).

TABLE 4
ANNUAL GROWTH OF INDUSTRIAL PRODUCTION IN AUSTRIA, BY SECTOR, 1960–1980
(percent)

	1960/1970	1970/1980	1960/1980
Total industrial output	5.5	4.0	4.7
Mining	−2.0	2.6	0.3
Magnesite	2.7	−2.2	0.2
Oil	6.0	−0.8	2.9
Ironworks	3.5	1.1	2.3
Metallurgical products	3.6	4.7	4.1
Building materials	5.3	2.7	4.0
Glass	3.7	7.5	5.6
Chemical industry	9.6	6.7	8.1
Paper	5.1	4.1	4.6
Paper industries	8.5	4.5	6.5
Wood	8.5	5.5	7.0
Food and drink	4.4	3.4	3.9
Leather manufacturing	1.1	0.1	0.6
Leather industries	5.3	3.4	4.3
Textiles	5.3	1.3	3.3
Clothing	5.1	2.2	3.6
Foundries	2.4	−0.1	1.1
Machinery	6.4	5.3	5.9
Vehicles	1.4	3.9	2.7
Fabricated metals	5.1	4.6	4.8
Electrical industries	8.1	6.5	7.3

SOURCE: Austrian Institute for Economic Research, Vienna.

TABLE 5

SECTORAL SHARE OF VALUE ADDED FOR INDUSTRY IN AUSTRIA,
1960, 1970, AND 1980
(percent)

	1960	1970	1980
Basic industries (mining, raw materials, paper)	25.4	22.2	18.9
Chemical industry	9.1	12.7	16.7
Investment goods and technical products (machinery, fabricated metals, electrical goods, vehicles)	25.4	27.1	30.0
Traditional consumer goods (food, textiles)	30.0	27.8	24.0
Construction industries (building materials, wood, glass)	10.0	10.1	10.3
Total	100.0	100.0	100.0

SOURCE: Austrian Institute for Economic Research, Vienna.

Foreign Trade. In 1980, 40 percent of Austria's industrial output was exported. If indirect exports are included, more than 50 percent of Austrian industrial production is exported. It is worth noting that, contrary to the custom in countries like Japan, in Austria trading companies do not figure prominently in the export business. They account for only 15 percent of total exports.

The sectoral structure of exports has undergone considerable change in the recent past. The percentage of basic goods in total industrial exports decreased from 44 percent at the end of the 1950s to 25 percent in the 1970s. In the same period the metal, machinery, and electrical sector raised its share of exports from 27 percent to 40 percent and the chemical industry from 8 to 12 percent. Thus the sectoral composition of Austrian exports today resembles more closely than was previously the case the average figures for the OECD countries as a whole, though the share of machinery and vehicles in Austrian exports is still below the OECD figures. (Table 6 shows the annual growth of Austrian exports and imports from 1960 to 1970.)

Between 1970 and 1979 Austria enlarged its percentage of total OECD imports. Austria's market share rose from 1.28 percent (1970) to 1.47 percent (1979). Austria's market share increased in most European countries (see table 7), whereas the tendency towards a slight deterioration of the Austrian competitive position in overseas industrial countries first became evident in 1979 and continued in 1980. Slight

TABLE 6

THE DYNAMICS OF AUSTRIAN FOREIGN TRADE: ANNUAL GROWTH
IN REAL TERMS
(percent)

	Exports		Imports	
Group of Products	1960/1973	1973/1979	1960/1973	1973/1979
Machinery, vehicles	10.0	9.4	9.0	4.9
Chemical products	16.4	12.4	13.0	7.9
Finished products	7.4	6.8	11.3	5.2
Consumer goods	13.2	4.8	16.7	13.0
Raw materials and fuels	2.3	5.0	7.7	3.1

SOURCE: Jan Stankovsky, "Probleme des österreichischen Aussenhandels," in
Seidel and Kramer, eds., *Die österreichische Wirtschaft in den achtziger Jahren*
(Stuttgart, 1980), p. 42.

gains in the Japanese market were counterbalanced by market losses in
the United States and Canada.

Plant Size and Concentration. More than half of the industrial work
force in Austria can be found in plants that employ fewer than 500
employees. The average size of industrial plants has changed little during
the past twenty years. This relative stability—in the size of plants in
terms of the number of employees—is not only evident in Austria. Several studies confirm that in many industrial countries the size of plants
has not changed significantly during the past two decades.[2]

A comparison can be made, however, between the size of plants in
the Federal Republic of Germany and in Austria. In Germany 40 percent of the industrial work force is employed in large-scale plants—that
is, plants having more than 1,000 employees. In Austria the comparable
figure is close to 30 percent.

The size of companies and corporations has undergone greater
change than the size of plants. This is especially true in a worldwide
perspective. In a report on the state of competition in member countries
for the 1960s and early 1970s the European Economic Community
(EEC) Commission stated: "The concentration process comprising all
countries and sectors has been intensifying steadily. The number of
competitors has decreased."[3] In Austria major concentration processes
and mergers took place in the steel and specialty steel industries, nonferrous metals, the electrical industry, food and beverages, pulp and
paper, building materials, and the glass industry.

134

TABLE 7
AUSTRIA'S MARKET SHARE IN SELECTED COUNTRIES, 1970 AND 1979

	1970		1979	
	Market share	Percentage of total exports	Market share	Percentage of total exports
Western Europe	1.33	68.3	1.44	68.2
Federal Republic of Germany	2.11	23.4	2.91	30.4
Switzerland	4.48	10.4	3.76	7.4
Italy	1.79	9.7	1.95	9.7
Great Britain	0.87	6.1	0.72	4.5
France	0.36	2.2	0.51	3.2
Eastern Europe	7.58	12.9	5.22	10.3
Overseas industrial countries	0.25	6.5	0.17	4.6
United States	0.30	4.1	0.19	0.7

SOURCE: Institute for Economic Research, Vienna.

The Structure of Ownership. In 1946 several dozen Austrian companies and plants were nationalized. Thus nearly all mining (iron ore, lignite, lead, zinc, and oil) and basic industries (steel, aluminum, nonferrous metals, fertilizers, oil-refining products) came under the control of the state, as well as some of the more important machinery and electrical equipment manufacturers. After various mergers and reorganizations, today the state holding company Österreichische Industrieverwaltungs-Aktiengesellschaft (ÖIAG) owns 100 percent of the shares of eight corporations and has a minority participation in Siemens AG Austria. The ÖIAG group employs about 115,000 people at present.

The Nationalization Act also included three major banks[4] (among them the two largest ones) that had longstanding interests in Austrian industry. Today the main interests of the banks are in vehicles, tires, machinery, textiles, paper, glass, chemicals, and building materials. The industrial sector controlled by the banks employs about 60,000 workers.

After the Austrian State Treaty of 1955 direct foreign investment increased. During the 1960s, this process was strengthened as foreign capital was involved in numerous mergers and in the establishment of new companies in various fields. The integration of foreign capital in Austrian industry is still going on. Table 8 shows the structure of ownership of Austrian industry in relation to the work force.

TABLE 8
INDUSTRIAL MANPOWER AND THE OWNERSHIP OF AUSTRIAN INDUSTRY,
1969 AND 1977

	1969		1977	
Major Owner	Absolute nos. of workers	Percent	Absolute nos. of workers	Percent
State [a]	155,000	26	178,000	28
Foreign capital	111,000	18	172,000 [b]	28
Austrian private capital	343,000	56	276,000	44
Total	609,000	100	626,000	100

a. ÖIAG-group and bank-controlled firms.
b. Indirect foreign majority participations (estimated).
SOURCE: ÖIAG.

The share of foreign capital is very high in the electrical industry (about 70 percent), in the oil and chemical industries (about 50 percent), followed by wood and paper, building materials, food, and textiles. Of the thirty-six Austrian industrial companies listed on the Viennese stock exchange—which together employed about 65,000 people in 1980—three are controlled by nationalized industry and twelve by the nationalized banks. Thirteen companies are controlled by Austrian private capital, and eight by foreign capital. The shares of the nationalized industrial companies are not traded on the stock exchange, but 40 percent of the shares of the nationalized banks are.

Industrial Investment. During the 1960s, Austrian industry passed through a period of gradual integration into the European and world market that had been made possible by the liberalization of trade conditions. The adaptation of Austrian industry to this new situation was difficult, as the conditions prevailing at the time of reconstruction of Austrian industry (1945–1955/1960) allowed for only a limited volume of foreign trade. Thus the efficiency of Austrian industry at the beginning of the 1960s was one-third less than that of the Federal Republic of Germany, the main reason obviously being the limited scope of the small domestic market.[5]

Only in the second half of the 1960s did an impressive growth rate give proof of the rising international competitiveness of Austrian industry, which since 1960 had been involved in extensive efforts to

TABLE 9

TOTAL INDUSTRIAL INVESTMENT IN AUSTRIA, 1960–1980
(percent)

	1960/ 1965	1965/ 1970	1970/ 1975	1975/ 1980
Basic industry (mining, oil, ferrous and nonferrous metallurgy, foundries, paper)	29.5	25.0	29.9	31.1
Chemical industry	9.9	14.4	13.5	12.8
Investment goods and technical products (machinery, vehicles, fabricated metals, electrical industry)	22.1	22.8	24.8	28.6
Traditional consumer goods (textiles, clothing, paper products, food and drink)	24.9	23.4	18.2	16.7
Building materials	10.6	14.4	13.7	10.8

SOURCE: Karl Aiginger, et al., "Ergebnisse des Investitionstests vom Frühjahr 1981," *WIFO-Monatsbericht*, no. 7 (1981), p. 401.

produce more sophisticated products suitable for export. The use of economies of scale in industry helped to diminish Austria's efficiency gap with respect to other industrial countries.[6] As a result, the share of capital expenditures in the sector of investment goods and technical products has been rising steadily, whereas the percentage of investment in the traditional consumer goods sector has been showing a marked decline (see table 9). The percentage of investment in the basic industries is still rather high. In 1980 the sum of industrial investment reached AS33.3 billion (or about $2 billion). Basic industry's share came to AS9.5 billion (28.5 percent), and AS11.8 billion was invested in the sector of investment goods and technical products. Forecasts for 1981 predict a reduction in the share of investment in basic industries (down to 25.5 percent). Investments in the sector of investment goods and technical products are expected to reach a record of 44.3 percent. In the period from 1960 to 1978 Austrian industry invested AS20,200 per employee each year. In the same period, West German industry invested AS19,000 per employee each year.[7]

Comparative studies published[8] on the allocation of investment to branches in West Germany and Austria, respectively—the Federal Republic of Germany being Austria's most important commercial partner and one of the countries most integrated into international trade—show that the two countries' structure of investment in regard to sectors has become more similar. The structural gap existing between the two countries has thus been reduced. Of course, the huge investment by General Motors may exaggerate the real improvement in the Austrian investment pattern. Research in some areas of the investment goods and technical products industry[9] has shown that the added value in this sector still is relatively low.

Factor Composition. Between 1956 and 1976 fixed capital grew at an average of 5.5 percent per year, so its volume had almost tripled by 1976. The industrial work force grew only a half percent each year during that period. Thus the ratio of invested capital goods per employee grew considerably (4.9 percent annually). Though capital goods have shown a stronger growth than employment, the productivity of invested capital has not been reduced. In order to produce a given unit of industrial products in 1976, only one-third of the work force, and less capital, were required than in 1956. This could be seen especially in the chemical, pulp and paper, textile, and metallurgical industries, whereas the oil and some parts of the metalworking industries and the leather industry showed a very strong growth of fixed assets so that unit costs of capital have risen.

Compared with the annual growth of production—5.5 percent annually between 1956 and 1976—the input of capital investment and employment grew annually by 2.5 percent.[10] The increase in the efficiency of total inputs that may be observed here is attributable to improvement in the quality of the factors themselves, especially improved technology and a wider use of economies of scale. This increase in efficiency occurred mainly during the second half of the 1960s and the early 1970s. As for employment, one might say that between 1976 and 1979 it was reduced slightly (down by 1 percent), but in 1980, as a result of the upswing of cyclical trends in 1979/1980, it regained lost ground (up by 1 percent). For 1981 a distinct decline in employment is predicted, owing to the crises affecting the basic industries. Capital goods since 1976 showed an increase of volume (in real terms) because of strong investment in the basic and investment goods industries.

Instruments of Industrial Policy

Investment Promotion. There is no general macroeconomic planning within the Austrian economic system. Instead, the Austrian system uses various instruments designed to support industrial growth and to improve the structure of industry in regard to the following objectives:

- increase value added in relation to operating revenues and employees
- increase the export ratio of turnover
- increase the share of new products having a high standard of technology
- introduce new production lines requiring less energy
- improve environmental protection devices within companies

These instruments were adapted to the targets prevailing at a given time. One of the most important aims of the system of industrial promotion is that of supporting industry by means of direct and indirect investment incentives.

Direct investment incentives. An advantage of direct investment incentives is that they can be applied to specific projects. Among such incentives are low-interest loans, interest subsidy schemes, and loan guarantees. A financing tool that has been used successfully in Austria for many years is the so-called ERP funds. These funds originate from the countervalue of goods supplied by the United States to Austria under the European Recovery Program (ERP). Since 1962 these funds have been administered by the Austrian government. Loans at low interest rates (2–6 percent) are granted for investments creating high added value, investments in sophisticated technologies, and investments in regions suffering from labor market problems.

ERP loans are granted to all sectors of the economy—that is, to manufacturing, agriculture, and service industries (especially tourism). ERP loans may cover up to 50 percent of the total investment. Between 1963 and 1979 industry has been granted ERP loans totaling AS49 billion, which amounts to 16 percent of all industrial investment in Austria during this period.[11]

Furthermore, the Österreichische Investitionskredit AG, a bank jointly owned by important Austrian banks, offers support for industrial projects by granting long-term loans at a low cost. This institution is also entrusted with administering direct federal investment supports. During the 1970s, special subsidies were granted to certain branches of industry. Between 1973 and 1978, the pulp and paper industry received interest subsidies for credits totaling more than AS2 billion, when the government granted a subsidy of 4 percent on interest due on loans for investment projects. This subsidy scheme was to improve the competitive position of the paper and pulp industry following Austria's association with the EEC. In addition, investment projects for environmental protection within companies were to be carried out under the subsidy scheme.

Between 1978 and 1980, a general subsidy scheme to reduce interest costs was made available to all branches of industry. It provided for an annual subsidy of 3 percent for investments promising structural improvements and an increase in exports. Continuing this support is being considered for the future.

The previously mentioned instruments for promoting industry are the most important ones. Beside these, however, a large number of special activities are carried out by diverse authorities. They meet the specific needs of various branches and regions and of enterprises of various sizes. A study published by the Austrian National Bank in 1979 stated that 40 percent of the total credit and loan volume granted to enterprises and private individuals is subsidized.[12]

In addition to these direct investment incentives, state loan guarantees are available to companies. The guarantees are handled by the Finanzierungsgarantie-Gesellschaft (FGG), which was established at the beginning of the 1970s. This institution covers long-term loans with its guarantee and is backed by the guarantee of the Republic. The idea is to help companies that wish to start new activities or to undertake risky investments, but that do not have the necessary venture capital at their disposal.

Indirect investment incentives. Indirect incentives for promoting investment are aimed at improving internal funding by reducing taxes on profits and income. In Austria a large part of actual profits can be deducted from taxable income so that in spite of high tax rates, taxation of actual profits and income is relatively low compared with other industrial countries. Tax revenues on profits and income amount to 11.2 percent of the GNP, which is lower than the European average of 14.4 percent and also lower than the average of the OECD countries (see table 10). The most important tax incentives are accelerated depreciation reserves for investment, and investment allowances. All of these incentives may be used simultaneously. For each investment project, however, only one type of incentive may be used.

Besides normal depreciation, a certain percentage of capital costs may be written off in the year of acquisition: 50 percent for movable fixed assets and 25 percent for unmovable fixed assets. Thus, by anticipating normal depreciation, an enterprise can take advantage of an interest-free tax credit. Furthermore, there are special allowances for investments in environmental protection, research, energy production, and energy-saving devices.

Investment allowances act as a support for capital formation. They can be deducted in addition to normal depreciation up to 20 percent of the cost of fixed assets. The tax advantage of this incentive is final, as the amount deducted from profits is not taxed in subsequent years

TABLE 10

TAXES ON PROFITS AND INCOME AS A PERCENTAGE OF GNP, 1978

Country	Taxes (as % of GNP)
France	7.1
Italy	9.6
Japan	9.7
Austria	11.2
Switzerland	13.4
Federal Republic of Germany	13.5
Canada	13.9
Great Britain	13.9
United States	13.9
Netherlands	15.3
Belgium	18.1
Norway	19.4
Sweden	24.2
OECD	14.5
OECD-Europe	14.4
EEC	15.1

SOURCE: OECD, *Revenue Statistics of OECD Member Countries 1965-1979* (Paris, 1980).

(depreciation at 120 percent). Investment allowances have to be listed in the balance sheet in a separate total for each fiscal year. At the end of the fifth fiscal year following utilization of the investment allowance, it has to be transferred either to a capital account or to voluntary reserves subject to taxation. A reserve for investment can be formed with up to 25 percent of taxable profits. Unlike accelerated depreciation and the investment allowance, this device can also be used in years when there is no actual investment.

These instruments promote profitable enterprises and foster a steady high level of investment because the interest-free tax credit can be perpetuated only in case of permanent reinvestment. In the event of increasing investments the tax credit is even enlarged. Despite the importance of these instruments, enterprises faced with continuous recession and new companies facing start-up costs need different forms of support that do not depend on the income of the enterprise. Therefore, in Austria indirect investment incentives are being partially substituted for direct supports. The target is to make greater investment supports available to those branches and sectors whose development is desired—especially in the area of sophisticated technologies.

Research Promotion. The Research Promotion Fund for Industry supports research projects by means of loans, grants, and loan guarantees. Its funding comes from the federal budget. In line with the increasing importance of industrial research, support for research increased considerably during the 1970s. The volume of support (measured in Austrian schillings) given to enterprises in 1980 was six times higher than the amount in 1970. In spite of this, the fund accounts for only 5–6 percent of the total research expenditures of industry. Compared with international figures on research promotion, this percentage is rather low, and it will be necessary to increase it.

Labor Market Promotion. The Labor Market Promotion Act tries to ensure full employment. Enterprises facing difficult employment situations due to changes in production programs or production processes or other internal problems can receive subsidies. Priority is given to enterprises in areas having regional employment problems. Support is given for labor force training and the creation of new jobs. The aid is granted either through subsidies or low-cost or interest-free loans.

Export Promotion. Under the Export Promotion Act federal aid is given to foster the export activities of enterprises. A system of diverse guarantees is managed by the Österreichische Kontrollbank AG, an institute specializing in export financing. Another measure of export promotion is offered within the tax system. Fifteen percent of receivables originating from exports may be deducted from taxable income. This temporary adjustment of the value of receivables provides an interest-free tax credit.

Structure and Conduct in the Public Sector. As has already been mentioned, there is an important state-owned sector within Austrian industry employing 110,000 workers out of an industrial labor force of 630,000. Furthermore, there are 60,000 people working in enterprises controlled by state-owned banks. It should be asked if and to what extent this sector is used in industrial policy.

The original purpose of nationalization in 1946 and 1947 was undoubtedly determined by the postwar situation. In order to ensure economic recovery and to avoid seizure by the occupation forces, it was necessary to reestablish a clear ownership and management situation. In addition, fundamental attitudes about the role of economic policy and ideological motives played a certain role. During the parliamentary debates at that time, speakers of all parties pointed out that nationalization should also act as a stabilizing force in the economy. Furthermore, nationalization was intended to be the basis of overall planning in this sector.

To understand the role of state-owned industry within the Austrian economy, one should consider its legal and organizational basis. An important fact is that these enterprises remained registered joint stock companies—that is, they operate under Austrian corporation law. The influence of the state was limited to the rights of a shareholder. According to Austrian corporation law, the supervisory board and the board of executive directors act rather autonomously. Since 1946 there have been no major changes in this respect or in the extent of nationalization.

The administration of owners' rights was entrusted to ministries or to trustee companies until 1970. In that year, a state-owned holding company—the ÖIAG—was established. It is run as a joint stock company, and it owns the shares of companies formerly held directly by the state. The federal chancellor represents the Republic in the annual general meeting of the ÖIAG. Austrian state-owned firms—like any other enterprise—aim for growth and profit, publish their accounts, are members of the Chamber of Commerce, and do not have a special position in collective bargaining with the trade unions.

The state-owned enterprises do have a few special characteristics. The performance and the economic situation of the group must be reported to parliament. State-owned enterprises are audited by the federal audit office. The Republic has guaranteed certain liabilities of the holding company and also of subsidiaries, and the sale of a subsidiary has to be approved by a parliamentary committee. It should be added that the supervisory directors of ÖIAG are elected by the shareholders' meeting in accordance with the distribution of parliamentary seats to political parties. This gives some influence to the political parties in nominating people to the top positions in the state-owned enterprises.

In past decades, the policies of the state-owned industries always resembled in some way the general economic policy of the country. Therefore, in the 1950s state-owned corporations helped considerably to stabilize prices; through their investments in the 1960s and 1970s they contributed to the growth and restructuring of the Austrian economy. Nevertheless, the direct connection between the government's economic policy and the policies of state-owned industries is rather loose. Neither the government nor any planning office or similar body sets up quantified goals for this industrial complex. There is no overall top-down planning outside the group. The revolving five-year plans worked out by ÖIAG are based on the bottom-up plans of the subsidiaries of ÖIAG. These plans are not part of an overall macroeconomic plan, which virtually does not exist.

Direct intervention by the government—especially by the federal chancellor—took place in the early 1970s in connection with the extensive mergers that created the biggest companies of Austrian industry. At that time, the Austrian steel complex VÖEST-ALPINE and VEW (Vereinigte Edelstahlwerke), one of the most important specialty steel makers in the world, was established. The petrochemical and nonferrous metal activities of state-owned industries were also merged. It might come as a surprise that these mergers had to be accomplished against the resistance of management, shop stewards, and the labor forces of the companies in question. These mergers were possible only through the authority of the federal chancellor and the president of the Federation of Trade Unions.

The mergers took place at the end of a period during which all European countries tried to strengthen the competitiveness of their industries by mergers. In the Federal Republic of Germany and Sweden the initiative was taken by the industries themselves and the banks, whereas in France and Great Britain the state played a dominant role.

Since the beginning of the steel crisis, the most important question in the discussions between government and corporations has been to secure full employment. Government's attitude in this respect may be characterized as follows: The government is, of course, interested in maintaining each job in each location. Nevertheless, the government properly understands that nonviable structures cannot be maintained. Management, however, tries to change outdated structures, but managers must take into consideration that for social reasons and regional matters they cannot reduce the labor force extensively.

The employment policy of the steel companies during the first years of the steel crisis was piecemeal reduction of the work force. Thus, sudden increases in unemployment in regions with almost no job opportunities outside the steel sector were avoided. As a consequence, however, productivity could not be raised at the rates then prevailing in the West German steel industry. The policy objectives are aptly demonstrated by the example of VÖEST-ALPINE. When a corporation is forced to give up parts of its production and close some of its plants, it must create new jobs and new plants in the affected regions. This is done by means of planned diversification, as in the diversification of VÖEST-ALPINE into electronics, in the course of which a joint venture with American Microsystems, Inc., covering the production of semiconductors, was established. Other examples are the diversification into synthetic marble and glass finishing. Although both plants were originally opened to provide employment opportunities, they are, of course, profit oriented.

The iron and steel industry has invested AS20 billion during the past six years for the modernization and renewal of fixed capital. Today

VÖEST-ALPINE is, to a very large extent, using advanced methods of steel production. The percentage of continuous casting applied in its steelworks—which usually is taken as a criterion for the standard in steel making—comes to 58 percent, which is a very high percentage when compared internationally (Japan, 60 percent; United States, 20 percent). The Austrian specialty steel producer VEW, having incurred losses in the past, is at present carrying out the restructuring program recommended by an international consulting company.

Sectoral Industry Policy. Whereas regional industry policy as well as general economic promotion is hardly questioned, sectoral industry policy is controversial politically and theoretically. Austrian economists carefully studied the Japanese and the French models and repeatedly discussed the establishment of some central planning institution. The arguments against such an institution can be summarized in the contention that a planning bureaucracy cannot better judge the dynamics of present and future markets than entrepreneurs.

The supporters of sectoral industry policy look at this question from a different point of view. The arguments for sectoral industry policy are based on the specific economic conditions prevailing in Austria—namely, the lack of large internationally based corporations, and the relatively small domestic market, which are all unfavorable for the development of modern industries.

The promotion of certain industries such as pulp and paper, textiles, and specialty steels might be considered a first step in the direction of sectoral industry policy, though these measures had mainly a defensive character. Another step in this direction were the efforts of the Austrian government to establish industries that would contribute positively to the Austrian balance of payments and rank among the key industries in the industrial world. In the absence of military, nuclear, space, and aeronautics industries, which in other countries provide incentives for the development of new technologies such as electronics or laser techniques, the government wanted to give a stronger base to these industries in Austria, by supporting specific projects. At present, two major projects are going to be realized. The first is a joint venture of Siemens and ÖIAG that is partly financed by funds from the Research Promotion Fund. The second is a joint venture of American Microsystems, Inc., and VÖEST-ALPINE.

Another initiative was directed to car production in Austria. Because there was no automotive production in Austria and because imports of cars figure importantly in Austria's import statistics, the government gave priority to projects in this area. After evaluating several options, the government was successful in attracting General Motors to establish a large engine plant in Vienna. Since Austria had to compete with other European countries for this investment, Austria had to grant considerable aid. Furthermore, the government tried to use the purchasing power of the country with respect to car imports and persuaded the main car producers to increase their imports from Austria.

Industrial Performance

Since the end of World War II, Austrian industry has shown enormous growth. This process has not been a linear one. There were long- and short-range cyclical movements. Clearly, the medium-term variations of growth can be explained as difficulties in adapting to new conditions in the world economy or changing conditions within the Austrian environment.

After the postwar boom years that lasted until the end of the 1950s, there was a phase of depressed growth during the 1960s when industry had to adapt to the conditions of a peacetime economy. The continuing liberalization of foreign trade brought about hitherto unknown competitive pressures for many producers and a rapidly increasing import volume. Moreover, it took some years to compensate for the export discrimination created by the formation of the EEC in these traditionally important markets. New markets had to be found in the European Free Trade Association (EFTA) and in overseas countries.

When Austria signed its agreement with the EEC, the readjustment to the new conditions (mutual reductions of duties) was mastered quite successfully. The positive effect of these efforts resulted in accelerated growth, from the end of the 1960s until 1975, at an outstanding pace compared with the performance of most Western industrial countries. People spoke repeatedly of a second wave of industrialization in Austria.

The worldwide recession of 1975 inaugurated a medium-term accommodation process accompanied by reduced growth rates. Contrary to the situation in the 1960s, at present considerable doubt exists about the best way to adapt Austrian industry for the future. This doubt can be illustrated by the conclusion of an OECD analysis: "a large part of the comparative advantage of the advanced industrialized countries lies in products and processes which are hard to describe because they are either rather intangible or do not yet exist."[13]

The critical analyses began as early as the 1950s when a study revealed that Austrian industry did not invest enough in branches that determine the position of Austria as an advanced industrial country.[14] (Examples of such modern branches in 1958 were: nuclear technology, electronic equipment, and petrochemicals.) It is this argument that has been used repeatedly during the past twenty years and that is still valid. It is one of the unexplained phenomena of the economy that in spite of all these structural defects the Austrian economy has performed quite satisfactorily.

At the beginning of the 1960s K. W. Rothschild pointed out a certain weakness of Austrian industry in his study of Austria's export structure.[15] In another study, Stephan Koren pointed to the insufficient degree of specialization of many enterprises and to a strong protectionist mentality among Austria's industrialists.[16] All these doubts regarding the efficiency of Austrian enterprises were expressed again during the discussion of the competitiveness of Austrian enterprises in the common market (*Integrationsreife*). Needless to say, most enterprises were more successful than the economists had predicted.

Toward the end of the 1960s, a quantitative aspect emerged. Because of the strong growth of the service sector, some economists feared that Austria's economy might reach the postindustrial stage without having fully developed its secondary sector. As a reaction, a new wave of industrialization was called for, and this became one of the most important objectives of the economic program of the Bruno Kreisky government. Competitiveness and the potential for development were also main points in discussions of the hard currency policy. Once again criticism was focused on the "weakness" of Austria's industry.

At the beginning of the 1980s, the threat of de-industrialization was again discussed. In the recent past, several spectacular bankruptcies had occurred. This revived the debate about the appropriate structure of industry in the new conditions of the world economy. There is a close connection between the inadequacy of the statistical data and the problem of defining optimal industrial structure. Whereas politicians and economists want to have as much industry as they can get, ideas about the desirable structure of the economy differ widely. To show how difficult it is to find the right approach, originally the discussion dealt with growth branches, then turned to growth firms and growth products. The most fashionable term in today's debate is the so-called intelligent product.

The origin of the whole discussion lies in the fact that from the period of reconstruction Austria had inherited a structure characterized by the dominance of basic industry and the self-sufficiency of the consumer goods industry. The sector of sophisticated, "brain-intensive" investment and consumer goods, however, was less developed compared with that in West Germany, Switzerland, and Sweden.

Although it has been shown that the situation has improved considerably, in some aspects—industrial research and development, internationalization, the integration of production, consulting, engineering, distribution, and the equity-capital ratio—parts of Austria's economy still lag behind. With the introduction of direct investment incentives, massive efforts to attract foreign investments, and the increase in the budget for research promotion in industry, the government has shown that it is prepared to develop a coherent strategy for industrial policy, the objectives of which are to improve further the competitive position of Austrian products on world markets and to contribute positively to the Austrian trade balance.

For the realization of these objectives it will be necessary (1) to support the production of technology-intensive products; (2) to reduce the energy consumption of industry; (3) to support these and other efforts with direct and indirect federal investment incentives that continue the incentives already in place; and (4) to encourage management and workers to use all their capability and flexibility in the switch to new production processes and new organizational structures.

Notes

1. See *Industriestatistik 1979,* pt. 1 (Vienna, 1980), pp. 8-24.

2. See, for example, *Factors and Conditions of Long Term Growth, Industrial Specialization and Trends in Industrial Policy* (Paris: United Nations Economic Commission for Europe, 1973).

3. European Economic Community, *Zweiter Bericht über die Wettbewerbspolitik* (Brussels, 1973).

4. The three banks are: Österreichische Länderbank AG, Creditanstalt-Bankverein AG, and Österreichisches Credit-Institut AG.

5. See H. Seidel, *Struktur und Entwicklung der Österreichischen Industrie* (Vienna: Österreichischer Wirtschaftsverlag, 1978), p. 46.

6. Ibid., p. 47.

7. A. Kausel, "Die Österreichische Wirtschaft ist kerngesund," in *Quartalshefte* der Girozentrale und Bank der Österreichischen Sparkassen AG, Sonderheft 1, 1979, pp. 11-39.

8. K. Aiginger, M. Czerny-Zinegger, and K. Musil, "Ergebnisse des Investitionstests vom Frühjahr, 1981," *Monatsbericht* des Instituts für Wirtschaftsforschung, no. 7 (1981), pp. 396-411.

9. H. Kramer, *Industrielle Strukturprobleme Österreichs dargestellt am Beispiel der Eisen- und Metallverarbeitung* (Vienna: Signum-Verlag, 1980).

10. Weighting factor for capital: 0.4; for labor: 0.6. Cf. Seidel, *Struktur und Entwicklung,* p. 42.

11. M. Karger and H. Kepplinger, *Investitionsförderung in Österreich. Eine Volkswirtschaftliche Analyse* (Vienna: ORAC-Verlag, 1981), p. 107.

12. See "Sondererhebung über subventionierte Kredite," *Mitteilungen* des Direktoriums der Österreichischen Nationalbank, no. 6 (1979).

13. OECD, Report by the Secretary-General, *The Impact of the Newly Industrializing Countries on Production and Trade in Manufactures* (Paris, 1979).

14. *Investitionspolitik und Investitionsfinanzierung in Österreich,* Studie der Wirtschaftswissenschaftlichen Abteilung der Wiener Arbeiterkammer, *Arbeit und Wirtschaft,* no. 3 (1958).

15. K. W. Rothschild, "Wurzeln und Triebkräfte der Entwicklung der österreichischen Wirtschaftsstruktur," in W. Weber, ed., *Österreichs Wirtschaftsstruktur Gestern—Heute—Morgen,* vol. 1 (Berlin: Duncker & Humblodt, 1961), pp. 1-157.

16. S. Koren, "Die Industrialisierung Österreichs—vom Protektionismus zur Integration," in Weber, *Österreichs Wirtschaftsstrukur Gestern,* pp. 223-549.

Commentary

Peter J. Katzenstein

Listening to a discussion between Americans and Austrians about the remarkable economic performance of the Second Republic in the 1970s reminds me of one of George Bernard Shaw's characterizations of Ireland and England as two countries divided by a common language. Around this table all the Austrians speak the kind of English that is understood and appreciated in the Washington of the 1980s. At lunch, for example, I was surprised to learn that supply-side economics has been practiced for years in Austria. At this rate, supply-side economics will suffer the fate of the sewing machine: every country claims to have invented it. So much unexpected convergence between America and Austria, however, should be treated with some caution. Although Americans are very eager to learn how Austria has managed its economy, Austrians are not really able to share their secrets. That inability is not so much a matter of deception but of the ambiguity surrounding the term "political economy." Many Americans assembled around this table assume that the economy shapes politics. The Austrians however know— they do not assume—that politics shapes the economy.

The paper by Oskar Grünwald offers an excellent overview of both the character of Austria's changing industrial structure and its variegated industrial policies. The paper is also wise. It does not try to define the term "industrial policy," choosing instead to discuss investment policy, research and development, the public sector, export promotion, labor market policy, and sectoral industrial policy—all of which have numerous direct and indirect effects on Austria's industrial structure. The paper raises for me a particularly interesting question when it asserts that Austria is now prepared to develop a coherent strategy for industrial policy. This assertion is made in what one might call the third cycle of a debate on Austria's industrial policy since the end of World War II. These cycles have a periodicity—the late 1950s, the late 1960s, and the late 1970s—which is reassuring to someone like myself who has

150

developed a comparative advantage in trying to learn about the politics of industry in different countries; the current boom of literature on industrial policy will generate excess capacities, rigidities, and a depression which, judging by the Austrian experience, will give way to another boom in the late 1980s. Why is it that Austrians still wish to pursue a coherent strategy for industrial policy if, judging by the experience of the first three cycles of political interest, such a strategy is apparently beyond their reach?

In trying to answer that question, I am less interested in the primary than in the secondary effects of policy. Primary effects are economic performance measures such as rates of inflation, unemployment, and economic growth. We are all agreed that primary effects are important, but, speaking as a political scientist, I think they are less important than economists would want us to believe. Listening to the Austrians on this subject, I am tempted to conclude that they would concur with me. What interests me and, I think, what interests the Austrians are the secondary consequences of policy on the future range or political choice that the country has. These secondary consequences are shaped greatly by the character of Austria's domestic political arrangements.

I shall try to develop my argument in two parts. First, I shall try to make the case for Austria as a likely candidate for pursuing a coherent industrial policy: "Austria as a Number Two" if I may borrow Ezra Vogel's title for Japan. Certain characteristics in Austrian politics and policy and certain international comparisons suggest indeed some plausibility for the call for a coherent industrial policy. Second, I shall then argue that the way power is organized and distributed in Austria simply does not permit the adoption of such a coherent policy and that judging by the experience of other small European states, Austria's inability is not unique. Austria shares with them open economies similarly placed in the international division of labor and an industrial policy that is incremental, flexible, and reactive, not coherent. To deny the domestic and international constraints operating so forcefully on Austria's political economy and inhibiting the adoption of a coherent industrial policy can be likened to what one might call the Peter Pan approach to economic policy prescription. Adherents of that approach have been seen, even in this town, to close their eyes and wish really hard.

For several reasons, it could be argued that Austria is a European incarnation of Japan. In terms of the performance of the Austrian economy in the 1970s and the rapidity with which its industry has changed since 1960, Austria surpasses all countries except Japan. Furthermore, Austria approximates Japan in that it is, to my knowledge, the only European country that has a stable one-party dominant regime evolving in the 1970s, with the temptation of socialist hegemony now built into it. The manner in which the Austrians will react to that temptation in the 1980s will determine whether the Second Republic will evolve as gradually as it has in the past three decades or whether Austria will move from the Second Republic to its Third.

Furthermore, apart from a political regime dominated by the Socialist party, Austria has a very considerable capacity to steer investment capital in what remains a capitalist economy. Forty percent of Austria's investment is affected by various government programs. Investment policy is articulated self-consciously and implemented haphazardly. Austria more than all other capitalist states I know of has chosen to socialize investments rather than send political signals, as does Japan's Ministry for Industry and Trade, to the city banks. Furthermore, unlike Japan, Austria has a very large public sector. Delineating precisely the size of that sector is a tricky business, but by whatever measure one chooses, it is, in the area of industry, larger than the public sector in any other major industrial country. Considering these features of Austria's economic and political life, if one were to expect a coherent industrial policy anywhere in the world outside of Japan, one would expect to find it in Austria.

This expectation is reinforced by comparing Austria with other countries. Three in particular have shown a great reluctance to engage in coherent industrial policies: the United States, the United Kingdom, and Switzerland. All three have located a larger fraction of their productive capacities beyond national borders than all the other industrial states. All three have therefore the option of adjusting to change abroad rather than implementing a coherent industrial policy at home.

In contrast, Austria does not own any significant productive assets abroad. The reasons are largely historical. The Austrians lost their empire at the end of World War I, and they ended up on the losing side of World War II as well. There simply exists no opportunity for developing an industrial adjustment strategy outside national borders. Instead Austria relies on an active investment and employment policy as critically important components in its industrial policy. Furthermore, Austrian politics features a tightly integrated network of institutions linking all of the important political actors. This, too, is characteristic of Japan and to a lesser extent of the Federal Republic of Germany, two societies that have adopted different though similarly coherent strategies of industrial policy in the 1960s and 1970s. Finally, Austria has a powerful trade union movement that is willing to accept the costs of change because it defines its interests in the medium and long term. In other countries, such as the United Kingdom, the unions' willingness to accept change was smaller than in Austria and the inclination to pursue short-term interests was greater. Such a political constellation

PETER J. KATZENSTEIN

turns out to be quite adverse to a coherent industrial policy. A long-term definition of interest accords Austria, Japan, and West Germany a margin of choice that other countries, such as Britain, France, and Italy, do not have. In sum, both Austria's domestic political arrangements and comparison with the politics and policies of industry in other countries predestine Austria for a coherent industrial policy modeled in Japan's image.

The interesting question is why such a coherent policy has not been adopted. This reluctance is not the result of insufficient exhortations. The Social and Economic Advisory Council repeatedly has called for coherence in this area of policy. Throughout the 1970s the political rhetoric in Austria has reflected this wish. Rather than assuming that we are dealing here with a prolonged fit of absent-mindedness or communal stupidity on the part of the Austrians, it is probably wiser to search for an explanation for this paradoxical omission. Part of that explanation lies in Austria's system of social and economic partnership which ties together business and labor representatives with party leaders and bureaucratic elites. Since it is the subject of another set of papers in this volume I shall pass over it here.

The system of social and economic partnership reflects and shapes a policy process built around an equilibration of power differences not as an end in itself but as a means of assuring that the process of small-scale political conflict over carefully factored issues never ends. In Austria political opponents are engaged in a domestic version of protracted conflict which requires an ability of measuring the victory or defeat today against the prospect of defeat or victory tomorrow. No one battle and no one site is judged to be as important as the process of readjusting and relegitimizing the mode of conflict itself through the very process of policy.

Austrians thus fight politically as much over their politics as over any particular policy issue such as industrial policy. No coalition of actors has to date acquired sufficient political power to force an opposing coalition to accept far-reaching deviations from the established policy of muddling through. This is true of Austria's industrial policy as much as of all major economic and social issues. Although it looks like a series of tactical moves and incremental adjustments, in fact, political conflict over policy requires the ability to think strategically. Political leaders on both the red and the black side of the fence that still divides Austria's political life are always calculating the ramifications of incremental policy change on the future range of choices for themselves and for the society at large.

The impediments that Austria's social and economic partnership and the policy process create for the adoption of a coherent industrial

153

policy are reinforced by the organizational interpenetration of the unions by business organizations and of business by union strongholds. Which other country, after all, features as significant a faction of "black" socialists as does Austria? The Federation of Employees and Workers (Österreichischer Anglestellten-und Arbeiter-Bund, or ÖAAB) is the largest of the three federations that form the conservative Austrian People's party (Österreichische Volkspartei, or ÖVP) and enjoys the broadest electoral appeal. The ÖAAB's ideology is shaped more by the corporativism of the 1930s than the neoliberal currents of the postwar years. Furthermore it is an important bridge to Austria's union movement. It represents the Christian Democratic unions, which, in terms of sheer size rather than power, are a force to be reckoned with in Austria's centralized trade union movement. Conversely, which other country features a vast nationalized industry organizationally present, though politically impotent, in the peak association of big business? Austria's nationalized industries are formal members of the Federation of Industry (Österreichischer Industriellen Verband, or IV) without to date exercising significant influence. The methods and institutions of collective bargaining in the public and private sectors do not differ. The consequence of organizational interpenetration is to tie political opponents closely together in the policy process. It leads to a subtle politics not easily appreciated by outsiders. It inhibits unilateral initiatives and the formulation of a coherent industrial policy.

Besides the social and economic partnership, the policy process, and the institutional interpenetration of the black with the red camp, the neutralization of state power is a fourth factor inhibiting a coherent industrial policy. The assertiveness of Austria's political parties is the main reason for the astonishing passivity of the state bureaucracy. Conflicting conceptions of the purpose of economic power of Austria's two major parties blunt both the potential for state intervention in the economy and the potential for invigorating further competition in Austrian markets. Students of Austrian politics are familiar with the partisan penetration of Austria's nationalized industries and nationalized banks throughout the postwar period. In the 1970s that penetration incorporated the institutional requirements of an industrial policy. The major reason for the astonishing passivity of the state is the Austrian self-consciousness in using all sorts of policies, including industrial policy, not only as an instrument for achieving certain objectives but also as a way of perpetually re-creating the legitimacy for the manner in which Austria conducts its politics.

International comparisons reinforce the impression that Austria is ill-suited to adopt a coherent industrial policy. Like the other small European states with open economies (Switzerland, the Low Countries and Scandinavia), Austria confronts the problems posed by industrial adjustment with two options foreclosed.

The economic openness of Austria and the small European states makes these countries so vulnerable to retaliation that, in contrast to the large industrial countries, protectionist policies are not entertained. Furthermore, Austria shares with the other small European states domestic structures that tie political opponents closely together in a dense institutional network and a recurrent policy process. These structures make politically infeasible the typical response of the large industrial states: political indifference to industrial change on the one hand and coherent industrial policies on the other. Instead these domestic structures encourage the adoption of reactive, flexible, and incremental industrial policies.

Americans interested in Austria's economic success should never forget that there exist two sorts of people interested in Austria's political economy. There are those who can explain it, but do not really understand it; and there are those who can understand it, but do not really explain it. Speaking to an international audience this essay runs the risk of convincing the Americans that I cannot explain and the Austrians that I do not understand. My cryptic message will then resemble that of the owl in the story of snake and frog. Almost beside himself in fear of being devoured by the snake, the frog asked the owl how he might be able to survive. The owl's response was brief and cryptic: learn how to fly. Like the frog, on questions of industrial policy, Austria has learned how to fly. Unlike the eagle, it does not soar high above the Alps; and it does not adopt a coherent industrial policy. Instead Austria has an amazing capacity to jump. While often Austria, like the frog, appears to land on its stomach, in fact it lands on its feet, retaining the ability to jump again and again in different directions, correcting its course as it goes along. Frogs can escape snakes. In a world of high-risk choices, Austria's industrial policy is an authentic and intelligent response to accelerating changes in the international economy. Austria does not know how to solve the problem of industrial change. Nevertheless, it has found a way of living with it.

The Competitiveness of the Austrian Economy

Karl Vak

Austria's Present Competitiveness

The competitiveness of Austria's economy cannot be measured only by individual economic indicators; it should be judged by historical, social, and economic developments as well. The fall of the Austro-Hungarian empire in 1918 marked the end of a state that had encouraged stability and peace. The occasion brought the abrupt and drastic breakup of a large economic entity, of the structure and division of labor it had developed, and of a well-balanced domestic economy into the separate economies of various countries. The economic crisis and the domestic and foreign policy problems of the interwar period and the later orientation of industry toward a war economy considerably limited the structural development of the Austrian economy and its adjustment to new circumstances. In the postwar period the pressure to introduce structural changes has clearly been reduced by favorable conditions in the raw materials market and by the considerable increase in international tourism, from which Austria in particular has benefited.

Comparison of Economic Data of Austria's Main Trading Partners. Although economic growth, wealth, and employment in Austria have not only kept up with but actually overtaken certain countries in the international community, structural problems exist that can and must be solved. Among these problems are the preponderance of primary production with a corresponding low contribution of high-value finished goods to total national product, productivity levels that could be improved, and the low level of exports of the medium-sized firms predominant in Austrian industry.

The present problems of adaptability of the Austrian economy are basically the same problems that confront many other industrial coun-

TABLE 1

ECONOMIC GROWTH (REAL GDP) IN SELECTED OECD COUNTRIES,
1970–1980

Country	1970	1975	1980[a]	1979 1980[a]	1975/ 1980	1970/ 1980
				(yearly growth in percent)		
Japan	100	128	169	5.9 5.0	5.7	5.4
Austria	100	121	147	5.1 3.6	3.9	3.9
West Germany	100	111	132	4.6 1.8	3.6	2.8
Sweden	100	110	118	3.8 2.3	1.5	1.7
Switzerland	100	104	110	2.2 2.5	1.1	0.9
EEC	100	114	133	3.4 1.3	2.9	3.1
OECD	100	116	138	3.3 1.0	3.3	3.5

a. Preliminary data.
SOURCE: OECD.

tries. Essentially, the problem is domestic industry adapting to changing relative prices between energy, raw materials, and finished products and making wise use of the cheap labor from developing countries.

Industrialization. Of all the countries in the Organization for Economic Cooperation and Development (OECD), only Japan matches Austria's economic performance. Since 1970, Austria's annual growth rate has exceeded that of the European Economic Community (EEC) by 0.8 percent, that of West Germany by 1.1 percent, and that of Switzerland by 3 percent per year (see table 1). Japan's 1.5 percent advantage amounts to only 0.3 percent per year when viewed on a per capita basis. This trend has continued despite the current world recession, as shown by the noticeable improvement in the real trade contribution, as well as by the remarkable increase in industrial production (particularly of final production) in the first quarter of 1981.

Increased industrial production has also contributed to the Austrian growth pattern (see table 2). While the industry of OECD countries is expanding at a rate that is in almost all cases below the average GDP growth rate for the world, Austria's industry is expanding faster than the world rate—4.2 percent per year versus 3.9 percent for 1979/1980. The notion of deindustrialization has proved to be false in Austria. As a result of vast structural improvements, Austria's industrial production has, since 1970, increased twice as much as that of West Germany and the EEC and four times as much as that of Sweden and Switzerland, falling short of Japan's performance by only 2 percent over a ten-year period (0.2 percent per year).

TABLE 2
INDUSTRIAL PRODUCTION IN SELECTED OECD COUNTRIES, 1970–1980

Country	1970	1975	1980 [a]	1979	1980 [a]	1975/ 1980	1970/ 1980
				(yearly growth in percent)			
Japan	100	108	153	8.2	6.9	7.2	4.4
Austria	100	118	150	7.3	4.5	4.9	4.2
West Germany	100	105	124	5.6	0.2	3.5	2.2
Sweden	100	115	114	7.3	0	−0.2	1.3
Switzerland	100	97	111	1.4	4.7	2.7	1.0
EEC	100	108	127	4.4	0	3.3	2.4
OECD	100	110	137	4.9	0.2	4.4	3.2

a. Preliminary data.
SOURCE: Organization for Economic Cooperation and Development.

Currency stability. Austria has maintained its currency stability better than the other OECD countries, except for Switzerland and West Germany. When viewed over a longer period, however, these two countries appear to have only a moderate advantage over Austria in currency stability, which has little competitive significance. This advantage is solely the result of greater price increases in the tertiary (or service) sector, not of increases in industrial prices. Austria is not at a disadvantage in the primary (food) and secondary (material goods) sectors, which are externally more important. Table 3 shows the increases in consumer prices in selected OECD countries.

TABLE 3
INCREASE IN CONSUMER PRICES IN SELECTED OECD COUNTRIES
(annual percentage rate)

Country	1979	1980	1981	1970/ 1975	1975/ 1980	1970/ 1980
Switzerland	3.7	4.0	5.8	7.7	2.3	5.0
West Germany	4.1	5.5	5.6	6.1	4.1	5.1
Austria	3.7	6.4	7.0	7.3	5.3	6.3
Netherlands	4.2	6.5	6.6	8.6	6.0	7.3
Belgium	4.5	6.7	7.2	8.5	6.4	7.4
United States	11.3	13.5	11.1	6.7	8.9	7.8
Norway	4.7	10.9	14.5	8.4	8.4	8.4
Japan	3.6	8.0	6.7	11.5	6.5	9.0
OECD	9.7	12.9	11.3	8.3	9.7	9.0

SOURCE: OECD; Institute for Economic Research, Vienna.

TABLE 4
UNEMPLOYMENT IN SELECTED OECD COUNTRIES, 1970–1981
(percent)

Country	1979	1980	1981	1970/ 1975	1975/ 1980	1970/ 1980
Switzerland	0.4	0.2	0.2	0.1	0.4	0.3
Norway	1.4	1.3	2.0	0.9	1.3	1.1
Austria	2.0	1.9	2.0	1.5	2.0	1.7
Japan	2.1	2.0	2.1	1.4	2.1	1.7
Sweden	2.1	2.0	2.5	2.1	1.9	2.0
West Germany	3.8	3.9	4.9	1.9	4.2	3.0
France	5.9	6.2	6.9	2.2	5.3	3.6
Finland	6.2	4.9	4.7	2.1	5.8	3.8
Netherlands	5.0	5.8	8.1	2.8	5.4	4.0
Great Britain	5.4	6.8	9.9	3.3	6.3	4.6
Denmark	6.0	6.9	8.9	3.3	6.8	4.9
United States	5.8	7.1	7.3	5.9	6.7	6.3
Italy	7.7	7.6	NA	6.1	7.3	6.6
Belgium	10.9	11.8	13.8	4.0	10.3	6.9
EEC	5.4	5.9	NA	2.6	5.2	3.9
OECD	5.0	5.5	NA	NA	5.3	NA

NA = not available.
SOURCE: OECD; Institute for Economic Research, Vienna.

Employment. Austria has successfully carried out its policy of full employment during the past few years. Between 1970 and 1980, the unemployment rate varied between a mere 1.5 and 2.4 percent. Only Switzerland and Norway have better employment statistics than Austria for this period (see table 4). Switzerland's performance, however, pales somewhat when one considers that, since 1970, it has eliminated 250,000 jobs (a loss of 9 percent), while Austria has created 400,000 new jobs (an increase of 16 percent), though half of them were at the expense of the self-employed. In Switzerland the *Gastarbeiter* (foreign workers) bore the burden of the job loss when their numbers were cut back, and Norway owes its relatively favorable position primarily to natural gas discoveries. Despite the recent recession, the number of employed workers in Austria has not only been maintained, but has actually increased considerably.

Austria has avoided youth unemployment, one of the most serious problems of industrial nations, because of its intensive education and job-creating policy. Austria's labor market in the past has had little

TABLE 5
MARKET SHARE OF OECD EXPORTS IN SELECTED OECD COUNTRIES, 1970–1980
(percent)

	Exports of Goods					
					1975/ 1980	*1970/ 1980*
					(average annual percentage rate	
Country	*1970*	*1975*	*1979*	*1980*[a]	*of change)*	
Japan	8.78	9.82	9.79	10.50	+1.3	+1.8
Austria	1.30	1.32	1.46	1.41	+1.3	+0.8
Switzerland	2.32	2.27	2.51	2.38	+0.9	+0.3
West Germany	15.54	15.85	16.30	15.51	−0.4	0
Sweden	3.08	3.07	2.62	2.48	−4.2	−2.1
EEC	50.9	52.1	54.6	53.3	+0.2	+0.5

	Export Ratio including Services					
					1975/ 1980	*1970/ 1980*
					(average annual percentage rate	
Country	*1970*	*1975*	*1979*	*1980*[a]	*of change)*	
Japan	7.79	9.00	9.20	9.87	+1.9	+2.4
Austria	1.66	1.79	1.94	1.96	+1.9	+1.7
West Germany	13.80	14.66	15.06	14.41	−0.3	+0.4
Switzerland	2.43	2.40	2.60	2.37	−0.3	+0.2
Sweden	2.82	2.84	2.48	2.34	−3.8	−1.8
EEC	50.6	51.8	54.0	52.7	+0.3	+0.4

	Machinery and Transport				
				1975/ 1979	*1970/ 1979*
				(average annual percentage rate	
Country	*1970*	*1975*	*1979*	*of change)*	
Japan	10.04	12.99	15.67	+4.8	+5.1
Austria	0.88	0.97	1.17	+4.7	+3.2
Switzerland	2.09	2.18	2.26	+0.9	+0.9
West Germany	20.37	19.83	20.64	+1.0	+0.1
Sweden	3.46	3.59	3.03	−4.2	−1.5
EEC	51.6	50.9	52.0	+0.5	+0.1

a. Preliminary data.
SOURCE: OECD.

problem absorbing layoffs resulting from structural change. Although this is becoming increasingly difficult, it is nevertheless a further indication of the adaptability of the Austrian economy.

Export intensity. Austria's economic competitiveness can best be seen in its market shares of OECD exports. Table 5 shows Austria's market position in comparison with its closest competitors in exports of goods, total exports, and technology exports (UN code 7). According to table 5, Austria's market-share increases have since 1970 fallen short of only those of Japan, which acquired its lead before 1975. Austria matched Japan's performance between 1975 and 1980.

In comparison with that of its European competitors, Austria's performance was positive. Its performance in total exports (including tourism and allowing for statistical discrepancy) was particularly impressive. Austria's market share of OECD exports has grown 1.7 percent per year since 1970 (1.9 percent since 1975), while West Germany's has grown only 0.4 percent (−0.3 percent since 1975); Switzerland's, 0.2 percent (−0.3 percent since 1975); and that of the EEC, 0.4 percent (0.3 percent since 1975). Japan's shares (2.4 percent since 1970 and 1.9 percent since 1975) are only slightly better than Austria's and are worse when considered on a per capita basis. The main cause of Austria's penetration into the world market is clearly the industrial structural change in the direction of high-value products, as seen in the export performance of the most technology-intensive product group, machinery and transport (UN code 7). In contrast with the stagnating performance of the EEC, Austria's market share increased 3.2 percent per year between 1970 and 1979 (4.7 percent from 1975 to 1979). Japan was the only industrial country that was more successful (5.1 percent from 1970 to 1979, and 4.8 percent from 1975 to 1979). The structural improvement increased strongly in the second half of the 1970s in relation to Austria's main European trading partners, and in view of the present situation, it should increase even more in the future.

Export quota. Since 1970, Austria's export quota (current account minus factor payments) has developed at a rate almost equal to that of the EEC, West Germany, and Switzerland. Since 1975 Austria appears to have adjusted more successfully to the oil price shock than have West Germany, Switzerland, and Sweden. Austria's export quota has decreased slightly, at 1.4 percent per year since 1975, compared with 2.0 percent, 2.5 percent, and 3.9 percent for Sweden, West Germany, and Switzerland, respectively. In 1981 a positive reversal of the trend set in. The increasing export intensity that resulted is expected almost to balance the relation between exports and imports (see table 6).

161

TABLE 6
RATIOS OF EXPORTS TO IMPORTS IN SELECTED OECD COUNTRIES, 1970–1980

Country	1970	1975	1979	1980[a]	1975/ 1980 (average annual percentage rate of change)	1970/ 1980
Austria	103	102	97	95	−1.4	−0.8
West Germany	111	112	102	99	−2.5	−1.1
Switzerland	95	110	99	90	−3.9	−0.5
Sweden	98	99	96	90	−2.0	−0.8
EEC	104	103	100	96	−1.4	−0.8
Japan	113	100	93	93	−1.4	−1.9

a. Preliminary data; EEC and Japan approximate.
SOURCE: OECD.

Productivity. The determining factor of the economic strength of a country is the absolute and relative level of labor productivity. Austria is below Japan in productivity increases, but is far above the other OECD countries, surpassing the OECD average in the decade 1967–1977 by 33 percent. West Germany surpassed the average by only 18 percent and Switzerland by only 3 percent, while Sweden was 14 percent below the OECD average (see table 7). In 1980 the differences increased even more.

Because Austria has been able, in recent years, to increase its growth rate and, at the same time, decrease its rate of energy consumption, its competitive position has improved considerably. Although Austria's gross domestic product in 1980 rose by 3.6 percent, total energy consumption declined by 2 percent and in industry by 4.5 percent.

Labor costs. The restrictive incomes policy combined with strong gains in productivity led in mid-1981 to a significant cost advantage for Austrian industry in the OECD sphere (see table 8).

Considering labor costs per unit of production since 1967 (on a 1978 basis), Austria achieved a labor cost advantage in 1981 over Sweden, the United States, Belgium, West Germany, Switzerland, and the Netherlands ranging from 37 to 69 percent (see table 9). Austria clearly surpassed the soft currency countries of France, Italy, and

TABLE 7
PRODUCTIVITY IN SELECTED OECD COUNTRIES, 1967–1977
(OECD = 100)

Country	1967/1973	1973/1977	1967/1977
Japan	138	106	146
Austria	121	109	133
Spain	114	108	123
Finland	115	103	118
West Germany	109	108	118
Belgium	109	105	114
France	107	106	114
Netherlands	109	104	113
Italy	110	98	109
Switzerland	101	102	103
Norway	99	103	102
Denmark	102	100	102
Australia	97	97	94
Great Britain	99	95	94
Canada	95	96	92
Sweden	93	92	86
United States	80	93	74

NOTE: Data are for real GDP per worker as a percentage of the average labor productivity of the other OECD countries (changes for the base period).
SOURCE: H. Dicke, "Relative Preisverschiebungen und Strukturanpassung im Welthandel," *Wirtschaftspolitische Blätter*, vol. 1/81, Vienna.

Great Britain. Austria was able to stabilize costs more than the degree to which the schilling was revalued, so that Austria's labor cost position improved, particularly in relation to the EEC countries. As shown in table 9, Austria's relative position from 1967 to 1981 improved 36 percent vis-à-vis Great Britain and the following percentages vis-à-vis these countries: West Germany, 16 percent; Switzerland, 15 percent; France, 10 percent; Italy, 10 percent; and Japan, 20 percent.

Despite the upward revaluation of the schilling and the strong structural and productivity improvements, Austria has become once again a de facto "lower-income country," with all the positive (exports, employment) and negative (terms of trade, imported inflation) consequences. The thesis of the "over-hard schilling" (with respect to Austria's competitiveness), can therefore be refuted. Figure 1 shows the exchange rate fluctuations in the currencies of Austria's most important trading partners.

TABLE 8
REAL EARNINGS AND LABOR COSTS IN SELECTED OECD COUNTRIES, 1980–1982
(percent changes)

Country	Real Earnings[a]			Real Labor Costs[b]			Productivity[c]		
	1980	1981	1982	1980	1981	1982	1980	1981	1982
United States	−1.2	1¼	−½	0	½	0	−0.5	1	−½
Japan	0.7	2½	3	4.5	2½	3	3.2	2½	2¾
Germany	1.0	0	½	1.3	1¼	1	1.1	−¼	3
Austria	0.9	¼	1¼	2.7	1¾	1¾	3.5	0	2¾
Switzerland	3.8	1½	1¼	6.7	2¾	1½	1.7	1¼	2¼
Total OECD[d,e]	0.3	1	¾	1.3	1	¾	0.7	1	1

a. Wages and salaries per employee deflated by private consumption deflator.
b. Total compensation per employee deflated by GDP deflator.
c. GNP or GDP per employed person.
d. 1980 GNP and GDP weights and exchange rates.
e. Excluding Greece, Iceland, Luxembourg, Portugal, and Turkey.

TABLE 9
INDEXES OF LABOR COSTS PER HOUR PER INDUSTRIAL WORKER IN SELECTED OECD COUNTRIES, 1967–1981
(Austria = 100)

Country	1967	1978	1980	1981[a]	1978/ 1981 percent change	1967/ 1981 percent change
Sweden	181	144	151	169	+17	−7
United States	223	122	128	157	+29	−29
Belgium	145	148	153	154	+4	+6
West Germany	131	144	152	152	+6	+16
Switzerland	124	142	142	142	0	+15
Netherlands	150	147	147	137	−7	−9
France	113	101	118	124	+23	+10
Italy	109	98	110	120	+22	+10
Great Britain	80	63	94	109	+73	+36
Austria	100	100	100	100	—	—
Japan	73	87	70	88	+2	+20

a. Estimated for the first half of 1981.
SOURCE: For Austria, Austrian Federal Chamber; for other countries, German Institute for Economic Research.

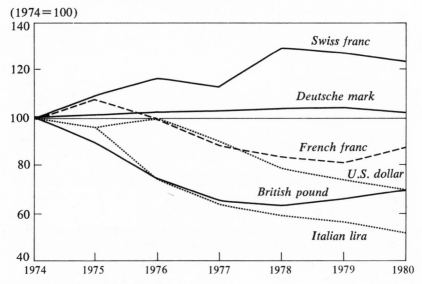

FIGURE 1

EXCHANGE RATE FLUCTUATIONS IN THE CURRENCIES OF AUSTRIA'S
MOST IMPORTANT TRADING PARTNERS, 1974–1980

(1974 = 100)

SOURCE: Austrian National Bank.

The indicators of the competitiveness of a country—economic and industrial performance, productivity, currency stability, employment situation, export performance, balance of payments, and labor costs—point to a positive future for Austria. Austria has not only largely caught up with the other industrial countries; it has in some cases even surpassed other countries. Through its economic policies, Austria will overcome social tensions and avoid environmental damage and will therefore be in a position to continue improving its desired competitive advantage.

Analysis of the Competitiveness of the Austrian Economy

High Industrial Quota. Industry contributes 29 percent to Austria's total national product (see table 10). Austria thereby exhibits an industrial quota equal to that of Japan and higher than that of France, Belgium, Great Britain, and Sweden. The average of the industrial nations of OECD is 27 percent. Austria's service sector quota, however, is 53 percent, 6 percent lower than the comparative figure for the industrial countries.

Austria has for a long time taken a middle position regarding regional economic factors, for example, raw materials, energy supply,

165

TABLE 10
INDUSTRIAL QUOTA OF SELECTED OECD COUNTRIES AS A
PERCENTAGE OF GNP, 1979

Country	Manufacturing Industry
Austria	29
West Germany	38
United States	24
Japan	29
OECD	27

SOURCE: World Bank, *World Development Report,* 1980.

wage levels, and distance from important markets. This allows industry a broad range of production possibilities, free from any pressure to specialize. Economic measures have partly compensated for relative disadvantages. The Austrian system of social partnership, an institutional framework representing employers and employees, also helps resolve problems of structural adaptation in specific sectors.

High Flexibility. Austria's industrial structure is based predominantly on medium-sized enterprises (see table 11). Experience shows that this does not cause a competitive disadvantage because medium-sized firms are, as a rule, more flexible than large corporations. With less capital tied up in their operations, it is easier for them to switch to new products and new production processes. They must, however, strive to utilize their advantages fully, by overcoming such difficulties as bottlenecks in

TABLE 11
NUMBER AND SIZE OF AUSTRIAN FIRMS, BY NUMBER OF EMPLOYEES

Number of employees	Number of Processing Firms, Industry	Total Number of Firms
1–4	21,343 (50.5%)	124,459 (62.3%)
5–49	17,842 (42.3%)	67,801 (33.9%)
50–99	1,480 (3.5%)	4,196 (2.1%)
100–499	1,831 (3.2%)	2,972 (1.5%)
500 and over	220 (0.5%)	399 (0.2%)

SOURCE: Austrian government statistics.

management and staff capacity (in marketing, export facilities, accounting, etc.).

Of the approximately 10,000 firms that produce industrial or technical products, less than 1 percent, or fewer than 100 firms, employ more than 1,000 workers. At the other end of the scale, almost one-half (47 percent) have either no or a maximum of four employed workers. Yet, more than one-fourth the number of wage earners work in large firms with over 1,000 employees, about 14 percent in firms with 500 to 1,000 employees, and more than 25 percent in companies with 100 to 250 employees. Two-thirds of all wage earners are therefore in medium- and large-sized firms.

Continuity in Economic Policy and Long-Term Planning. Unlike other western industrial countries over the past twenty years, Austria has developed with a continuity and an independence from cyclical problems and from international economic trends. Economic growth and price stability have been and remain principal economic objectives in Austria. Full employment, however, always takes precedence over other objectives. This policy not only facilitates the maintenance of a peaceful society, but also assures market power and thereby improves capacity utilization in industry as a whole. The resulting lower costs have an immediate effect on competitiveness.

Austria enjoys an atmosphere of discussion. Worker-employer problems are traditionally resolved through negotiation; strikes are rare. Consensus is sought in the economic sphere and elsewhere, producing, over all, an atmosphere of peace, security, and prosperity in which economics, like other activities, may proceed without problems. The most important institution for cooperation between interest groups is the Joint Commission on Wages and Prices. On this commission, representatives of labor and of employers—the so-called social partners—try to resolve questions by negotiation, an approach that has almost eliminated social conflicts and strikes in Austria (see table 12). This social partnership is a typically Austrian invention symbolizing the atmosphere conducive to compromise and the ability of the two sides of industry to negotiate effectively such issues as the development of wages and prices.

Competition and Flexibility in an Open Economy. The Austrian economy, like most small economies, is much more oriented toward foreign trade than larger countries with their domestic markets. Exports in 1979 accounted for 7.7 percent of gross domestic product in the United States and 22.6 percent in Austria (see table 13). The comparatively small size of Austrian export firms means that they cannot influence world market prices. Austrian business therefore feels constant pressure to adjust to

TABLE 12

AVERAGE NUMBER OF STRIKE MINUTES PER EMPLOYEE IN SELECTED
OECD COUNTRIES, 1975–1979

Country	Strike Minutes
Austria	0
United States [a]	200
West Germany	39
Switzerland [a]	1

a. Estimated.
SOURCE: International Labor Organization.

new conditions and must try to confine the effects of any mistakes to the short term. In the long term, this pressure proves advantageous and serves to compensate for possible conservative elements of economic policies that center on full employment and continuity. For a small country like Austria to hold its own in international markets, it must constantly adjust to new developments in technology and react quickly to changes in market conditions.

High Propensity to Invest and to Save. A lively investment rate was partly responsible for the favorable development of the Austrian economy. (Table 14 compares Austrian investment quotas with those of several other OECD countries.) Never in recent decades did the investment ratio in Austria fall below 25 percent. This high level will have to be maintained to keep up with future requirements and with the rising capital intensity. Roughly AS1.1 million of investments in plant and

TABLE 13

EXPORT INTENSITY AS A PERCENTAGE OF GDP IN SELECTED
OECD COUNTRIES, 1979

Country	Export Intensity
Austria	22.6
West Germany	22.5
United States	7.7
Switzerland	27.9
Japan	10.5

SOURCE: OECD, *Economic Outlook*, July 1981.

TABLE 14
INVESTMENT QUOTAS AS A PERCENTAGE OF GROSS NATIONAL PRODUCT
IN SELECTED OECD COUNTRIES, 1960 AND 1978

Country	1960	1978
Austria	28	28
West Germany	27	22
Switzerland	29	22
United States	18	19
Japan	34	31
OECD	21	22

SOURCE: OECD.

equipment were needed in 1978 to create one new job; by 1985 the figure will be AS1.5 million (at 1978 prices), and in 1990, AS1.9 million. A continuing high saving rate by private households, as shown in table 15, will contribute significantly to the funds required for these investments.

Technical Skill in Austrian Industry. Austrian technicians, engineers, and scientists enjoy a high reputation. Despite certain structural problems and technological gaps not unique to Austria, this country ranks among the most highly industrialized countries of the West. The Austrian education system is a good example of combining practical instruction and academic education, as in the training of apprentices and technicians. Funds spent on education amount to about 9 percent of Austria's federal budget. The education system also strives to make its graduate engineers highly versatile for future employment. The system undoubtedly contributes to the high technical skill displayed by workers in Austrian

TABLE 15
PRIVATE SAVING AS A PERCENTAGE OF DISPOSABLE INCOME IN
AUSTRIA, 1977–1981

	Savings Rate
1977	6.4
1978	8.5
1979	9.2
1980	8.0
1981	8.0

SOURCE: Institute for Economic Research, Vienna.

169

industry and promises the rapid elimination of the technological gaps and productivity backlogs still evident in some sectors. Efforts toward further improvement of the level of training in certain sectors will certainly be of great benefit.

Austrian Research and Development Departments. Because of the efficiency of Austrian research and development departments, Austrian enterprises have competitive advantages in many fields and can compensate for competitive disadvantages. The lower wage bill in many of these departments is only a minor aspect of the cost advantage. This advantage results primarily from the versatility of Austria's engineers, which enables innovative departments to limit bureaucracy and to operate wtih comparatively small staffs.

Policy Measures to Improve Competitiveness

Promotion of Investment and Plant Construction. The Austrian revenue system offers a considerable range of investment incentives to encourage investment activities, including accelerated depreciation allowances, investment allowances, investment reserves, transfers of latent (hidden) reserves to new investment goods, and specific tax incentives for exporting enterprises. In addition, there are special credit drives and direct investment subsidies. These investment incentives are also available to Austrian subsidiaries of foreign firms based in Austria, who enjoy, by and large, the same support as domestic firms. General Motors Corporation has responded to this investment program and is installing an engine assembly plant near Vienna. The company receives substantial subsidies from the Austrian federal government and from the city of Vienna and has been granted industrial sites at favorable terms.

An Efficient Export Financing System. An excellent system of export financing has been built up in Austria because exports are so important to the economy. Cover is available for export risks at comparatively modest cost, and funds are available at preferential terms for financing exports. Various other export promotion schemes have been established to supplement government export financing and to provide expert advice to exporters.

Steps toward Structural Improvement. An existing economic structure cannot be changed by mere discussion. In view of the Austrian trade deficit, due to long-term price increases in energy and raw materials, Austria attaches particular importance to structural policy. The measures for improving the economic structure, as stated by the finance minister, require Austria to pursue immediately an economic policy geared toward innovation. High-priority programs aimed at structural improvement are classified in a four-point scheme.

1. *Financial support for "priority" investment designed to improve the current account.* Investment designed to produce internationally competitive goods, to improve economic structure, and to further the current account will be encouraged through loans.

2. *Financial support for product development.* The development of prototypes and pilot production series from research findings is to be promoted under this category.

3. *Improved funding for small- and medium-sized firms through the provision of secondary capital.* Risk capital is to be made available to small- and medium-sized firms for investment designed to adapt to changing technology.

4. *Insolvency support.* Support is to be made available to small- and medium-sized firms adversely affected by the bankruptcies of large concerns, provided that the continuation of the firm is deemed desirable for economic and social reasons.

Further Measures Needed to Improve Competitiveness

Increased Export Intensity and Export Structure. Small economies, having relatively small domestic markets, are considerably dependent on foreign trade. Their export quotas are therefore correspondingly high— over 20 percent in Austria, with forecasts by the Austrian Institute for Economic Research predicting a rise to about 30 percent by 1990. Taking exports of services into account, Austria's export intensity over all is comparable to that of countries of similar size and development level, such as Sweden, Switzerland, Denmark, Norway, and Finland. Not including exports of services, per capita exports in Austria amounted to only about 58 percent of per capita exports of comparable countries (although per capita GNP in 1976 was over 80 percent of these countries'). An examination of the more promising technical goods sphere brings a less favorable picture of the Austrian situation. The value of technical exports per worker in Austria reached $14,000 in 1971. This figure is 3 percent below the average figure for the EEC and 45 percent below the average figure for the small countries of Western Europe.

One of the main reasons for the inadequate export performance may be that large sectors of production have not yet entered the international market. Firms that are quite able to export fail to do so. Most exported goods are technical products, which approach or equal the quality of goods from the highly industrialized nations. One important

TABLE 16

EXPORT STRUCTURES OF SELECTED OECD COUNTRIES, 1977
(percent)

Country	Share of Total Exports for Product Group:				
	I	II	III	IV	V
Austria	25.9	7.8	5.6	10.7	50.0
West Germany	24.5	11.6	5.1	6.4	52.4
Japan	31.5	5.0	5.2	13.1	45.2
Switzerland	35.0	20.6	7.0	1.3	36.1

NOTE: Product Group I: highly skilled labor and labor intensive production; Product Group II: highly skilled labor and capital intensive production; Product Group III: less skilled labor and labor intensive production; Product Group IV: less skilled labor and capital intensive production; Product Group V: chiefly raw material production.
SOURCE: OECD.

influence on exports may be that smaller firms have difficulty gaining a foothold in the risky export markets. Supportive services such as engineering, consulting, and marketing, which could make an important contribution particularly in helping small- and medium-sized firms to export, clearly remain inadequate in Austria. Table 16 compares Austria's share of total exports with that of West Germany, Japan, and Switzerland.

Increased Research Intensity. Expenditures for research and development must be considered one of the significant factors influencing technical development. As late as the 1960s, the share of such expenditures in Austria was under 1 percent of GNP, and the target envisaged at that time, of raising this to 2 percent, has yet to be attained (see table 17).

TABLE 17

EXPENDITURES FOR RESEARCH AND DEVELOPMENT IN AUSTRIA, 1970–1980

R & D Expenditures	1970	1975	1980
In AS millions	3,492	7,861	13,600
As a percentage of GNP	0.94	1.20[a]	1.37

a. In the United States and in West Germany, R & D expenditures were more than 2 percent of GNP.
SOURCE: OECD.

TABLE 18

RESEARCH AND DEVELOPMENT FUNDS AS A PERCENTAGE OF GDP IN
SELECTED OECD COUNTRIES, 1977

Country	Percentage of GDP
United States	2.4
West Germany	2.1
Great Britain	2.0
Switzerland	2.3
Japan	1.9
Austria	1.2

SOURCE: OECD.

In 1980 the share of GNP spent on research was 1.37 percent, that is, AS13,600 million. Table 18 compares research and development funds as a percentage of GNP in several OECD countries.

The major share of industrial research in Austria is financed from the enterprises' own resources. About 70 percent of R & D is concentrated in four branches of industry—chemicals, petroleum, iron and steel, and electrical products. In highly industrial countries, however, these "key industries" account for an average of 80 to 90 percent of all expenditures on industrial R & D. Other branches, too, are not yet sufficiently research intensive. The relatively high research expenditure in the established branches of production cannot, by any means, compensate for the below-average research expenditure in the modern and innovation-prone branches. Expenditures in Austria on industrial R & D still lie far below those hypothetical values that were expected, in view of the stage of development attained, in relation to per capita GNP. The absence of prestige research projects (military, space travel) is only one of the causes of this situation (see table 19).

Better Cooperation between Research Institutions and Industry. The trend in scientific research to withdraw from the major fields of application in the industrial sector will have to be reversed. Experts have made suggestions concerning cooperation between science and industry: there should be more mobility, both in personnel and in subject matter, between the sectors; dialogue should be encouraged between researchers in many fields, from problem solving to reorganization; research consortia, joint ventures, and commercialization companies are to be instituted—either jointly by universities and industry or as service organizations. University research experts, too, recognize the new challenge.

TABLE 19
PUBLIC EXPENDITURES FOR RESEARCH AND DEVELOPMENT
COMPARED INTERNATIONALLY, 1979
(millions of counting units)

Country	Civil Research	Civil and Military Research
Belgium	965.2	966.3
Denmark	255.2	257.2
West Germany	5,588.1	6,318.3
France	2,907.2	4,499.5
Ireland[a]	38.8	38.8
Italy	822.9	855.2
Netherlands	1,026.6	1,059.1
Great Britain	1,440.4	3,219.6
Austria	332.1	332.1

a. 1977.
SOURCE: For Austria, Austrian Federal Ministry of Science and Research; for other countries, EEC Statistics Office, Luxembourg, 1980.

A better utilization of research findings and close cooperation between research and practical application might eliminate barren activity and more than compensate for comparatively low expenditures on research.

More Readiness to Innovate. Declining competitiveness is predicted for Austrian enterprises unless they show greater willingness to innovate, but it is possible to encourage innovation. Promotion of innovation is, however, more complicated than merely offering grants for research to a firm. It begins by introducing innovative thinking in education and cultural policy. The promotion of innovation requires the creation of a climate conducive to innovation. Innovation must be publicly discussed and publicized, so that employees develop a certain awareness of its important role. This process must begin at the education and training levels.

Gaps in Investment Financing. The funding of innovative products and processes may fail for four reasons. (1) The financial risk may seem an insupportable burden for the individual enterprise or for the funding bank. (2) Young firms are often unable to obtain the necessary bank guarantees and sufficient backing to raise outside funds. (3) Enterprises wishing to raise equity in the capital markets are often confronted with potential investors' preference for secure, quick returns. Profits from innovative investments can only be expected after a certain setting-up

174

period. (4) Austria lacks suitable organizations to provide venture capital to finance profitable technological innovations by small- and medium-sized firms. In addition, a private venture capital market must be developed.

Solutions to these problems may be available through innovation corporations, innovation loans, and special facilities for the assumption of liability. Several steps in this direction have already been taken.

A Strategy for Reindustrialization. The life cycle theory distinguishes among the development, growth, and maturity phases of a product. For each phase, different combinations of factor inputs are best. Small industrial countries like Austria should specialize in the first phase of the product cycle. This means that Austria must specialize in technologically advanced, high-value products. In order to exploit the comparative advantage inherent in such products, technical skill must be available.

A reindustrialization strategy along these lines requires considerable cooperation among private and public firms, banks, and government. Also needed are increased public awareness, improvements in infrastructure (firms are needed to provide research, development, information, and marketing assistance to Austria's relatively small- and medium-sized businesses), and greater use of modern electronics in production so that smaller Austrian firms may economically produce small-production series.

Awareness is growing, and a variety of efforts have been initiated. These include establishment of engineering consulting firms; of export companies and export promotion firms to assist first-time as well as established exporters and to provide low-interest credit; of innovation promotion companies to provide risk capital and assist in product development and in the marketing of innovative products; and of economic information centers to provide information and counseling on commercial law, finance, and the formation of new businesses. These measures are seen, in view of the emerging international division of labor, as essential if Austria is to realize its economic potential and remain competitive.

Trade, Trade Finance, and Capital Movements

Helmut H. Haschek

Trade

Developments in Austria's Trade. For a small country, the development of Austria's economy heavily depends on its foreign trade. This is true for the middle and large enterprises with a highly specialized production structure as well as for those in the field of mass production. The domestic market is too small to offer the required economies of scale for these types of company.

In addition to foreign trade in goods, tourism plays an important role. The income from tourism amounts to one-third of that from the export of goods. Receipts from tourism are two to three times larger than expenditures, so Austria is able to bear a structural deficit in its trade in goods.

Especially in the reconstruction years after World War II, Austria, with an export structure similar to that of a developing country (raw materials and semifinished products as primary goods) and ranking, as far as per capita income was concerned, well below the level of other industrial countries,[1] chose a strategy of economic growth centered on foreign trade. Exports became the driving force of the Austrian economy.[2] Their growth rate since 1960 (11 percent per annum nominally, 8 percent per annum in real terms) not only exceeded the high growth rate of gross domestic product, or GDP (table 1), but also was remarkable in comparison with other nations. Whereas some industrial countries were able to achieve a similarly high export growth, only Japan showed a substantially higher increase in its exports.[3] As shown in figure 1, extremely high export rates were recorded in 1969, 1974, and 1979.

The division of Europe, however, into two trade areas—the Common Market and the European Free Trade Association (EFTA)—in the

TABLE 1
AUSTRIAN EXPORTS AND ECONOMIC GROWTH, 1960–1980

	1960	1970	1980	Growth (%) 1960–1980	Growth (%) 1970–1980
Exports, nominal (AS billion)	29.1	74.3	226.2	10.8[a]	11.8[a]
GDP, nominal (AS billion)	162.9	375.7	995.9	9.5[a]	10.2[a]
Exports/GDP (%), nominal	17.9	19.8	22.7	4.8	2.9
Exports, in 1964 prices (AS billion)	30.0	76.8	136.7	7.8[a]	5.9[a]
GDP, in 1964 prices (AS billion)	189.2	301.8	442.5	4.3[a]	3.9[a]
Exports/GDP (%), in real terms	15.8	25.4	30.9	15.1	5.5

a. Growth per year.
SOURCE: Oesterreichische Kontrollbank AG (OKB).

early 1960s damaged Austria's economic development. Although its foreign trade was heavily directed to this region, for political reasons Austria was prohibited from becoming a member of the Common Market. Thus exports suffered. Austria's market share of the total imports of the Common Market fell, and the Common Market's share of Austria's total exports shrank to only 39 percent in 1972.

Trade with EFTA countries did not compensate for the losses in trade with the Common Market, because the Austrian economy had been only slightly intertwined with those of the EFTA countries. Furthermore, since some members of EFTA (the Scandinavian countries and Portugal) are far away, Austria could reach their markets only with goods that were relatively insensitive to transport costs. Thus, on the one hand, Austria's integration into the EFTA region has helped to bring about a structural change in Austrian production toward more sophisticated investment and consumer goods.[4] On the other hand, only minor changes could be recorded in the regional structure of Austria's exports. The poor regional diversification is shown by the fact that Austria not only exported less than 1 percent of its total volume of exports into the most rapidly growing countries of the third world, but also suffered a loss in its market share in some of these countries (table 2).

FIGURE 1

DEVELOPMENT OF AUSTRIA'S EXPORT RATES, IN NOMINAL AND REAL TERMS, 1961–1980

(1964 prices)

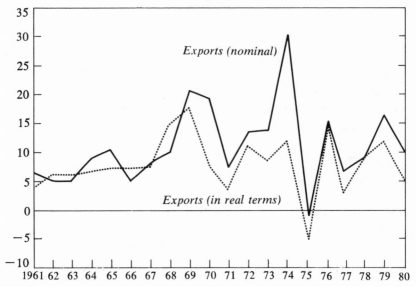

SOURCES: Austrian Institute for Economic Research; Oesterreichische Kontrollbank Aktiengesellschaft.

Austria was one of the few industrial countries that could at least temporarily avoid an explosive rise in its trade deficit immediately after the first energy crisis. In 1975 Austria experienced a recession caused by losses in exports as well as reduced investment in industry and increased household savings. Since 1976, however, Austria's trade deficit has increased. In the 1960s and the first half of the 1970s the deficit was 5–6.5 percent of the gross domestic product, and it increased 7–9 percent in the second half of the 1970s. Austria imports about 80 percent of its oil, half of its natural gas requirements, and all of the pit-coal, so the energy bill contributed significantly to the increasing deficit. Energy imports rose from 2 percent of the gross domestic product in the 1960s to 3–3.5 percent between 1974 and 1979. The figure was 5 percent in 1980. It was possible to pay for part of this by increasing exports to the Organization of Petroleum Exporting Countries (OPEC).

The deterioration of the trade balance that is not related to the oil price increase is estimated at approximately 2 percent of gross domestic

TABLE 2

AUSTRIAN EXPORT STRUCTURE, BY COMMODITY AND REGION,
1960–1980

(percentage share of the total volume of exports)

Commodity	1960	1970	1980	Increase/ Decrease, 1960– 1980 (percent)
Raw materials, food, and beverages	25.6	17.0	14.4	−11.2
Semifinished products	28.9	22.9	22.7	−6.2
Finished goods	45.5	60.1	62.9	17.4
(Machinery and transport equipment)	16.3	24.1	27.7	11.4
Regional structure of Austrian exports				
OECD countries	72.0	74.9	72.6	0.6
Europe	66.4	68.3	68.8	2.4
Eastern Europe	13.7	12.9	9.4	−4.3
Other countries	14.3	12.2	18.0	3.7
OPEC	2.1	1.8	5.6	3.5

SOURCE: Austrian Institute for Economic Research.

product.[5] This deterioration was caused by: (1) the appreciation of the Austrian schilling (AS) in real terms; (2) a change in the quality of Austria's high economic growth from one driven by exports to one maintained temporarily by budget deficits; (3) a rather slow adaptation of the Austrian production structure to the new domestic and external economic situation; and (4) diminishing import demand in the Eastern bloc countries.

The Austrian Institute for Economic Research has recently projected the development of foreign trade until 1990, concluding that under certain conditions an external balance (a deficit in the expanded current account[6] of not more than 1.5 percent of the gross domestic product) could be achieved.[7] Among these conditions was the expectation that exports would grow at an annual nominal rate of 10.1 percent, or 7.3 percent in real terms, from 1979 to 1990. This means a deceleration of growth caused primarily by an expected slower growth of world trade, and the absence of further impulses from Austria's economic integration in the European Economic Community (EEC).

Regionally, an increasing export share to developing countries and a decreasing export share to Eastern bloc countries are expected. The total volume of Austrian exports at current prices will amount to AS600 billion (1979: AS206 billion). Thirty-seven percent of Austria's exports in 1980 will be related to machinery and transportation equipment (1979: 28 percent).

Austrian imports are expected to grow at a rate of 9.4 percent annually in nominal terms (5.9 percent in real terms) from 1979 to 1990. The total value of imports is expected to reach AS722 billion (1979: AS270 billion). Despite a slower growth rate for imports than for exports, Austria's trade deficit will grow from AS64 billion in 1979 to AS128 billion in 1990. In relative terms, however, it will decrease from 7 percent of the gross domestic product to 6.2 percent. The deficit resulting from energy imports will grow from AS30 billion to nearly AS100 billion (4.8 percent of the gross domestic product).

Prospects are that there is relatively little room to maneuver on imports. The efforts to contain the trade deficit within tolerable limits must, by necessity, be centered on exports. Apart from basic measures at the grass-roots level (making foreign language courses compulsory again at the business university; emphasizing international law at the universities, in particular the law of contract and commercial law; and so forth), a concentrated effort should be made to penetrate more thoroughly the markets of the newly industrialized countries in Asia and Latin America. More attention should be given to the effective marketing of exports. Indeed, a successful international marketing organization could be an outstanding promotion tool to induce companies to produce increasingly for exports.

Export Promotion in General. Organizations for the promotion of exports (the provision of guarantees against political and commercial risks as well as the financing of exports) play a vital role, particularly for countries such as Austria that largely depend on foreign trade. Before going into the specific properties of the Austrian export guarantee and financing system, it is useful to consider the evolution of export promotion in general.

Export financing as a special tool for trade promotion is the result of the interwar period. It originated in the industrial world and is based on export credit insurance systems created at the turn of the century to diversify the credit risks of suppliers in international trade. During the interwar period, exchange restrictions helped promote supplier credit as the main financing tool in international trade. The exporter became the main creditor in international exchange. The banks' role was reduced to refinancing the exporter.

Export financing was originally designed to bridge the financial requirements of the exporters when they sold on extended terms. Terms were extended to allow the importer to reimburse the exporter after the importer sold the goods. It financed the distribution of goods over national boundaries. The additional risk—mainly the political risk associated with exchange difficulties—was assumed by the various governments because it was one that could be neither commercially reinsured nor sufficiently diversified and export insurance was identified as an important tool for export promotion. Over the years, however, the combination of export insurance and export financing developed into a normal tool in international trade for selling manufactured goods on short terms and on extended terms of up to two and three years.

Capital goods exports developed differently. In the early 1960s, export financing assumed a role that is still growing: export credits were used as investment credits in project financing. The tool was the buyer credit formula combined with credit insurance now offered by banks in the exporting country for credits extended to importers. From an institutional point of view, the administration of the credits and insurance is usually handled by commercial banks and credit insurance organizations insuring supplier credits.

Any type of effective export financing requires an export insurance scheme of one sort or another. In most countries, the functions of export financing and insurance are divided.[8] The exceptions are few: institutions that handle both in a more or less integrated fashion are the Export-Import Bank of the United States, the Export Development Corporation (EDC) in Canada, the Oesterreichische Kontrollbank Aktiengesellschaft (OKB) in Austria, and the Export Finance and Insurance Corporation (EFIC) in Australia in the industrial countries and the Export-Import Bank of Korea among the less developed countries. There is, however, a tendency toward centralization that can also be seen in the new organizational structure of the Sezione Speziale Assicurazione Credito all' Esportazione (SACE) in Italy.

Export transactions that involve extended terms are usually handled by exporters—in many cases comparatively small enterprises—who are not used to international financial transactions, their normal contact being the commercial banks. The logical setup, therefore, would involve the commercial banking system in both the financing and the insurance part of export transactions. The commercial bank, however, should not share the foreign credit risk, because, again, this requires additional decision making and administrative delays. The only further decision that is necessary concerns interest rates and other fees.

Another reason for an integrated system concerns funding procedures, which require that export financing be made available only on insured business. Commercial banks should be used as intermediaries so that in case of default, where lengthy procedures must be set up to establish whether payment will be effected under the insurance cover, the financing agency has the funds available on the due date in order to plan its funding activities.

Export Promotion in Austria. The outstanding feature of export promotion in Austria is a systematic and integrated approach to the provision of export guarantees and finance. A brief description of the various systems might be useful before examining some of the details of the integrated approach.

Austria provides three major export financing schemes. All are operated with the Republic's assistance and handled through the commercial banking system. In the majority of cases financial assistance is provided on the basis of guarantees issued by the Republic of Austria and in the context of an elaborate export and investment insurance system adopted by the Export Promotion Act of 1964 and amended from time to time.

The three major schemes are: (1) Export Financing Scheme operated by the OKB; (2) Rediscount Facility of the Austrian National Bank; and (3) "Exportfonds"—credits. The second and third schemes deal exclusively with the refinancing of supplier credits made available to Austrian exporters. These short-term refinancing credits extend for a maximum of eighteen months and cover both the production and the repayment period granted to the foreign buyer.

Accounting for almost 90 percent of all outstanding disbursements, the Export Financing Scheme of OKB is by far the most important in volume as well as comprehensiveness (see table 3). It covers many credit maturities, with emphasis on medium- to long-term credits. The actual lending operations are carried out by Austrian commercial banks. OKB makes loans available to the commercial banks for all export contracts, buyer's credits, or Austrian investments abroad, provided the transaction to be financed is guaranteed by the Republic for political and commercial risks. The credit period, the portion of the transaction for which financing is provided, and the security required for the loans are determined by the terms and conditions of the guarantee issued by the Republic, according to the Export Promotion Act. Institutionally, OKB is charged (on behalf of and as the agent of the Republic of Austria) with the administration of export guarantees and the responsibility to procure and provide export financing on its own account. This integration is based on the principle that the guarantee backing an export claim is a necessary and sufficient condition for the provision of export finance under OKB's scheme.

TABLE 3

AUSTRIAN EXPORT FINANCING SCHEMES, VOLUME OF
DISBURSEMENTS OUTSTANDING, 1978–1980

(AS billion)

	December 31, 1978		December 31, 1979		December 31, 1980	
	Amount	%	Amount	%	Amount	%
Loans (Österreichischer Exportfonds) Ges.m.b.H.	1.3	2.6	2.5	3.5	3.4	3.4
Loans extended through Statutory Export Financing Scheme operated by Kontrollbank	45.7	88.8	61.7	86.7	91.1	89.7
Start-up loans and investment financing operated by Kontrollbank	0.1	0.2	0.1	0.2	0.1	0.1
Acceptance credits under guarantee of the Republic of Austria with rediscount facility of the Austrian National Bank	4.3	8.4	6.9	9.6	6.9	6.8
Total volume of disbursements outstanding	51.4	100.0	71.2	100.0	101.5	100.0

SOURCE: OKB.

The financing for individual export projects is channeled through the commercial banking system, so no distortions from competition emerge and the full range of services of the commercial banking system is untouched. This achieves considerable economies of scale in administration. Furthermore, there are the possibilities of risk diversification as well as economies of scale in the procurement of refinancing in domestic and international financial markets. Visible expressions of these advantages are seen in the lower-than-average refinancing costs in those markets (including risk premiums) and in the speed with which decisions can be reached.

The Export Refinancing Scheme is to be self-liquidating and self-supporting. Table 4 contains a synopsis of the interest rates currently in force. In considering the prevailing interest rates, which range from

183

TABLE 4

AUSTRIA'S STATUTORY EXPORT FINANCING SCHEME, INTEREST RATES,
AS OF AUGUST 15, 1981
(percent)

Repayment Period of the Credit	Tranche A of the Loan (floating-rate portion)	Quarterly[a] OKB Export Finance Rate (current annual rate)[b]	Tranche B of the Loan (fixed-rate portion)	Prevailing Fixed Interest Rate[b] (per year)	Blended Rate (approx.) (per year)
Less than two years	85	9.00	15	8.75	8.95
Two years or more but less than five years	70	9.00	30	8.25	8.65
Five years or more but less than eight years	40	9.00	60	8.50	8.60
Eight years or more	15	9.00	85	8.75	8.76

NOTE: The Export Financing Scheme is operated by the Oesterreichische Kontrollbank Aktiengesellschaft, or OKB.

a. As of July 1, 1981.

b. Interest is payable quarterly in arrears.

SOURCE: OKB.

8.6 percent to 8.95 percent per year (exclusive of a ½ percent guarantee charge), there are two factors to be highlighted: first, these rates are relatively low in comparison with the cost of capital in international markets; and second, these rates are self-supporting. Subsidies have not been necessary, because interest rates charged on export credits should slightly exceed the average cost of funding. Thus it is of considerable importance that a portion of the export credit be made available at a floating interest rate. This ensures that the effective interest rates are adapted to market conditions. Furthermore, because about half of OKB's portfolio is subject to the floating rate, OKB's blended lending rate need not reflect the full extent of changes in the marginal cost of funds. The floating-rate feature, therefore, stabilizes the overall level of interest rates for export finance.

These facts are relevant for the discussion that has been going on within the Organization for Economic Cooperation and Development (OECD) regarding the so-called consensus, the arrangement regarding officially supported export credits. Two facts stand to be criticized in this respect—namely, the low level of interest rates and the fact that the OECD's interest rate matrix contains uniform interest rates irrespective of the currency in which export finance is to be denominated.[9] Austria has made several contributions to remedy the situation, arguing that a system that allows differentiation by currencies is the only sensible one.

Currency Denomination of Trade

International Trade. The shift to floating exchange rates and the recent gyrations in exchange rates have led to increased interest in the composition of the currencies used to invoice and finance merchandise trade. Based on 1979 figures, it was found that over half (50.5 percent) of world trade is priced in U.S. dollars. The deutsche mark is used for about 14 percent of the total, followed by the pound sterling and the French franc, at around 7.5 percent and 6 percent, respectively.[10] The deutsche mark is the most important currency in Europe.

A number of factors determine whether exports are paid for in the currency of the exporting nation or in another one. Most important seems to be the demand structure for the goods that are to be exported. Others are the international character of the relevant currency, the expected exchange rate developments, and the practices and traditions in various sectors of international trade. The choice of currency is frequently determined by the bargaining position of the trading partners, which in turn is crucially influenced by the commodity to be exported. Generally, it was found that importers are more willing to accept the exporter's currency as payment the more monopolistic an element the product contains. Thus, simple mass products that are exposed to tough international competition are often traded in the currency of the importer, whereas products with a high technological content are often traded in the currency of the exporter.[11] Larger firms, however, are more willing to use the currency of the trading partner, or third-party currencies, than small firms, because of their access to sophisticated know-how regarding forward exchange coverage.

The Situation in Austria. There are no statistics available as to the currency in which exports and imports are invoiced.[12] Since the Austrian schilling is not an international trading currency, it is possible that the volume of exports invoiced in Austrian schillings could be larger than the payments received in Austrian schillings. This question is relevant for the determination of the exchange risk borne by the exporter. It seems safe, however, to assume that at least those export transactions that are paid for in Austrian schillings are also invoiced

185

TABLE 5

THE SHARE OF CURRENCIES USED IN PAYMENT FOR AUSTRIAN EXPORTS AND IMPORTS, 1973–1980

	Exports						Imports					
	1973		1974–1977		1978–1980		1973		1974–1977		1978–1980	
Currency[a]	Ø	%	Ø	%	Ø	%	Ø	%	Ø	%	Ø	%
US$	12.5	11	18.6	11	25.2	11	18.7	13	36.0	17	57.9	20
£	3.6	3	3.3	2	4.7	2	7.2	5	7.2	3	6.1	2
DM	24.6	22	36.3	22	58.5	25	55.8	38	76.8	37	109.2	38
SFr	10.4	9	9.7	6	10.0	4	11.8	8	13.6	7	12.5	4
Lira	2.3	2	2.0	1	4.0	2	6.4	4	6.85	3	8.5	3
AS	53.0	47	89.6	53	119.4	51	32.6	23	49.95	24	71.3	25
Hfl	2.6	2	3.4	2	4.3	2	3.1	2	4.3	2	5.4	2
SK	1.3	1	1.4	1	1.4	1	2.4	2	3.2	2	3.3	1
FF	1.0	1	1.4	1	3.4	1	2.7	2	3.3	2	5.0	2
Others	2.2	2	2.1	1	3.2	1	4.7	3	6.1	3	7.7	3
Total	113.5	100	167.8	100	234.1	100	145.4	100	207.3	100	286.9	100

a. The names of the currencies appear unabbreviated in table 6.

Ø = the average annual value (in AS billion) for the periods 1974–1977 and 1978–1980; for 1973, the value given is for that year. No data are available for earlier years.

SOURCE: OKB calculations from data published by the Austrian National Bank.

in the national currency. On the import side, a divergence between the currency of payment and invoicing seems to be less probable. The observations that follow refer to payments made or received.

About half (50.6 percent) of the payments received for Austrian exports in 1980 were denominated in Austrian schillings. The second most common currency was the deutsche mark (25.3 percent). The U.S. dollar was third (10.8 percent), followed by the Swiss franc (3.8 percent). None of the other currencies achieved a share in excess of 2 percent. This is to be noted in particular for the Italian lira, the pound sterling, and the French franc since Italy (accounting for about 10 percent of trade) as well as France and the United Kingdom (accounting each for about 4 percent of trade with Austria) are some of Austria's most important trading partners.

In regard to payments for Austrian imports, a different picture emerges of the currency composition. Given Germany's dominant position as the originating country of Austrian imports (accounting for 41 percent in 1980), it is not surprising that payments made in 1980 for imports showed a large (37 percent) share of the DM as denomination currency. The Austrian schilling was second, with 24.4 percent, followed by the U.S. dollar (22.6 percent) and the Swiss franc (3.8 percent). The Italian lira, the pound sterling, and the French franc each had a 2 percent share.

An analysis of the use of currencies in trade finance over time yields interesting results. Data are available in Austria from 1973 to 1980 that suggest some conclusions on the use of currencies before and after the oil price shock in the fall of 1973 (table 5). In regard to exports, the most interesting result is the significant drop, as payment currency, in the use of the Swiss franc, from a 9 percent share in 1973 to an average of 4 percent from 1978 to 1980.[13] The dollar, surprisingly, showed no increase from 11 percent. The deutsche mark and the Austrian schilling, however, did show an increase of a few points (the DM increased from 22 to 25 percent and the Austrian schilling from 47 to 51 percent).

The modest increase regarding the Austrian schilling, however, is surprising because the Austrian export promotion system is geared to using the schilling as the payment currency. An increasing share of Austrian exports was covered by the export promotion system operated by OKB, and it reached about 40 percent of total exports by 1980. There is an important lag effect because at the same time, the payment terms offered in the marketing of Austrian exports had to be lengthened. Thus it may be anticipated that there will be a rise in the near future in the Austrian schilling share of payments received for Austrian exports.

TABLE 6

CURRENCY COMPOSITION OF PAYMENTS RECEIVED AND MADE
IN CONNECTION WITH AUSTRIAN TRADE, 1973–1980

	1973	1974–1977	1978–1980
Average annual currency balance[a] (AS billion)	−32.0	−39.5	−52.7
Individual currency as a percentage of total			
U.S. dollar	−19	−44	−62
Pound sterling	−11	−10	−3
Deutsche mark	−98	−102	−96
Swiss franc	−4	−10	−5
Italian lira	−13	−12	−8
Austrian schilling	64	100	91
Dutch guilder	−2	−2	−2
Swedish krona	−3	−5	−3
French franc	−6	−5	−3
Other currencies	−8	−10	−9
Total	−100	−100	−100

a. The currency balance is the payments received for exports (including related items) minus the payments made for imports (including related items). A minus sign (−) indicates a deficit.

SOURCE: OKB (computed on the basis of table 5).

In regard to the currency composition of imports, the most dramatic though not surprising change because energy prices have increased, is the use of the U.S. dollar as payment currency. The dollar increased its share from 13 to 20 percent. The pound sterling, Swiss franc, and lira declined in relative importance, with the drop in the Swiss franc share, from 8 to 4 percent, being particularly pronounced. A most welcome development from the domestic point of view is the increase in the use of the Austrian schilling as payment currency for imports (the AS share increased from 22 to 25 percent).

The implications of these changing patterns in currency usage can best be illustrated by reviewing the currency balance (the difference between receipts for exports and related items and payments for imports and related items in various currencies) from 1973 to 1980 (table 6). It is to be noted that the currency deficit increased from AS32 billion in 1973 to an average of AS40 billion from 1974 to 1977 and to an annual average of AS53 billion from 1978 to 1980. The shifts in currency composition, however, are more relevant. The most dramatic change concerned the U.S. dollar. The dollar payments deficit, as a percentage of the overall currency deficit, increased from 19 percent in 1973 (before the oil price shock) to an average of 44 percent from 1974 to 1977 and to 62 percent from 1978 to 1980. All other currencies for which there is a deficit in payments showed declines. The declines were particularly pronounced for the pound sterling (from 11 percent to 3 percent) and the Italian lira (from 13 percent to 8 percent). Regarding the use of the Austrian schilling as a payment currency, it is noteworthy that its currency surplus on average corresponded to the overall currency deficit (the AS surplus showed a remarkable growth rate in this period).

The Capital Account and Its Relation to the Current Account

Analysis of the Current Account. To highlight some of the interdependencies between the capital account and the current account, an attempt will be made to expand on some conclusions in the earlier sections. A recent study by the Austrian Institute for Economic Research analyzed the effect of economic growth and Austria's competitive position on the development of the expanded current account,[14] which consists of the current account and errors and omissions. The latter are added to the current account because they are believed to represent largely misrecorded goods-and-services transactions. A recent attempt by the Austrian Institute for Economic Research to verify this failed because of the quality of the data. The institute concluded that about two-thirds of the items could be explained by trade transactions and one-third by capital movements.

The development of the expanded current account in the past fifteen years is characterized by two different phases. As a percentage of gross domestic product, it was roughly in balance during the first phase (1966–1973), a period of high international economic growth. In the next period, which was characterized by slower economic growth and the oil crisis, the deficit on average in the expanded current account (see table 7) was 1.5 percent of GDP. Beginning in 1976 and interrupted only in 1978, the current account deficit became one of the most important and controversial issues in shaping economic policy in Austria.

The medium-term deficit of the current account cannot be explained by growth differentials alone, since Austria maintained a growth rate in both periods higher than the average for the other European OECD countries. There has been a change, however, in the competitive position of Austria and in the size of its energy bill. It has been estimated that

189

TABLE 7

DEVELOPMENT OF AUSTRIA'S CURRENT ACCOUNT, 1970–1981

	Trade	Services	Transfer Payments	Current Account	Errors and Omissions	Expanded Current Account
			(AS billion)			
1970	−18.4	17.6	0.2	−0.5	2.8	2.3
1971	−25.5	22.6	0.2	−2.7	4.7	2.0
1972	−30.9	27.2	−0.8	−4.5	5.1	0.6
1973	−33.8	28.2	−1.6	−7.2	5.6	−1.6
1974	−32.3	26.4	−3.0	−8.8	2.9	−5.9
1975	−30.6	27.6	−2.6	−5.6	5.2	−0.4
1976	−52.5	28.1	−1.9	−26.4	10.1	−16.2
1977	−71.3	24.4	−2.3	−49.2	20.3	−28.9
1978	−50.7	30.5	−0.1	−20.3	14.1	−6.2
1979	−58.7	34.9	0.4	−23.4	6.3	−17.1
1980[a]	−87.5	39.7	1.0	−46.8	25.9	−20.9
1981[b]	−84.7	47.2	−1.0	−38.5	20.0	−18.5
			(as a % of GDP)			
1970	−4.90	4.69	0.06	−0.14	0.75	0.60
1971	−6.10	5.41	0.04	−0.65	1.12	0.47
1972	−6.48	5.71	−0.17	−0.94	1.07	0.13
1973	−6.30	5.26	−0.30	−1.34	1.04	−0.30
1974	−5.26	4.31	−0.49	−1.44	0.47	−0.96
1975	−4.66	4.20	−0.40	−0.85	0.80	−0.06
1976	−7.25	3.87	−0.26	−3.64	1.40	−2.24
1977	−9.01	3.09	−0.29	−6.22	2.56	−3.66
1978	−6.06	3.64	−0.02	−2.43	1.69	−0.74
1979	−6.42	3.81	0.04	−2.56	0.69	−1.87
1980[a]	−8.86	4.02	0.10	−4.74	2.62	−2.12
1981[b]	−8.13	4.53	−0.10	−3.70	1.92	−1.78

a. Preliminary figures.
b. Forecast of the Institute for Economic Research (June 1981).
SOURCE: Oesterreichische Nationalbank.

one-third of the deterioration in the current account can be tied to increased energy costs and two-thirds to losses in competitive position. At the same time domestic demand was kept at high levels by economic policy.[15]

The main reason for the worsening in the current account balance was the inconsistency between the competitive position of the Austrian economy (in regard to its structure and its price competitiveness) and the growth rate desired for employment reasons. The structural side of the weakness in the competitive position is highlighted by the fact that Austria produces a relatively large share of intermediate products and too small a share of finished goods with high domestic value added in areas of rapidly growing demand. This is shown by the fact that markets for Austrian exports grew at a slower pace in the 1970s than markets of other industrial countries. Since 1977, however, some significant improvements have been achieved. At the same time there has been an improvement in price competitiveness since 1977, after years of significant deterioration. Still, it is to be noted that relative unit labor costs were by international comparison 17 percent higher in 1980 than in 1970.

Short-term influences, including increases in the cost of energy and the appreciation of the U.S. dollar as well as business cycle effects, have dominated in certain years the development of the current account. If one disregards these factors, there was a deterioration in the current account until 1977 and there has been improvement since then. Despite this tendency, a current account deficit of AS18.5 billion is expected in 1981.

An attempt was made through econometric analysis to estimate the short-term, medium-term, and long-term effects of economic policy on the development of the current account. In the short run, a 0.3 percent elasticity between the economic growth differential to the other OECD countries and the current account was estimated. Thus, an increase in the economic growth rate by one percentage point above that of the OECD countries would worsen the expanded current account balance as a percentage of GDP by about 0.3 percentage points (AS3 billion). For the medium term, it was estimated that the reduction by 1 percent in the unit cost of labor compared with the average of the competing countries would improve the current account balance by AS1 billion. For the long term, the emphasis must be on structural improvements. Austria's competitive position in the world will depend on the successful maintenance and development of high-grade technologies.[16]

Development of the Capital Account. Table 8 compares the development in the expanded current account with movements in the capital account and changes in the stock of official reserves. From 1976 to 1980 Austria accumulated a current account deficit totaling AS90 billion (AS18 billion annually, on average), equivalent to about 2 percent of GDP. This deficit was financed by net foreign borrowings amounting to AS93 billion, of which almost three-quarters (72 percent) was short-term borrowings by the banking sector. Long-term net capital inflows accounted for only 28 percent of the total.

191

TABLE 8

SELECTED BALANCE-OF-PAYMENTS ACCOUNTS, 1970–1980
(AS billion)

	Expanded Current Account	Reserve Creation and Valuation Changes	Capital Account		Capital Account[b]	Errors and Omissions	Official Reserves[c]	Short-Term Capital Transactions on Nonofficial Account
			Short-term	Long-term				
1970	2.3	0.8	−3.4	0.4	−3.0	2.8	−5.5	2.1
1971	2.0	−0.7	−0.8	−0.4	−1.2	4.7	−8.0	7.2
1972	0.6	0.5	−3.1	1.9	−1.7	5.1	−8.6	5.5
1973	−1.6	−1.3	6.7	−3.8	2.9	5.6	+5.1	1.6
1974	−5.9	−2.1	0.6	7.4	8.0	2.9	−3.9	4.5
1975	−0.4	2.2	−20.1	18.2	−1.9	5.2	−22.7	2.6
1976	−16.2	−3.6	21.2	−1.3	19.9	10.1	+6.9	14.3
1977	−28.9	−2.2	21.3	9.8	31.1	20.3	+9.2	12.1
1978	−6.2	9.3[a]	−23.5	20.4	−3.1	14.1	−26.4[a]	2.9
1979	−17.1	7.9[b]	16.3	−7.2	8.9	6.3	+9.1[b]	7.2
1980	−20.9	4.4	9.6	6.9	16.5	25.9	−26.1	35.7

a. Including an increase of AS11.4 billion in the valuation of gold.
b. Including an increase of AS9.8 billion in the valuation of gold.
c. Decrease (+); increase (−).
SOURCE: Austrian National Bank.

In addition to the AS93 billion inflow on capital account, there were AS16 billion of valuation changes (notably revaluation of the official gold stock at the end of 1978 and 1979) and reserve creation (allocation of International Monetary Fund [IMF] Special Drawing Rights), resulting in an AS19 billion rise in Austria's official reserves from 1976 to 1980. This increase in official reserves, therefore, was not earned (this would have required a current account surplus) but borrowed.[17]

Borrowing for Export Finance. Among long-term capital imports, foreign borrowing for budgetary expenditures as well as for the refinancing of Austrian exports and capital movements on account of foreign investments is particularly relevant. This section examines in detail export funding and the effect of foreign investments.

OKB funds its lending operations by borrowing in national and international capital and money markets. Total borrowings, mainly from international sources, have expanded rapidly, as illustrated by the following statistics. Total net borrowings have increased from AS4.4 billion in 1975 to AS13 billion in 1977 and to AS29 billion in 1980. The share of domestic net borrowings in these years has decreased, from 52 percent to 31 percent to 5 percent, respectively, whereas the share of foreign net borrowings has shown a corresponding increase, from 48 percent to 69 percent to 95 percent. At present, substantial portions of OKB's net borrowings for the Statutory Export Financing Scheme, therefore, are foreign borrowings.

OKB has increasingly relied on foreign capital markets for its funds since the mid-1970s, both because its requirements were too large to be accommodated in the relatively small domestic market and because the immediate inflow of foreign funds from its borrowings abroad was felt desirable because of balance-of-payments conditions. As of December 31, 1980, OKB had outstanding borrowings of AS91.9 billion (equivalent) for export financing activities, of which AS66.7 billion (73.3 percent) was in foreign currencies. The breakdown of the foreign currencies is: deutsche marks, 49.4 percent; Swiss francs, 43.6 percent; U.S. dollars, 5.2 percent; Dutch guilders, 1.5 percent; and all others, 0.3 percent.

Funds are borrowed as required to meet disbursement schedules, and OKB frequently arranges standby credits to be drawn down when needed. Most of OKB's foreign borrowings are through medium-term and long-term bonds (public issues and private placements) and loans ("Schuldscheindarlehen" and bank-to-bank credits). OKB also uses the Eurocurrency market for short-term funding. OKB generally matches average maturities on its assets and liabilities.

Most of OKB's foreign borrowings are guaranteed by the Republic for the payment of principal and interest. The Republic is also authorized to guarantee that OKB will not have to pay more principal and interest expressed in schillings than was contemplated at the time of the foreign borrowing on the basis of prevailing exchange rates. Although most of OKB's foreign borrowings carry such an exchange risk guarantee, OKB has tried to achieve a balanced performance in exchange rate gains and losses. Cumulative gains, in fact, exceeded losses by AS800 million as of December 31, 1980.

Thus an important feature of foreign borrowings to finance Austrian exports may be highlighted. In contrast to a situation where such borrowings are used purely for domestic expenditures, the capital imports for export financing schemes are being used to create receivables abroad. The economic effect of these receivables is a capital export in a capital account. Whereas OKB's foreign borrowings have a neutral effect on the capital account,[18] because of the positive interest differential between the interest charged and the interest incurred, there is a positive effect on the current account.

Direct Foreign Investment. Direct foreign investments in Austria are important links between the capital account and trade. Foreign capital investments began flowing into Austria after the ratification of the State Treaty in 1955. There are currently about 3,000 companies with 420,000 employees that are directly or indirectly under foreign ownership. The value of total foreign investment in Austria at the end of 1980 is estimated at AS56 billion.[19]

A hypothesis recently tested on Austria is that direct foreign investments are having a short-term positive effect on the balance of payments of the receiving country, but the long-term effects are negative. It was concluded that direct foreign investment had a positive effect on the Austrian balance of payments only until 1970 and 1971, and that the situation changed thereafter to Austria's disadvantage. One comes to this conclusion by comparing the net capital inflow from foreign direct investments to the corresponding net capital outflow. From 1967 to 1971 the net capital inflow of foreign direct investments in Austria was AS7.5 billion, whereas the net capital outflow was AS5.2 billion. In this period the balance (AS2.3 billion) was still positive, but from 1972 to 1979 the net capital outflow from Austria exceeded the net capital inflow by AS4.1 billion.[20] Foreign ownership of stocks and participation rights in Austrian industry is about 25 percent of the nominal value (especially high shares were found for insurance companies, 64 percent; trade and retail business, 50 percent;

industry, 31 percent). Most of the investments were made by Germany, Switzerland, and the United States.

Whereas foreign capital investments typically have a positive effect on the balance of payments in their first stage, it was found that subsidiaries of multinational enterprises were producing relatively import-intensive goods and were often bound, at least informally through worldwide company guidelines, to export restrictions.[21] Furthermore, it was found that in several cases a larger share of the production-palette could have been transferred to Austria. This includes finished-goods production with a high value-added component generally reserved for the mother company.

Earlier studies by Grünwald/Lacina[22] and Jurkowitsch[23] were also critical, but they acknowledged a number of positive effects, including the transfer of managerial know-how and structural improvements in output. The employment effect, due to Austria's low unemployment rate, was minimal but probably negative because foreign firms tended to choose locations where the labor situation was already tight. In regard to the structure of output, it was shown that foreign direct investments in Austria had led to efficient import substitution in the food, textile, and electric industries. (This conclusion was reached in 1971 and no longer applies to the textile industry.)

The balance-of-payments effect of foreign investments is seen in table 9, which shows the flow of funds on account of companies owned directly by foreigners. It can be seen that the positive balance-of-payments effect has gradually been eroded because of increases in the amount of yearly remittances of profits, licensing, and management fees, which were AS4.5 billion in 1980 compared with an inflow that year of AS2.9 billion. The cumulative effect since 1967 amounts to an estimated outflow of AS7 billion.

Some Interdependencies among Economic Policy Variables

Some of the interdependencies between trade and capital movements have already been indicated. They include the structural and regional composition of exports, the currency composition of Austrian trade, the organizational implications for efficiency in the management of export promotion, the competitive elements that need to be improved in order to check the current account situation, and the implications of foreign investment. It can also be shown that without export promotion the commodity structure of exports would not have shown as large a change in favor of high value-added goods and that there would be much less regional diversification.[24]

TABLE 9
BALANCE-OF-PAYMENTS EFFECT OF DIRECT FOREIGN INVESTMENTS, 1969–1980
(AS billion)

Year	Net Capital Inflow from Foreign Direct Investments	Dividends Remitted Abroad from Foreign Direct Investments	Net Effect	Remittances Abroad for Patents, Licenses, etc.	Total Effect
1969	1.3	1.0	0.3	0.3	0.0
1972	1.8	1.8	0.0	0.6	−0.6
1974	3.2	2.5	0.7	0.8	−0.1
1975	1.7	2.9	−1.2	1.0	−2.2
1977	1.9	3.0	−1.1	1.2	−2.3
1980[a]	2.9	3.0	−0.1	1.5	−1.6
Cumulative effect since 1967	27.6	29.5	−1.9	5.4[a]	−7.3

a. Estimated.
SOURCE: J. Peischer, "Multinationale Konzerne in Österreich: Auswirkungen auf die Zahlungsbilanz und Finanzierungsgewohnheiten," *Quartalshefte,* no. 1 (1981), Girozentrale, Vienna, and OKB estimates.

Nothing has been said so far in regard to the monetary effect of substantial capital imports. Instead of a detailed analysis it may be mentioned that the Austrian National Bank has attempted to neutralize the monetary effects of capital imports as part of its anti-inflationary policy. This has led to tight liquidity since the second half of 1979, but it is the Austrian National Bank that may be chiefly credited with stabilizing the Austrian schilling.

Tight liquidity and the recent decline in real income, which have led to an increasing gap between the volume of savings and credit demand, have resulted in the need to finance budget expenditures through borrowings from abroad. A large borrowing program was undertaken in 1980 and in the first half of 1981 by Austrian issuers. The problems arising in this connection stem from the attempt to neutralize the monetary effects of such capital imports that add to the monetary base if spent domestically. With its internationally integrated economy, Austria cannot afford to pursue an interest rate policy that disregards the international situation. When a policy attempt was made in 1980 to stimulate investment by slightly easing the money supply and to push domestic interest rates below those in Germany, there was an immediate and substantial outflow of short-term capital.

Given the tight domestic liquidity, the goal of improving the current account would seem to imply that foreign borrowings would have to be selective. A production structure with high technology and high value-added content would lead to important changes in the commodity and regional structure of exports that would require longer-than-average repayment terms. This feature will tend to increase the net amounts to be borrowed abroad to meet the disbursement demands that arise from exports in these areas of priority. There will have to be increased attention given to capital imports showing high yields in terms of positive current account effects over time.

In aggregate terms it may be noted that Austria, through its export financing scheme entailing a gross funding program abroad for Austrian capital exports on the order of some US$3 billion in 1980, has made a contribution in correcting the imbalance in the current account situation of surplus and deficit regions in the world. Of all the official export financing institutions, including those in large countries, Austria has made one of the most sizable recycling contributions in assuming the transformation of risks and maturities.

Notes

1. In 1950 Austria's per capita income amounted to US$350, compared with US$500 in the Federal Republic of Germany, US$750 in Great Britain and Belgium, and US$1,000 in Switzerland.

2. In real terms, exports almost doubled their share of GDP (16 percent in 1960, 31 percent in 1980).

3. See H. H. Haschek and E. Löschner, *20 Jahre Exportfinanzierung 1960–1980* (Vienna: Österreichische Kontrollbank AG, 1981).

4. Finished goods accounted for 63 percent of total exports in 1980 compared with 46 percent in 1960.

5. See H. Handler and J. Stankovsky, "How to Prolong Economic Stability?", *Austria Today,* vol. 7, no. 2 (1981).

6. Including "errors and omissions."

7. See J. Stankovsky, *Struktur und Tendenz des österreichischen Aussenhandels und der Leistungsbilanz in den achtziger Jahren* (Vienna: Österreichisches Institut für Wirtschaftsforschung, May 1980).

8. This organizational division from an administrative point of view is neither useful nor logical. Export financing requires two decisions: one on the risk involved and one on the availability of funds at given costs. These two decisions are interrelated. The credit period that is required influences the risk involved and the cost at which funds can be provided.

9. This provision would seem to imply that different capital markets with vastly different costs of capital (the differences at present being well over one thousand basis points) did not exist at all!

10. See S. A. B. Page, *The Choice of Currencies of Invoicing in Merchandise*

Trade (London: National Institute of Economic and Social Research, April 1981).

11. See H.-E. Scharrer, "Die Währungsstruktur im Welthandel," *Wirtschaftsdienst,* vol. 9 (1979).

12. The published data refer to the currencies in which exports and imports are paid in any particular year. The data refer to the total of exports and imports, including transit trade and transactions with gold as well as allocations to trade from the errors and omissions account.

13. Only part of this decline can be explained by the diminished trade between Austria and Switzerland following their conclusion of treaties with the EEC in 1973.

14. See E. Smeral and E. Walterskirchen, "Der Einfluss von Wirtschaftswachstum und Wettbewerbsfähigkeit auf die Leistungsbilanz," *Monatsberichte* des Österreichischen Institut für Wirtschaftforschung, no. 7 (1981).

15. Ibid.

16. Ibid.

17. Austrian National Bank, *Annual Report 1980* (Vienna, 1980), p. 30.

18. In spite of this neutral effect economically, the capital account in the past has reflected only tied loans and the financing of assignment agreements as capital exports. Sales on extended terms that were undertaken on a supplier credit basis did not run through the capital account but were shown in the trade account as well as in errors and omissions.

19. By comparison, the value of Austrian investments abroad is estimated at AS13.5 billion.

20. See J. Peischer, "Multinationale Konzerne in Österreich: Auswirkungen auf die Zahlungsbilanz und Finanzierungsgewohnheiten," *Quartalshefte,* no. 1 (1981), Girozentrale, Vienna.

21. Ibid.

22. O. Grünwald and F. Lacina, *Auslandskapital in der Österreichischen Wirtschaft* (Vienna: Arbeiterkammer, 1970).

23. See F. Jurkowitsch, *Die deutschen Direktinvestitionen in der österreichischen Industrie* (Dissertation an der Hochschule für Welthandel, Vienna, 1971).

24. See E. Löschner, "Volkswirtschaftliche und internationale Bedeutung der Exportfinanzierung," *Österreichisches Bank-Archiv,* vol. 29, no. 1 (1981).

Commentary

William H. Branson

I found the papers by Karl Vak and by Helmut Haschek to be two interesting and fairly complete pieces that lay out the facts on Austria's trade and competitiveness. The discussions in the papers range from topics as broad as the Austrian social contract on income distribution to the details of trade finance. Having selected a few points to focus on, I have four items on my list. One is export credits; one is the problems raised by the current account deficit; a third is some interactions between the durability of the social contract and the current account problem; and the fourth, if I get to it at the end, is a bit of discussion of the role of Austria in the changing structure of world trade.

First, let me discuss export credits. This was mentioned in the paper by Vak, and there is a substantial section in Haschek's paper that describes export finance schemes and argues that these schemes are nondistorting and self-financing. Also, there is a discussion of the attempt by the Organization for Economic Cooperation and Development (OECD) to put together a consensus scheme limiting competition by export financing. I think it is fair to say that both papers approve of export credit subsidies wholeheartedly.

The first thing I would like to take issue with is the view that export credits and guarantees are not subsidies, which is argued in Haschek's paper. The argument that they are not subsidies because the scheme is self-financing is a familiar one here in the United States. The Export-Import (Ex-Im) Bank uses it every time it goes to the Congress to obtain additional appropriations. I think that the argument is one we should banish from consideration. Basically, it seems clear to me that if the rate at which you are lending is lower than the market rate, then this is lost return to the savers who are supplying the funds ultimately. So to that extent, the transfer is from savers to borrowers, even if the intermediary is making a nice profit, and the amount of this transfer obviously depends on the spread. In the Haschek paper, we see export lending rates in August 1981 around 8.6 to 9 percent. In the Seidel paper, I noticed equivalent market rates around 12 to 13 percent in the same period. So a straightforward calculation says that the subsidy that is going from the ultimate savers to these export borrowers is approximately 4 percent.

Before coming back to a serious question about export subsidies, let me just mention my agreement with Haschek on the OECD consensus. The point that he makes is clear; an agreement about export financing that has uniform interest rates for all countries makes no sense. In a situation in which exchange rates are moving and are expected to move, you certainly want to take account of the fact that interest rate differences will roughly equal the rate of appreciation between the two currencies that you are comparing. Those obviously cannot be predicted. They obviously cannot be written into an agreement, but they cannot be ignored. So one would expect that it would be more productive to think in terms of recognizing that these are subsidies and to talk about maximum subsidy rates below market rates in the various centers.

Let me come back for a moment to the rationale for export subsidies. This is a question that is not addressed in the Haschek paper. This is certainly not a criticism of that paper. As the author may put it, since he is the administrator, it is not for him to reason why, it is just for him to make sure the system works. I suppose, however, that it is the function of an academic discussant to take a different and broader view. Why do we want to subsidize exports? One reason is that we simply like to export. That does not make sense. Exports are after all the output of the domestic economy that we refrain from consuming. So it is output that we are giving to other people. Then what is the purpose of exporting? Clearly it is to earn imports. Exports are something that we reluctantly give up in order to obtain the foreign exchange to buy the imports that we want to consume or invest. It is only in a world of international machismo that exports are a good thing because if we are out-competing the other guys on exports, somehow we are better than they are.

Second, do we subsidize exports to improve the current account balance? The answer is probably no. If the scheme is successful in stimulating exports, it will eventually lead to an appreciation of the currency which will reestablish current account balance. In any event, the current account balance is output minus absorption, and one would have to see how the export credits are going to influence those variables to have a convincing story about influencing the current account balance.

The third argument is that everybody else does it, so we have to do it to compete. Well, if everybody else is subsidizing exports at an average rate of 10 percent, as an example, then roughly a 10 percent change in your own exchange rate would give you the same degree of across-the-board price competitiveness that meeting them with 10 percent export subsidies would. So there is no argument in saying that because everyone else is foolish enough to subsidize their sales to us, we should be foolish enough to subsidize our sales to them. They are the ones that are following a policy of, in a sense, trying to give something away.

The result is that export credit subsidies basically subsidize the particular firms that receive them, and you need an argument about why those are the firms that need subsidizing. The standard answer in terms of the Export-Import Bank discussion in the United States is, why do you think that the firms that do exporting are at a disadvantage in credit markets relative to the other firms in the economy? The borrowers at the Ex-Im Bank are very big companies who obviously are not at a disadvantage in capital markets, so the question always comes down to, why do you want to subsidize International Harvester, and so on, who are doing the exporting? I will leave that as the question—where is the argument for export subsidies?

Let me take up the question of the current account balance. In Haschek's table 7, there are some nice data on Austria's current account balance that also appear in Hans Seidel's overview paper. We see in those data that the current account deficit has been at least 2½ percent of the gross domestic product (GDP) since 1976. If we scaled that to U.S. numbers, that would be a deficit of something like $75 billion in the current account, which to my mind is a very large number. There is an argument in the paper about why the errors-and-omissions item should be included in the current account to make an adjusted current balance, as the overview paper put it, or an expanded current account, as Haschek's paper puts it. Haschek says that there have been attempts to determine where the errors-and-omissions terms should go, but these have failed because of data problems, and so on. His guess is that about two-thirds of them are current account transactions that are missed. It is not clear to me why he adds all errors and omissions, then, to the current account to arrive at the expanded balance, but I gather that this is standard procedure as the same numbers appear in the overview paper.

I am skeptical about this for three reasons. I am not sure they are independent. One reason is that I have done some econometrics on errors and omissions from time to time and they generally look like capital flows. If you relate the errors-and-omissions term to changes in interest differentials and similar variables, it looks like capital movements. Maybe it is different in Austria; I do not know about that. Second, it is hard to reconcile this adjustment with the national income accounts. I am not sure whether this is done, and I just leave it as a question. When you try to reintegrate the adjusted current balance with the national income accounts, does it come out in adjusted private saving, or adjusted private investment, or the adjusted government deficit? The national income accounts have to add up; so if we are going to adjust the current balance here, we have to adjust some other balance in the national income accounts. Otherwise the whole accounting system becomes inconsistent and we lose the possibility of using the national income accounts to understand balance-of-payments problems. So there is a conceptual problem with doing an adjustment on one term and leaving all the rest alone. I guess I am just skeptical about the notion of the expanded current account balance. It seems to me that to a certain extent it is minimizing the problem of the current account deficit.

In terms of policy about the current account deficit, there seem to be three choices. One is devaluation. A second is structural policy to improve competitiveness. A third is reducing absorption. Both of the papers here focus on structural policy. They do not say anything about the output-absorption identity aspect of the current account deficit, and there is not much talk about exchange rates as a tool in that direction. It seems to me pretty clear from the evidence in the other papers that devaluation could help. There is evidence in Helmut Frisch's paper that Austria is not so open that internal price reactions quickly undo the effects of exchange rate change. In fact, he shows something like a 15 or 16 percent real devaluation since 1977; his index goes from 116 to around 100. In terms of the current jargon in this area of the exchange rate literature, it seems possible to change the real exchange rate by changing the nominal exchange rate in Austria. In fact, both of them have been changing, so one cannot argue that in the past the exchange rate has not been changed.

I have my doubts about structural policy. Obviously, it is a good thing to be efficient, but it is a rare case where someone has been able to produce evidence that improving efficiency will change output by 3 percent or reduce absorption by 3 percent in order to eliminate a current account balance. So it is not clear to me, until more evidence is in, that structural policies—whatever their other virtues are—are going to have much effect on the current account problem. That leaves me thinking that it is probably necessary to operate directly on absorption, and that says increase taxes. The problem is that Austria seems to have an unsustainably high excess of absorption over output. There is a discussion in Frisch's paper of fiscal policy effects on demand. This is also supported by Felix Butschek, who noticed that fiscal policy actions do have an effect on aggregate demand. This seems to be established, and therefore the question is raised: Why not increase taxes in order to reduce absorption and get the economy back into balance? This is a hard prescription to follow, so it is no doubt tempting to fall back on discussion of structural policies as a way to deal with the problem.

Let me now turn to the question of the social contract. I thought the discussion in Vak's paper was really quite interesting. One nice point is that the organization of the social contract seems to recognize the open-economy aspect of the problem, which is that there are competitive price pressures from abroad. I have spent some time in Sweden, and I noticed that they forget this occasionally and get into trouble. They get everything right except that a problem arises where unit labor costs in the export sector are rising rapidly. There are questions that I have that are not dealt with in Vak's paper. I would like to see how the income shares are implicitly determined: What is the mechanism inside the system that determines who gets 75 percent of income and who gets 25 percent? How did that mechanism swallow the oil price increase? There was substantial variation across countries about how they dealt with that. Does attributing the stability of Austria to this mechanism imply that it is necessary to aggregate business and labor into single units so that they can deal effectively with each other as conscious economic agents in setting wages and prices? The argument seems to drift in the direction of saying the way to deal with wage and price decisions is to monopolize fully the economy. Then you can identify who the decision makers are, talk with them, and get agreement. I am not sure that this way of going about dealing with inflationary pressures is exportable.

I have a final question for people who think about the social contract, which is linked to the current account balance. Is it possible that the viability of that social contract depends on the current account deficit? It seems to me that it might be much easier to maintain social relations in a situation where the country is consuming 3 percent more than it is producing than if it were constrained only to consume what it produces. So I am wondering what happens to the social contract when the time comes that the current account balance has to be reduced to zero. Where is that 3 percent of gross national product that you can no longer consume going to come from in terms of real incomes? I would be concerned about what happens when the social contract collides with external balance, rather than feeling easy about the durability of the social contract. I echo the uneasiness that Hella Junz expressed in that it is a little unnerving to see a situation in which there is a large current account deficit that people do not seem to be worrying about, and it is in a situation in which perhaps 40 percent of exports are being subsidized. It seems to me that this is a situation that could be very dangerous.

Jan Tumlir

Tom Sowell was quoted in the *Washington Post* as stating categorically that problems have no solutions. I read it at breakfast and did not quite know what he meant, but then I came here and listened and I realize now that he must have been talking from a deep knowledge of the Austrian economy. I mean, you do not solve problems, you live with them; and from its economic performance, I would say that Austria has been living it up with them.

What strikes me most in this discussion is the sheer number of economic policies being conducted in Austria. There are not merely the three monetary policies that Jacob Dreyer wondered about earlier. We have now heard about the famous incomes policy, closely integrated with a labor market policy; besides an agricultural policy, there is also an industrial policy, further subdivided into technology policy, structural improvement policy, an import and an export policy, the latter including an export-finance policy—I could go on and on. This enumeration of policy is to explain the admirable performance of the Austrian economy. Yet when our Austrian visitors try to explain to us how each of these policies actually works in practice, and how all of them together produced the result we find so enviable, there are difficulties. We cannot quite see it. I at least have a feeling of being lost in a magical policy forest.

Isn't there a simpler explanation? Aren't we putting the cart before the horse? Theirs is an economy that performs outstandingly. Wouldn't a political government be naturally tempted to claim credit for this performance—to latch on to a good thing going—and to proffer all these policies in evidence of how economic growth has been generated by its own enlightened effort? By this I do not mean to say that economic policy is irrelevant, only that it takes very little policy to make a free enterprise economy perform well.

Austrian monetary policy, if one judges by price statistics, must have been quite tight, cautious, and conservative—which is not surprising in an economy bordering on and closely involved with West Germany and Switzerland. The public budgets of the past quarter century were on the whole—though not perhaps in the past few years—fairly closely balanced. What more is needed in the way of explanation? Austria is a small, highly open economy. So what if its industrialists talk to each other and with the government? They still have to compete. It is, in other words, quite plausible to think that all the other policies we have been discussing, especially the microeconomic ones aimed at "industrial structure," were either make-believe and harmless—*Augenwischerei,* as they say in that clever capital—or that, to the extent that they were pursued in earnest, they detracted from rather than contributed to the good performance of the economy.

Yesterday's discussion culminated in the question whether all these various microeconomic policies can be integrated into an effective effort to restructure the economy. This is the talk of the place where I work, and I should be inured to it, but the sublime absurdity of this transitive phrase never fails to excite me. There is a national economy, an object, on which some purposeful agent will perform this act of restructuring. Where I come from, everybody talks as if restructuring national economies were the prime function of governments. Erich Spitäller gave me an idea yesterday when he mentioned the possibility of a constitutional conflict. Let us look at industrial policies from that angle. Whatever it is in detail, industrial policy has to do with industrial structure: relative sizes of different industries and perhaps their spatial distribution within national frontiers. From a constitutional viewpoint, this is a surreptitious policy. It is a purely executive or administration policy that the legislature cannot control. To control the policy, the legislature would have to have an agreed, at least a majority, conception of an optimal industrial structure for the nation—something an assembly of individuals representing different regions of the country and different interest groups in it is, so to speak, constitutionally unable to agree upon. To put it still more bluntly, there cannot be an industrial policy, no matter what governments may pretend.

Peter Katzenstein suggested another idea as he was comparing Austria with other countries, the large and the small ones. One country was conspicuously missing in his comparisons—namely, Italy, an economy in its own way almost as mysterious as that of Austria. So it seemed to me that this comparison could be particularly enlightening. The most striking similarity is in the industrial structures of the two. Both Italian and Austrian industries are predominantly composed of relatively small or medium-sized firms that are highly efficient, highly inventive, internationally competitive in the sense of securing for themselves profitable niches in the interstices of the international market. They operate with technologies that are neither highly science intensive nor standard and can only be described as highly intelligent technologies. The productivity of their labor is very high, even in international comparison. Superimposed on this large sector of efficient small and medium-scale firms, there exists, certainly in Italy and I suspect also in Austria, a thick, perhaps thickening, layer of large-scale, largely publicly owned enterprises operating in the red—firms that the governments can only subsidize but not control. It seems to me that social welfare in Austria would be even higher than it is today if in the past decades the country had contented itself with collecting royalties on the steel-making process it once invested, instead of trying to be a large-scale steel producer itself. Similarly the automotive facility, for which the government so cleverly secured export orders from foreign firms exporting automobiles to Austria, looks to me like becoming something of a drag on the country's welfare in the years to come, when the whole Western automobile industry will be going through the wringer. A case of bad timing, you may say, but to my mind it is the logical case. When have governments shown a *good* sense of timing?

It takes no prophetic gift to foresee considerable difficulties for Austria, past performance notwithstanding, simply because all Western Europe already has very serious difficulties that I do not see ending in this decade. These difficulties are the result of two contradictory tendencies in the world economy. In the Western world, sometime in the mid-1960s, governments have come to believe that it is their policies that produce economic growth at 4–5 percent year after year; and on this assumption they started making political promises. Unsurprisingly, the best political payoff was found to attach to promises to alleviate or delay the pain of industrial adjustment. It seemed at the time that at the attained level of welfare, we could well afford to trade some additional efficiency for the comfort of slower adjustment. The world, however, does not work that way. There are too many countries in it whose people can ill afford to sacrifice additional efficiency. This is the second tendency of the world economy, contradicting the assumptions on which our corner of it has been operating. There is a panic today in the West about the competitive force of Japan. I am trying to tell all these panicky people that Japan is not *the* problem but only the pioneer of the second wave of industrialization. Nothing, not even time, is gained by obtaining promises from Japan's industries that they will export less to us. There is a line of equally if not more competitive economies entering the world market in Japan's wake. In particular markets, even Japanese industries are already having problems.

The result of this clash of two tendencies is that the economies of different regions now differ greatly as to their capacity for adjustment. The adjustment capacity of the United States as well as of the Western European economies was severely impaired in the past fifteen years or so, but it seems that in the United States the impairment occurred by means that will be politically more easy to correct than those by which Western European governments crippled the economies of their peoples. In this situation Austria, and perhaps Italy also, may be privileged by the relatively large size of their efficient small and medium-scale industrial sector. At any rate, it is their main asset, which a forward-looking economic policy would concentrate on cultivating. What this sector needs most is stable money and stable, predictable policies—that is, governments operating by means of general laws instead of discretionary interventions.

Thus I would conclude on the constitutional theme raised by Spitäller. The basic function of democracy is to make change possible without a revolution; and that requires that democratic governments operate by means of general rules, indeed largely procedural rules, with only a minimum of substantive content. Substantive policies—as distinct from simple administration—invariably require discretionary power, which has an inherent tendency to expand. When, by virtue of these expanding powers, democratic governments get so involved in the private economy that they have become the necessary props of existing social and industrial structures, well, then they are a part of, identified with, the status quo. Then, however, their essential function— making change possible without upheaval—has become undischargeable.

Hella B. Junz

We have been told that almost everything in Austria is not quite what it seems to be. This remark was made in connection with the hard currency policy, in connection with industrial policy, and in some other ways as well. In addition, it seems to me, unfortunately, that the beautiful image of Austria as a small open trading nation, committed to international competitive cooperative behavior, is somewhat marred. I do not mean to be the wicked witch of the West who turns this beautiful prince into a frog, and can only hope that as this discussion proceeds, our Austrian colleagues will turn what looks suspiciously much like a frog, back into a prince.

As a recently recycled bureaucrat, I remember only too well the type of discussion we had today. We never find a country arguing that it is more competitive than anybody else. We never find a country arguing that it has more research and development than anybody else. When we add up the prospective export requirements that are expected to balance the economies of individual countries, we always find that total expected exports exceed total expected imports by large margins. It seems to me that we have gone through a similar exercise today, particularly with regard to our discussion of competitiveness.

The competitiveness question has been addressed almost entirely in terms of the statistical measurement of relative unit labor costs. These days, however, it is almost impossible to discern the basic facts and trends by measuring changes in some simple aggregate indicator. This is particularly true for countries in which there has been a fair amount of structural change. We have been told that the Austrian export bundle has moved considerably toward higher technology products. In such a case, one would think that labor inputs into exports must now also be considerably different, qualitatively and quantitatively, as compared with what they were before. Thus, even if one could measure unit labor costs in export firms separately from unit labor costs in the economy as a whole, one would find a considerable deterioration in Austrian relative unit labor costs. This apparent deterioration, however, stems from a change in industrial structure away from production requiring lower-skilled labor inputs to one needing higher skills. The adaptation of the economy to an environment requiring greater technological skills is a sign of improving competitiveness, though the unit labor cost measurement appears to be signaling the opposite.

Yesterday somebody defined what an entrepreneur is. That definition applies as well to what we mean by competitiveness. It is the ability to respond with considerable flexibility to the opportunities that are being created in the market. In that respect, I began to worry after what I heard today. After the first oil price shock, we began to have exercises within the Organization for Economic Cooperation and Development that concerned themselves with something called positive adjustment. In these discussions it became quite apparent that governments certainly are no better at picking the winners in economic development than is the private sector, and in most cases they actually did worse. In addition, it became clear that in our world, adjustment does not necessarily have to be totally export oriented. I worry when I read that official export finance of one sort or another applies to 40 to 45 percent of total Austrian exports. Whether it is structured as an interest rate subsidy or to deal with foreign exchange risk, it artificially cheapens exports. In addition, Austria has numerous investment incentives favoring export-oriented endeavors. These also involve competition to entice foreign investment into the country.

Yesterday we were told of the efforts to get General Motors to locate a plant in Austria, of the government telling other automobile makers that if they did not buy their replacement parts in Austria, the market would be closed to them—all this in conjunction with the pursuit of a "hard currency policy" in Austria. I have no idea, having heard of all the export-promoting policies, what the actual exchange rate is at which Austrian exports move in international trade. The statistical exercises which use so-called effective exchange rates, or real effective exchange rates, do not capture these subsidy elements. If one worries about competitiveness indicators in a basic sense, meaning the flexibility with which an economy responds to various stimuli and the efficiency with which it does so, then the government involvement we have heard about here tends to be totally counterproductive to the stated goals. Having said all this, I hope that I may have misunderstood some of the things that have been presented and that someone can turn this not-too-pretty frog back into a fair prince.

208

Discussion

The nature and activities of the social partnership drew a variety of questions and comments. Erich Spitäller, Sven Arndt, and Thomas Willett were interested in the details of decision making in the Prices and Wages Subcommissions. What were the objectives regarding relative prices and wages? What were the criteria? How did external conditions affect decisions? Did these decisions reduce divergent movements in relative goods and factor prices and thereby possibly inhibit desirable reallocations of resources? Did they create tendencies to asymmetric responses of money wages to changes in exchange rates? How in specific terms did the hard currency policy affect the conduct of incomes policy?

Johann Farnleitner responded by pointing out that the social partnership was a historical accident, that the fact of cooperation preceded the formulation of a concept or philosophy. In his words: "The politicians after 1945 decided to cooperate, to solve things by consensus. But they did not try to convince each other that one had the only reasonable concept of how to run the economy or how to conduct the politics. And so we stagger from one solution to another without an overall concept, except for the concept of consensus." Such an evolution may have been facilitated, according to Farnleitner, by a relatively underdeveloped civil service in the area of economic management.

Today the social partnership provides an important means of shielding ministers because they do not make decisions without the approval of the social partners. Oskar Grünwald and Erich Schmidt added that the social partnership performs the important role of integrating the labor movement into the Austrian state, making it part of the system and giving it substantial influence in its management.

In his summary Schmidt admitted that some mistakes have been made, especially in the wage policies of 1975. Heinz Kienzl agreed that the reaction had been one of panic. As for relative prices and resource allocation, Schmidt stated that the social partners have no control over capital investment and none over the introduction of new products and their prices. Only price revisions come under the purview of the Prices Subcommission.

Farnleitner illustrated the flexibility of the system by its response to the inflation of the mid-1970s. Instead of indexing money wages, contracts that had been running for an average of eighteen months were shortened to reduce the impact of changing inflation rates on real wages. When prices subsequently became more stable, efforts were made to lengthen contract periods. Similarly, when an appreciation of the schilling reduces import prices, representatives of the Federation of Trade Unions or the Chambers of Labor will invite firms to come before the Prices Subcommission to explain why the savings were not passed on.

In elaborating the management perspective on the social partnership, Farnleitner noted that Austrian entrepreneurs have been concerned about the growing influence of labor organizations. Cooperation with labor was initially accepted, he observed, as necessary for postwar reconstruction, but it was expected that in the long run the market would determine prices and the social partners would oversee collective bargaining for wages. Eventually, however, management and the Federal Economic Chamber became accustomed to price intervention.

Among the reasons for this acceptance, Farnleitner suggested the following: (1) Consent of the subcommission to price increases saved entrepreneurs from having to justify them to the public. (2) It quickly became apparent that this kind of control was feasible only in areas of mass production and that other prices, especially those in the service sector, would remain beyond the control of the social partners. Such prices include those in the very important tourism industry, as well as those of new products. (3) In the public sector, approval by the commission obviates the need to negotiate prices with individual agencies and institutions. (4) In practice the climate of control has been realistic and relatively free of politics. (5) For export-oriented Austrian industry, the record of social peace and uninterrupted production has developed into an important comparative advantage, making Austrian producers very reliable suppliers. (6) Entrepreneurs hoped that the rising influence of labor in the social partnership would relieve pressures for more codetermination; although these hopes were not realized, such pressures were reduced for a time. (7) Managements have found intervention by the presidents of the Federal Economic Chamber and the Federation of Trade Unions a useful means of settling disputes within an enterprise without strike action.

This is not to say that entrepreneurs are unconcerned about the thrust of developments. They see strong disadvantages in the emphasis of pricing policy on cost factors, for enterprises are usually not permitted to exploit favorable market situations simply to increase profits. Farnleitner felt that this constraint is especially binding during economic booms and may be one of the reasons for the insufficient equity capital of Austrian industry. Managers also worry about what they see as a radical change in the political structure of Austrian society, in which the political parties concentrate their efforts increasingly on the fate of wage and salary earners. Consequently, they see the social partnership as a means of influencing political developments.

There have been complaints from time to time that the commission's prices were too low, but the evidence suggests that actual prices tend to lie below those it recommends. Farnleitner attributed this mainly to the competition from import prices. He saw Austria's very liberal import policy as an important counterweight to the cartel-like effects of the Joint Commission.

The Labor Market

The discussion of Felix Butschek's paper began with the demographic aspects of employment in Austria. Barry Bosworth, Jacob Dreyer, Gottfried Haberler, and Peter Katzenstein noted the key role of foreign workers as a cyclical buffer: a substantial exodus of foreign workers relieves employment pressures. Erich Spitäller suggested that the tendency of nationalized firms to hoard labor helps keep unemployment figures low and that therefore demand pressures in the labor market are really much greater than those actually observed. This might explain the relatively high sensitivity of wages to unemployment in Helmut Frisch's model, which had also been noted by Bosworth. In response, Frisch explained that Austria's impressive employment performance was related to (1) general stabilization policy, (2) reduction in the number of guest workers, and (3) the absorption of large parts of the labor force in the sheltered sector.

Haberler noted the likely contribution of the Austrian minimum wage policy to the remarkably low youth unemployment. Butschek agreed, pointing out that paying young workers less in recognition of their initially lower skills makes them very attractive apprentices and provides them with valuable training. He noted further that overall unemployment was probably lower in Austria because of the relatively low unemployment benefits.

Jacques Artus disagreed with Butschek's concern about the future of employment in Austria. He argued that since Austria did not need unemployment to reduce inflation, an increase in the labor force should lead to increases in real output that will keep the labor force employed. He did not, for analogous reasons, agree with Butschek's proposed solutions, such as reduced working hours and early retirement. Such policies may do little to solve the problem because they may reduce output and hence require cuts in real income; if they lead to growth in domestic demand in relation to output, they will worsen the current account deficit.

International Competitiveness

International competitiveness received considerable attention in this session. The notion of competitiveness was viewed from two alternative perspectives. In positive terms it referred to a country's ability to produce goods demanded on world and home markets with least-cost factor inputs. Here Austria's problems were seen to be similar in many ways to those experienced elsewhere in the industrialized West. Austria's comparative advantage was eroding for many standardized commodities. Inevitably the long-run solution would require reallocation of resources to areas of production and to services requiring relatively large inputs of skilled labor and high-quality capital.

Karl Vak and others noted that the small and medium-sized firms so characteristic of Austria offer special opportunities in this adjustment process because they tend to be flexible and have displayed substantial adaptability in the past. Vak could also see a potential difficulty in what he perceived as an inadequate supply of skilled young managers to run these small and numerous firms.

Several participants wanted to know whether Austria's institutions, including the social partnership, were an asset or a liability in the restructuring process. In a related discussion dealing with the measurement of competitiveness, Hella Junz observed that definitions of competitiveness that compare unit labor costs must take care not to overlook the effects over time of changes in the structure of exports and imports; she agreed on the need for more emphasis on the quality of entrepreneurship in evaluating a country's competitive position.

On the negative side of international competition, several participants criticized the widespread governmental efforts to stimulate exports by means of subsidies, export credit schemes, direct state aid, and even state-run production for export. Such schemes frequently encourage inefficient allocation of resources, which takes on the character of beggar-thy-neighbor policies. Moreover, when such behavior is widespread, it is essentially offsetting, counterproductive, and wasteful. In this context, Junz expressed her concern over what she saw as Austria's highly aggressive competitive schemes involving various credit, subsidy, and incentive programs. Katzenstein observed that Austria is one of the most sheltered and protectionist of the rich small countries. Many participants seconded these concerns, but also agreed with Frisch, who, having noted a certain European myth or ideology surrounding export surpluses, cautioned that once such measures were in place everywhere, a single country could eliminate its support efforts only at its peril. Austria, he asserted, could ill afford to stop if West Germany, Sweden, and others did not.

Hans Seidel raised a related issue when he observed that significant parts of commercial credit are subsidized in Austria. Although this does not stay the debate on the value of such aid, it suggests to him that export credits are not quite a special method designed to shift resources into export production.

The comments on Grünwald's paper focused on the incentives for structural change and on the relative positions of large and small enterprises in this process. Several participants raised questions about the criteria and standards to be used in the allocation of investment support. Would all firms have claims, or only firms in designated areas? What would be the approach to labor-saving capital formation? By what means would the authorities pick the "winners"?

In partial explanation, Frisch pointed out that Austria does need to acquire new technologies to counteract the competition associated with the spread of existing technologies to countries with low-cost labor. He felt that Austrian entrepreneurs were well positioned, that they were alert to new opportunities, and that they would import new technologies and put them to productive use in the industrial sector.

In his response, Grünwald listed several criteria pertaining to investment incentives. These were value added in the export sector, regional considerations, and structural improvement. Certain border regions would be given special credits, and the precise determination of structural improvement would be up to the various agencies involved. He noted that the General Motors plant was a special case involving the government and the municipality of Vienna.

The relative profitabilities of firms of various sizes are difficult to determine. Often an industry consists of only one company—one oil refinery, one vehicle producer, one tire company. Only about 10 percent of Austrian industry is listed on the stock exchange; the rest does not provide the kind of information that would permit an answer to the question. Grünwald pointed out, however, that internal calculations showed the nationalized sector to have been profitable in every year from 1970 through 1979; only the onset of the steel crisis brought losses in 1980 and 1981.

In his closing remarks, Helmut Haschek agreed that subsidies are undesirable, but maintained that the Austrian export credit scheme he had described was not a subsidy. It was profitable and did not require resource transfers among sectors; it was rather a scheme for risk diversification and for the exploitation of economies of scale in the financial market, designed to offset the disadvantages imposed on Austrian firms by their relatively small size.

The Austrian current account deficit was also closely scrutinized. Spitäller suggested that the composition of absorption might need to be shifted toward investment and away from private and public consumption. Then a current account deficit might more readily generate capital inflows and become sustainable. He inquired whether the financial system and the social partnership were capable of generating the right kinds of investment finance.

Seidel and Kienzl maintained that depreciation provides little more than short-term improvements in trade and payments in a country in which labor does not suffer from money and exchange rate illusion. They thus rejected exchange rate adjustments as instruments for managing the current account deficit. Seidel did, however, agree that something needed to be done and that the problem could no longer be safely put off to the future.

Appendix

The Organization of the Austrian Credit Economy

Introduction

In the Austrian credit system it is the universal banking principle that prevails. Most Austrian credit institutions are authorized to carry out all types of banking—accepting deposits, conducting transactions in foreign exchange, dealing in credits. This system is encouraged by a very liberal credit law that permits credit institutions to compete in almost all fields of business.

There are of course certain historically or regionally determined leaders in different types of business activity. The *Aktienbanken* (joint-stock commercial banks) predominate in both industrial finance and export trade; the *Raiffeisenkassen* (rural mortgage associations set up along lines proposed by Raiffeisen) continue to be especially significant in the rural sector; and the *Volksbanken* (people's banks) and *Sparkassen* (savings banks) are leaders in business finance and, in conjunction with the Raiffeisenkassen, in accepting savings deposits.

The federal Ministry of Finance is responsible for supervising the banks, a task in which it is supported by the Austrian National Bank. The national bank makes central-bank funds available to the credit system when necessary by purchasing foreign currency, discounting bills or hypothecating securities, and buying securities on the open market. The bank is also empowered by the Bank Law to control the liquidity of credit institutions by prescribing the percentage of minimum reserves that they must maintain.

Legislative Foundations

The Law of Credit. The legal basis for business activities conducted by the credit institutions is the Law of Credit of 1979,[1] which states that only institutions chartered by the Ministry of Finance have a right to receive remunerations or commissions, especially interest payments,

This appendix was provided by the Austrian National Bank.

215

from the conduct of banking activities. Credit institutions must also ensure reliability by maintaining resources proportionate to the assets entrusted to them. Such resources are deemed sufficient when they equal 4 percent of the obligations minus liquid assets of the first degree. To ensure constant liquidity the institutions must maintain liquid assets of the first and second degree, which are receivables that are considered especially secure and liquid. The minimum amounts of liquid assets of the first and second degree that must be maintained are established by decree of the Ministry of Finance in consultation with the national bank within the overall framework of 35 percent of liabilities in schillings. Credit institutions connected with a central bank must maintain a liquidity reserve in that bank equal to 10 percent of their savings deposits and 20 percent of their miscellaneous schilling deposits, but no more than 14 percent of their total schilling deposits.[2] Liquidity reserves are considered liquid assets of the first degree.

A credit institution's long-term investments in land and buildings and in participations, except for participations in central banks, must not exceed 100 percent of its resources. No individual debtor may be granted credits exceeding a certain percentage of liabilities, usually ranging from 5 percent to 7.5 percent and established by decree of the Ministry of Finance. (At present it is 7.5 percent.) Every lender must report the name and address of any debtor to which it extends credit of more than AS5 million or collateral of more than AS8 million to a documentation center, located at 1870 Kreditschutzverband (Credit Protection Association). Following a transition period of ten years subsequent to the effective date of the Law of Credit this center will be transferred to the national bank.

Although the Law of Credit permits credit institutions freedom of action regarding both interest on deposits and interest earned, it states that the associations of credit institutions *may* negotiate agreements on creditor interest rates. They are thereby legally entitled to avoid price competition for the deposits of noncredit institutions by mutually establishing rates of interest. The only such agreement in existence at the present time, however, is one (the Basic Interest Agreement) that sets a rate of interest (now 5 percent annually) for savings deposits with statutory rollover periods—the "little man's" savings—which can be withdrawn practically immediately. No agreements about other types of deposit have been made up to the present time.

The Law of Credit also enables the Minister of Finance to restrict by decree the expansion of credit by credit institutions under certain conditions. Up to now this provision has not had to be used, because the central bank's own powers to control liquidity have always proved completely adequate. What is known as the *limes* (Latin for "national borders") concept, one of assets-side credit control, should be mentioned in particular in this context. It means that the national bank will make central bank money in the form of discounts on commercial paper or hypothecated securities available only to those credit institutions that comply with its requirement of reporting maximum permissible credit expansion. Although there are at present no restrictions on *total* credit expansion, the central bank has, according to its policy of maintaining a balance of resources, informed the credit institutions that they may expect rediscounting assistance only when they do not exceed the prescribed level for credits to persons not self-employed and to persons of independent means (consumer *limes*). The intention of the monetary authorities in employing these measures is to restrict the credit financing of consumer goods, especially those that encumber imports. These "borders" for credit extensions have not, however, been fully used.

What must be especially emphasized is the protection extended to the confidentiality of banking transactions in Austria. Far more liberal in this respect than the law of other nations, including Switzerland, the Law of Credit even provides criminal sanctions against the betrayal of banking secrets.

The Minister of Finance is responsible for overseeing both the domestic credit institutions and the agencies of foreign institutions. Where legislation does not provide otherwise, the ministry must appoint a government commissioner and his representatives to exercise oversight over institutions with balance sheets exceeding AS5 billion. The commissioner and his representatives have access both to general meetings and to meetings of the board of directors.

The National Bank Law. The national bank, as the bank of issue of the Republic of Austria, regulates the circulation of money within the country, attends to the balance of payments with foreign countries, and attempts to maintain the domestic and foreign stability of the schilling (Law Concerning the National Bank, 1955). The government holds 50 percent of the bank's shares, the other half belonging equally to banks and institutions in close relationship to the "economic and social partners." The bank must also consider the economic policies of the federal government when establishing its overall guidelines for monetary and credit activities. The federal authorities may not on the other hand issue paper money on the government's behalf as long as the bank is in operation or take any measures that might hinder the bank in fulfilling its duties. The bank's organization and statutory position make it independent of the government; so does the fact that members of its General Board (the body determining monetary policy) cannot be recalled during the board's five-year period in office. With the exception of

APPENDIX TABLE 1
SELECTED BALANCE SHEET ITEMS, END OF 1980

Sector	Credits to Dom. Nonbanks		Domestic Securities		Foreign Assets	
	AS millions	Percent	AS millions	Percent	AS millions	Percent
Joint-stock banks	203,683	26.3	59,781	29.1	198,045	63.0
Private banks	10,953	1.4	2,064	1.0	7,795	2.5
Savings banks	197,629	25.6	68,492	33.3	69,222	22.0
Landes-Hypotheken-banken	74,849	9.7	9,798	4.8	855	0.3
Raiffeisenkassen	128,244	16.6	24,191	11.8	19,019	6.0
Volksbanken	42,950	5.5	13,404	6.5	3,395	1.1
Bausparkassen	74,176	9.6	115	0	937	0.3
Special credit institutions	40,993	5.3	27,662	13.5	15,204	4.8
Total credit system	773,477	100.0	205,507	100.0	314,472	100.0

SOURCE: Austrian National Bank.

professors of jurisprudence and economics (employed in the public universities), no one in public service may serve on the General Board.

The Law of Foreign Currency. Trade in foreign currency is subject to the Law of Foreign Currency.[3] The Austrian National Bank, through its official capacity in administering this law, authorizes credit institutions to trade in foreign currency. The law empowers the bank to establish both the value and the amount of foreign currency entering and leaving the country. Since the breakdown in 1973 of the fixed exchange rate system, it has of course been possible to buy and sell foreign exchange at freely arranged rates. While the Vienna stock exchange publishes exchange rates, contracting parties are not bound by them. Through its "promulgations," or regulations by which it carries out the law, the national bank has largely liberalized exchange transactions. Thus, both payments for goods delivered and the transfer of profits are generally permitted. In capital movements as well, increasingly permissive policies are the rule.

The Market Shares of the Individual Types of Credit Institutions

As measured by the balance-sheet totals (appendix table 1), the joint-stock banks (*Aktienbanken*), which account for 35.8 percent of the

APPENDIX TABLE 1   (continued)

Total Deposits, Dom. Nonbanks[a]		Own Domestic Issues		Foreign Liabilities		Total	
AS millions	Percent	AS millions	Percent	AS millions	Percent	AS millions	Percent
145,944	20.4	76,534	38.2	239,203	66.0	664,999	35.8
8,432	1.2	801	0.4	4,092	1.1	27,770	1.5
222,549	31.1	25,367	12.6	74,255	20.5	449,162	24.2
16,080	2.2	66,694	33.2	1,158	0.3	97,810	5.2
147,873	20.6	10,761	5.4	26,786	7.4	313,691	16.9
49,550	6.9	5,380	2.7	3,855	1.1	92,548	5.0
74,459	10.4	528	0.3	135	0	82,585	4.4
51,322	7.2	14,498	7.2	12,884	3.6	130,159	7.0
716,209	100.0	200,563	100.0	362,368	100.0	1,858,724	100.0

a. Including borrowed money.

credit system's bottom line, make up the most significant group, followed by the savings banks (*Sparkassen*) with 24.2 percent and the *Raiffeisenkassen* with 16.9 percent. The fifteen largest credit institutions as measured by the balance sheets are listed in appendix table 2.

The joint-stock banks lead in industrial finance and export trade. They, like the leading institutes of the multilevel sectors and like the Austrian Postal Savings Bank (Postsparkasse), also play an important part in federal finance. The predominant part played by the joint-stock banks in export trade is also demonstrated by their shares of 66 percent in foreign liabilities and 63 percent in foreign assets.

It must of course be kept in mind that the Austrian Kontrollbank is also included in the joint-stock sector. This institution specializes in export finance, raising significant amounts of capital in foreign countries every year, from which export credits are granted either to Austrians or to foreign purchasers of Austrian goods. Austrian exporters of domestic products have the option of protecting themselves against many types of risk, whether economic or political, by availing themselves of guaranties offered by the republic. The Kontrollbank acts, according to the Law to Promote Exports, 1981, as an agent of the republic in handling such cases. Austrian credit institutions and exporters may submit guaranteed foreign receivables to the Kontrollbank for refinancing. The Kontrollbank itself may replenish its resources when necessary from

APPENDIX TABLE 2
THE FIFTEEN LARGEST CREDIT INSTITUTIONS AS OF DECEMBER 31
(AS millions)

Institution	Totals		Percent Change
	1979	1980	
1. Creditanstalt-Bankverein	164.3	199.6	21.5
2. Österreichische Länderbank	113.2	133.5	17.9
3. Girozentrale	120.9	128.0	5.9
4. Zentralsparkasse u. Kommerzbk.	89.4	104.7	17.1
5. Österreichische Kontrollbank	73.7	102.6	39.1
6. Österreichische Postsparkasse	80.7	87.1	7.9
7. Genoss. Zentralbank	72.3	81.2	12.3
8. BAWAG	63.3	72.1	13.9
9. Erste Österr. Spar-Casse	60.1	70.5	17.3
10. Österr. Volksbanken AG	25.7	31.7	23.2
11. Raiffeisen Bausparkasse	21.7	27.4	24.9
12. Bausparkasse d. Österr. Spark.	23.2	25.5	9.7
13. Österr. Credit-Institut	22.7	25.1	10.4
14. Bank für OÖ und Salzburg	20.7	22.6	9.2
15. Bauspark. Gem. d. Freunde Wüstenrot	19.2	22.1	14.7

NOTE: Institutions are ranked according to balance sheet totals.
SOURCE: Austrian National Bank.

domestic and foreign money markets, its own credit operations guaranteed through the law by the Republic of Austria. Thus, the Kontrollbank is able to obtain capital under relatively favorable conditions and to pass it on to the export sector in the form of low-interest credits.

The system is self-supporting. No subventions from the public sector are necessary. To avoid the danger of foreign political conditions encroaching on the solvency of the Republic of Austria, the Kontrollbank tends to refinance only readily marketable foreign receivables by incurring debts in foreign markets. As of the end of 1980 the republic had assumed a liability of AS250 billion for export receivables, about AS132 billion (53 percent) of which had been used. About AS91 billion worth of refinancing had been obtained from the Kontrollbank.

The private commercial banks (*Bankiers*) play only a subordinate part to the other sectors of the credit system. The largest firms of this type have left the sector and reorganized as joint-stock companies (*Aktiengesellschaften*).

The savings-bank sector, under the *Girozentrale* (clearinghouse) and the Bank of the Austrian Savings Banks, specializes in financing communities and home-building associations. The savings banks play a very important part as lenders. With 25.6 percent of credits to domestic nonbanking firms, they are just as significantly represented in this market as the joint-stock banks (26 percent) and, at 33.3 percent, participate to a greater extent as investors in the Austrian capital market than do the joint-stock banks (29.1 percent). In foreign transactions it is the two institutions at the top and the two major savings banks that predominate.

The mortgage banks (*Landes-Hypothekenbanken*) of the individual states (*Länder*) are corporate bodies established according to laws passed by each state. A large part of their financing activities is related to the states and communities. They meet their capital requirements mainly by issuing loans of various sorts.

The *Raiffeisenkassen* are cooperative associations headed by a Central Cooperative Bank. They are almost always found outside the cities and are integrated into the overall cooperative Raiffeisen System. Most of their capital needs are supplied by low-interest savings deposits with statutory rollover periods.

If the *Raiffeisenkassen,* which are mainly concerned with agricultural finance and are located in the country, can be characterized as rural credit cooperatives, the *Volksbanken* can be regarded as industrial loan companies. They are organized after the Schulze-Delitzsch System. The *Volksbank* sector is considerably smaller than the *Raiffeisen* sector.

The home-building associations (*Bausparkassen*) specialize in financing residential construction. Four of them are now active in Austria. They accept savings deposits from domestic nonbanking firms practically exclusively and pass these resources on for the financing of residential structures.

The sector of special credit institutions comprises a number of entities, of which only two, the Austrian Postal Savings Bank (*Postsparkasse*) and the Austrian Investment Credit Company (*Investitionskredit*), will be mentioned here. The Postal Savings Bank is a corporate body, whose obligations are secured by the republic.

Because of its participation in the check-clearing process, this bank is in a strong position in the Austrian money market. Through its close working relations with the post office it has access to a far-flung network of branches. Because of its importance in the Austrian monetary and credit system, the organization of this institution is subject to an individual law, the Law of the Postal Savings Bank of 1969,[4] which also specifies that in conducting its business it must consider the monetary and credit policy of the federal government and support the currency and credit policy of the national bank. The Board of Directors of the Postal Savings Bank is required to establish a committee to cooperate in administering the national debt. This committee makes its recommendations to the Ministry of Finance.

The Austrian Investment Credit Company owns the most important credit institutions and has the duty of financing investments under especially favorable terms. For projects that are to be especially furthered in terms of the national economy, additional low-interest resources are also available from the national bank.

Notes

1. Federal Law of January 24, 1979; *Official Gazette,* no. 63, concerning credit (Kreditwesengesetz: "KWG").

2. These are credit institutions of the "multilevel" sectors—savings banks, *Raiffeisenkassen, Volksbanken,* and cooperative societies—to the extent that they are authorized to accept savings deposits.

3. Federal Law of July 25, 1946; *Official Gazette,* no. 162, concerning the control of exchange (Devisengesetz).

4. Federal Law of November 26, 1969; *Official Gazette,* no. 458, on the reorganization of the Austrian Postal Savings Bank (Postsparkassengesetz, 1969).

Participants

Sven W. Arndt, *University of California, Santa Cruz*
Jacques R. Artus, *International Monetary Fund*
Barry P. Bosworth, *The Brookings Institution*
William H. Branson, *Princeton University; National Bureau of Economic Research*
Henry W. Briefs, *Georgetown University*
James Brown, *Pratt and Whitney Aircraft Company*
Felix Butschek, *Austrian Institute for Economic Research*
Benedicta Christensen, *International Monetary Fund*
Lindley H. Clark, Jr., *Wall Street Journal*
Fritz Cocron, *Austrian Institute*
Nicholas L. Deak, *Deak-Perera*
Adolf Denk, *Oesterreichische Nationalbank*
Robert Denton, *Booz, Allen and Hamilton International, Inc.*
Jacob S. Dreyer, *U.S. Treasury Department*
Klaus Emmerich, *Austrian Radio and Television*
Johann Farnleitner, *Austrian Federal Economic Chamber*
William Fellner, *American Enterprise Institute*
Michele Fratianni, *Council of Economic Advisers; University of Indiana*
Helmut Frisch, *University of Technology, Vienna*
David F. Good, *Temple University*
John W. Grimes, *General Dynamics Corporation*
Oskar Grünwald, *ÖIAG*
Gottfried Haberler, *American Enterprise Institute*
Helmut H. Haschek, *Oesterreichische Kontrollbank AG*
Horst Hoeller, *Austrian Press Agency*
Thomas F. Johnson, *American Enterprise Institute*
Jerry L. Jordan, *Council of Economic Advisers*
Hella B. Junz, *Townsend-Greenspan*
Peter J. Katzenstein, *Cornell University*
Heinz Kienzl, *Austrian National Bank*
Helmuth Klauhs, *Genossenschaftliche Zentralbank*
Adalbert Knobl, *International Monetary Fund*

Stephan Koren, *Austrian National Bank*
Marvin H. Kosters, *American Enterprise Institute*
Klaus Liebscher, *Genossenschaftliche Zentralbank AG*
Richard T. McCormack, *Office of Senator Jesse Helms*
Fritz Machlup, *Princeton University*
R. Timothy McNamar, *U.S. Treasury Department*
Marlene Manthey, *Die Presse*
Thomas Nowotny, *Consulate General of Austria (New York)*
Henry Owen, *The Consultants International Group*
Mark Perlman, *Institute for Advanced Study (Princeton); University of Pittsburgh*
Marion Powell, *Austrian Radio and Television*
David Redding, *Morgan Guaranty Trust Company*
Helmut Reincke, *Neue Zuercher Zeitung*
Joachim Riedl, *Profil*
Phillip Rieger, *Austrian National Bank*
Duncan M. Ripley, *International Monetary Fund*
Herbert Salcher, *Ministry of Finance, Austria*
Nikolaus Scherk, *Embassy of Austria*
Friedrich Schimpf, *Austrian Trade Commissioner*
Erich Schmidt, *Austrian Federation of Trade Unions*
Heinrich Schneider, *International Monetary Fund*
Karl Herbert Schober, *Ambassador of Austria to the United States*
Hanns Schwimann, *Booz, Allen and Hamilton International, Inc.*
Hans Seidel, *Ministry of Finance, Austria*
Eduardo Somensatto, *American Enterprise Institute*
Erich Spitäller, *International Monetary Fund*
Otto Steckelhuber, *Genossenschaftliche Zentralbank AG*
Herbert Stein, *American Enterprise Institute*
Jan Tumlir, *GATT Secretariat*
Horst Ungerer, *International Monetary Fund*
Karl Vak, *Zentralsparkasse und Kommerzialbank*
H. C. Wall, *General Electric Company*
Henry Wallich, *Federal Reserve System*
Thomas D. Willett, *Claremont Graduate School*
A. Woegoetter, *University of Vienna*
Milton Wolf, *Former U.S. Ambassador to Austria*

A Note on the Book

This book was edited by Claire Theune, Margaret Seawell,
Gertrude Kaplan, and Donna Spitler of the
Publications Staff of the American Enterprise Institute.
The staff also designed the cover and format, with Pat Taylor.
The text was set in Times Roman, a typeface designed by Stanley Morison.
Hendricks-Miller Typographic Company, of Washington, D.C.,
set the type, and R. R. Donnelley & Sons Company
of Harrisonburg, Virginia, printed and bound the book,
using paper made by the S. D. Warren Company.

$830173134

Selected AEI Publications

The AEI Economist, Herbert Stein, ed., published monthly (one year, $18; single copy, $1.50)

Policies for Coping with Oil-Supply Disruptions, George Horwich and Edward J. Mitchell, eds. (188 pp., paper $7.95, cloth $15.95)

The International Monetary System: A Time of Turbulence, Jacob S. Dreyer, Gottfried Haberler, and Thomas D. Willett, eds. (523 pp., paper $14.95, cloth $25.95)

Meeting Human Needs: Toward a New Public Philosophy, Jack A. Meyer, ed. (469 pp., paper $13.95, cloth $34.95)

The Gateway: U.S. Immigration Issues and Policies, Barry R. Chiswick, ed. (476 pp., paper $12.95, cloth $22.95)

Wage-Price Standards and Economic Policy, Jack A. Meyer (80 pp., $4.95)

Mergers in Perspective, Yale Brozen (88 pp., paper $6.95, cloth $14.95)

Low Pay, Occupational Mobility, and Minimum-Wage Policy in Britain, David Metcalf (83 pp., $4.25)

Unemployment Insurance Financing: An Evaluation, Joseph M. Becker (169 pp., paper $6.25, cloth $14.25)

Prices subject to change without notice.

AEI Associates Program

The American Enterprise Institute invites your participation in the competition of ideas through its AEI Associates Program. This program has two objectives:

The first is to broaden the distribution of AEI studies, conferences, forums, and reviews, and thereby to extend public familiarity with the issues. AEI Associates receive regular information on AEI research and programs, and they can order publications and cassettes at a savings.

The second objective is to increase the research activity of the American Enterprise Institute and the dissemination of its published materials to policy makers, the academic community, journalists, and others who help shape public attitudes. Your contribution, which in most cases is partly tax deductible, will help ensure that decision makers have the benefit of scholarly research on the practical options to be considered before programs are formulated. The issues studied by AEI include:

- Defense Policy
- Economic Policy
- Energy Policy
- Foreign Policy
- Government Regulation

- Health Policy
- Legal Policy
- Political and Social Processes
- Social Security and Retirement Policy
- Tax Policy

For more information, write to:

AMERICAN ENTERPRISE INSTITUTE
1150 Seventeenth Street, N.W.
Washington, D.C. 20036